REALITY, SPIRITUALITY, AND MODERN MAN

ALSO BY DAVID R. HAWKINS, M.D., PH.D.

Dissolving the Ego, Realizing the Self

Along the Path to Enlightenment

Letting Go

Healing and Recovery

Discovery of the Presence of God: Devotional Nonduality

Transcending the Levels of Consciousness: The Stairway to Enlightenment

Truth vs. Falsehood: How to Tell the Difference

I: Reality and Subjectivity

The Eye of the I: From Which Nothing Is Hidden

Power vs. Force: The Hidden Determinants of Human Behavior

Dialogues on Consciousness and Spirituality

Orthomolecular Psychiatry (with Linus Pauling)

Please visit:

Hay House USA: www.hayhouse.com®
Hay House Australia: www.hayhouse.com.au
Hay House UK: www.hayhouse.co.uk
Hay House India: www.hayhouse.co.in

REALITY, SPIRITUALITY, AND MODERN MAN

David R. Hawkins, M.D., Ph.D.

HAY HOUSE, INC.
Carlsbad, California • New York City
London • Sydney • New Delhi

Published in the United States by: Hay House, Inc.: www.hayhouse.com® • ***Published in Australia by:*** Hay House Australia Pty. Ltd.: www.hayhouse.com.au • ***Published in the United Kingdom by:*** Hay House UK, Ltd.: www.hayhouse.co.uk • ***Published in India by:*** Hay House Publishers India: www.hayhouse.co.in

Previously published by Axial Publishing Company
(ISBN 978-193339189-2)

Library of Congress Control Number: 2013947045

Tradepaper ISBN: 978-1-4019-4503-9

1st Hay House edition, January 2021
10 9 8 7 6 5 4 3 2 1

SFI label applies to the text stock

Printed in the United States of America

DEDICATION

Straight and narrow is the path . . .

Waste no time.

Gloria in Excelsis Deo!

TABLE OF CONTENTS

Appendices

TABLES AND CHARTS

FOREWORD

While in recent decades advances in technology have been in the public foreground, there has also been a simultaneous progression of human consciousness itself that was expressed as a rather sudden recent advance in its overall level. This enormously profound and salutary change, which occurred in the late 1980s, was not even noticed by the world at large, yet it was detected and documented by the new methodology of consciousness research that had made the seminal discovery of how to tell truth from falsehood and essence from appearance. Even more astonishingly, it could also detect and even calibrate the specific degree of truth or falsehood on a simple exponential calibration scale of 1 to 1,000, which included all possibilities of knowingness within the human domain and even beyond.

As can be seen through simple survey and observation, the sufferings of mankind, now as well as throughout history (with the exception of natural disasters), have been due primarily to the inability to differentiate truth from falsehood, reality from illusion, perception from essence, and opinion from verifiable reality. Thus, the discoveries of consciousness research provided a new paradigm from which to reassess the entire human condition over great periods of time because the scale provided a context and an expanded paradigm that simultaneously included both the linear and the nonlinear realms.

This discovery represented a major leap in human knowledge, which also clarified that a verifiable definition of truth is only possible by the simultaneous statement of both content (linear) and context (nonlinear). That content is only comprehensible within a stated context had already been recognized in the discipline of 'situational ethics' by which even the court system acknowledged the important influence of context (motive, situation, intention, mental capacity, and circumstances, etc.).

All historic attempts at defining verifiable truth lacked a standard for comparison that was absolute, invariable, definable, and confirmably demonstrable. Thus, the emergence of a confirmable, pragmatic means of identifying and corroborating truth presented an entirely new, enlarged dimension for the advancement of human understanding and comprehension.

Knowledge denotes an organized, systematic body of information or study, such as the natural sciences and their laws of operation as confirmed by application. In addition, information is theoretical (academic) as well as clinical, demonstrable, and confirmably pragmatic. In medical practice, for instance, there is the art (calibration level 445) as well as the science (calibration level 440) of the application of scientific principles and their inherent disciplines.

The study of the nonlinear domain has historically been referred to as ontology, metaphysics, theology, and philosophy, as well as historic religion. Modern religious organizations, such as Religious Science, Unity, New Thought, Christian Science, and nondenominational churches, focus on the commonality of the essence of spirituality rather than emphasize differences of classical, historical, ecclesiastical dogma.

An awareness has emerged of an intrinsic core of spiritual reality that lies behind the historic, seemingly divergent, revelations of religions. Thus, modern man is still seeking the core of verifiable spiritual truth that throughout history has often been sidetracked and obscured by ecclesiastical dogma or contentious promulgation.

Traditional religions were often naïvely inclusive of ancient cultural myths and legends that were expressions of allegorical folklore rather than verifiable, literal spiritual reality. It was the inclusion of these cultural legends within traditional religions that gave Clarence Darrow the ammunition with which he attacked William Jennings Bryan during the famous 1925 Scopes "monkey" trial. That historic conflict is now expressed in the current world as the 'evolution versus creation' argument. The concept of 'intelligent design' would seem to offer a possible, plausible, conciliatory, and balanced compromise between religionists and science.

It is rather obvious that if intelligence was not inherent, science itself would not even exist, nor would there be any science if there was no design in the universe, for science is essentially and primarily devoted to the detection and description of design (e.g., scientific laws). Therefore, rejection of the intelligent-design hypothesis could well be attributed to the proclivity and vanity of the human ego, which is more interested in being 'right' and proving others 'wrong' than it is in arriving at truth.

In this work, a means will be provided for the

resolution of issues as yet unresolved, such as those subsequent to the Scopes trial, and finally lay them to rest. The resistance to the resolution is not logic, as rationalists would like to think. The narcissistic core of the human ego that divides mankind into the Hatfields and the McCoys is not motivated by devotion to the truth but merely to the ego-inflated narcissistic payoff obtained from conflict and being 'right'. The ego is innately actively hostile to humility and would rather die (millions do just that) or kill others than relinquish its secret claim to sovereignty.

Interestingly, as we can see from the Map of Consciousness (see pg. xxvii), on a scale of truth from 1 to 1,000, science calibrates in the 400s, whereas, spirituality as such appears at level 500 and higher. The limitation of science is therefore primarily one of "paradigm blindness" (see Hawkins, 2006) and the lack of awareness of the consequences of paradigm limitation (which we will examine later). Paradigm blindness was originally understood by Jesus Christ in his terse statement, "Render unto Caesar the things which are Caesar's, and unto God the things that are God's," that is, do not mix levels of abstraction and confuse the realities of the linear and the nonlinear domains.

The inability to discern actual truth from illusion is the primary obstacle of humanity overall and accounts for the vast majority of human problems as well as war and personal and social suffering. Thus, an examination of the basic underlying problem would seem to be a pressing priority.

That the major riddles which confounded

mankind for centuries can now be resolved in a matter of seconds is confrontive to ordinary presumption and 'common sense'. All problems and seemingly complex issues actually break down to a simple" yes" or "not yes" ("no"). All that is needed to know then becomes simply how and what question to ask.

PREFACE

As described in this as well as the series of prior works, until very recently humankind has had no reliable, objective, confirmable, or verifiable means by which to identify or discern truth from falsehood. As a consequence, despite man's best efforts, for example, the conflict between spiritual faith and reason has remained a vexatious enigma for millennia. It challenged the great intellects of ancient Greece and Rome, as well as the great philosophers and thinkers over the centuries whose works constitute *The Great Books of the Western World*. It remained unresolved despite the efforts of even the greatest theologians, from Thomas Aquinas up to the present day, where the ongoing debate constituted the main theme of even *Time* magazine (Van Biema, 13 November 2006).

The crux of the impasse was presented eloquently at the famous hallmark Scopes trial in 1925, and the conflict was then further confounded in the political world by United States Supreme Court Chief Justice Hugo Black's "high wall between Church and State." That ruling, in 1946, which escalated the conflict, has been hotly contentious in today's society and is symbolized by the ongoing political war between the secularists and the traditionalists. In the academic world, it is currently expressed as 'creationism' versus 'intelligent design'.

The attempt to mix oil and water was not possible until the method of fractionated homogeneity was discovered. Analogously, because of new discoveries, there is now a methodology to synchronize and recontextualize both faith and reason without violating the integrity of either one. It is currently possible to remain scientific, rational, logical, and intellectually erudite while simultaneously spiritually very much inspired by a faith that is bulwarked by demonstrable verification.

A simple study of the nature of consciousness itself reveals an easily crossable bridge between what had previously seemed like very separate and disparate realms. The answer to the conflict and its successful resolution is a consequence of recognizing the importance of an expanded paradigm of reality that is inclusive of *both* science and spiritual realities instead of an 'either-or' partitioning of mutually separate, seemingly exclusive provinces or realms of inquiry. Because this verifiable expansion of context is simultaneously inclusive of both reason and faith, it is thus finally devoid of opinion, ambiguity, and conflict.

Historically, expansions of context have had salutary effects, such as the expansion of physics from the limited Newtonian paradigm to inclusion of subparticle physics, quantum mechanics, and ever-evolving quantum theory. A conceptual bridge was established by the critical discovery of the Heisenberg Uncertainty Principle. It explained the effect of the impact of observation by human consciousness, which thereby empowers and precipitates the 'collapse of the wave function' (explained later) as a consequence of intention (i.e., from potentiality to actuality). The field of astronomy similarly expanded from the study of just our planetary system to include infinite galaxies and multiple universes that are ever expanding and multiplying at the speed of light.

Spiritual realities and the inherent truths of revealed religion can also be examined in a manner that does not require deserting reason or violating the rules of logic and rationality. In fact, the very same context and methodology that is capable of validating spiritual realities also simultaneously validates scientific principles.

Until very recently, both science and religion seemed to be encased in very separate boxes. Now the boxes can be removed, put in a much larger container that includes both and gives them equal importance, credence, and balance.

Different points of observation do not thereby create separate conflicting 'realities' but merely represent different perspectives from within the all-inclusive, infinite field of consciousness itself. As an example, instead of artificially creating a fractious dichotomy between 'evolution' and 'creation', how simple it is to see from a higher, inclusive paradigm that evolution *is* creation. It becomes obvious that evolution is simply what ongoing creation looks like, and that they are actually one and the same thing (calibration level 1,000). Creation is innately evolutionary and emergently unfolding. Similarly, the intelligence of nature may seem to be only a linear, rudimentary trial-and-error system, but out of the prehistoric swamps has emerged *Homo sapiens* whose nonlinear consciousness provides context and meaning.

The seemingly conflictual 'faith versus science' conundrum is also simplified by the realization that a permanent, ever-present 'source' is different from a transitory, ostensibly single event, such as a 'cause'. The term 'cause' is a limitation of the restrictive Newtonian paradigm of reality, now outmoded by even science itself, which has gone on to nonlinear dynamics, probability theory, intermingling theory, emergence-and-complexity theory, and more.

Significantly, over time the greatest scientific geniuses, paradoxically, have been very religious in their personal lives in that their capacity for depth of comprehension was profound and inclusive. While, because of their innate genius, they intuited there was no conflict between religion and science, none of them actually explained the resolution of the presumable disparity, as theirs was the inexplicable knowingness of comprehension.

INTRODUCTION

The emergence of a pragmatic, objective elucidation of truth over the last few decades has provided new information and an enlarged paradigm of reality from which to reevaluate man's progress and current state of evolution. What is 'real' and what is not 'real', what is 'truth' and what is false presumption are now capable of reassessment and resolution from a higher, objective vantage point that is free of the distortion of human bias which has limited and contaminated human thought throughout history (e.g., opinion, rhetoric).

As has been noted in prior writings, the human mind, unaided, is intrinsically incapable of telling truth from falsehood and is limited by the inability to discern perception from essence and appearance from substance, as was famously stated by Descartes' paradox of *res interna cogitans* (subjective appearance) versus *res externa* or *extensa* (objective reality, i.e., the world as it is). Jesus Christ had already stated that sin is actually ignorance from which mankind needs salvation.

The great philosophers throughout history have made the same recurrent observation, from the skeptics of ancient Greece who held that the human mind was intrinsically incapable of discerning truth to Socrates' dictum that all men choose only the seeming good (perception) but are unable to differentiate the 'real' good (essence) from the false (illusion).

Enlightened sages from ancient as well as recent times, such as Ramana Maharshi or Nisargadatta Maharaj, have pointed out that the world we see (perception) is a mental projection. This limitation of dichotomous error has been confirmed by recent breakthroughs in quantum mechanics, which reveals that even time or position are merely projections of human consciousness. The limitation is also a primary postulate of the teachings of the Buddha who confirmed that the unenlightened human merely lives in a world of illusion *(maya)* composed of projected perceptions and, without enlightenment, repeats the same mistakes over and over.

Because of the limitation of the ordinary human mind, the teachings of the avatars and great spiritual geniuses have been historically honored as the highest available sources of truth. To be actually capable of knowing truth and being aware of its source reflects the radiation of Divinity, which alone is immune to subjective distortion. Yet even the highest teachings (calibration 1,000) of the greatest beings who have ever lived have failed to rescue civilization from constant error due to the inability and disinclination of the human mind to innately recognize and accept truth, even when it is spelled out and amplified by examples and parables.

All the great teachers have declared that man's primary defect is 'ignorance'. Research reveals rather quickly that the underlying basis of this ignorance is due to the limitation of the innate structure of the ego itself as a consequence of the still-ongoing evolution of consciousness.

With the discovery of a calibrated scale of consciousness (Hawkins, 1995), study groups formed spontaneously all over the world and the research expanded, resulting in the publication of the following books by this author in all the world's major languages:

Qualitative and Quantitative Analysis and Calibration of the Levels of Human Consciousness (1995); *Power vs. Force* (1995); *The Eye of the I* (2001); *I: Reality and Subjectivity* (2003); *Truth vs. Falsehood* (2005); *Transcending the Levels of Consciousness* (2006); *Discovery of the Presence of God: Devotional Nonduality* (2007); and *Healing and Recovery Lectures* (in publication).

Worldwide interest in the importance of the discernment of truth was intense and resulted in the presentation of more than one hundred major daylong lectures throughout the United States, Europe, and Asia, and at various universities, including the Oxford Union Forum in England. Dissemination of the information via study groups resulted in rapid expansion of the field. Startling discoveries were made in every area of human endeavor. The methodology was even successfully and pragmatically applied to the resolution of international conflicts that were bordering on ballistic-missile warfare. It also had very significant applications to scientific research and all other areas of human endeavor where previously inaccessible knowledge now became quickly available.

The human psyche was astonished that information not available, even with millions of dollars spent on research, could be discovered at no cost in a matter of seconds by well-motivated, integrous people. Application of the method resulted in the emergence of a new science of diplomacy. It has been used not only in daily life but also in engineering research, marketing, product development, employee selection, purchasing, crime detection, security intelligence, and the facilitation of integrous human endeavors around the globe, including economic and government planning.

Like other developing areas of new information, the limitations of consciousness research were not specifically known at first. It was naïvely assumed that by using the methodology, truth could be known by anyone. This was a consequence of the fact that during the first years of research, only very integrous people were utilized as test subjects. It later became apparent that test subjects themselves had to calibrate over level 200 on the Map of Consciousness, and specifics of the testing methodology as outlined in Appendix C had to be followed exactly. Thus, the technique is reliably usable by less than thirty percent of the U. S. population (but much less than that in countries and cultures that are as yet unevolved or still relatively primitive in nature). The testing technique requires objective dedication to truth rather than to personal opinion or desire.

As in previous books, the calibrated truth of the chapters, as well as the book overall, is stated in Appendix A. In addition, the levels of truth of important statements are included within the text. Also, as in prior works, important concepts are purposely re-presented so as to result in familiarity with and expansion of meaning and significance that arises from their presentation within different contexts. Of interest also was the discovery that merely becoming familiar with the basic concepts resulted in a measurable advance in the reader's own level of consciousness, often to a very significant degree, as attested to by many thousands of students of the work worldwide.

Inasmuch as modern man lives in a very complex

world, extensive references are provided in Appendix D. Each reference is concordant with a précis of its impact in a single sentence that denotes the relevance and theme of the reference. Documentation is provided by more than seven hundred references.

MAP OF CONSCIOUSNESS®

God-view	Life-view	Level		Log	Emotion	Process
Self	Is	Enlightenment	⇧	700-1000	Ineffable	Pure Consciousness
All-Being	Perfect	Peace	⇧	600	Bliss	Illumination
One	Complete	Joy	⇧	540	Serenity	Transfiguration
Loving	Benign	Love	⇧	500	Reverence	Revelation
Wise	Meaningful	Reason	⇧	400	Understanding	Abstraction
Merciful	Harmonious	Acceptance	⇧	350	Forgiveness	Transcendence
Inspiring	Hopeful	Willingness	⇧	310	Optimism	Intention
Enabling	Satisfactory	Neutrality	⇧	250	Trust	Release

Permitting	Feasible	Courage	⇕	200	Affirmation	Empowerment
Indifferent	Demanding	Pride	⇩	175	Scorn	Inflation
Vengeful	Antagonistic	Anger	⇩	150	Hate	Aggression
Denying	Disappointing	Desire	⇩	125	Craving	Enslavement
Punitive	Frightening	Fear	⇩	100	Anxiety	Withdrawal
Disdainful	Tragic	Grief	⇩	75	Regret	Despondency
Condemning	Hopeless	Apathy	⇩	50	Despair	Abdication
Vindictive	Evil	Guilt	⇩	30	Blame	Destruction
Despising	Miserable	Shame	⇩	20	Humiliation	Elimination

NOTE TO THE READER

There is a purposeful repetition of basic information for pedagogical purposes because abstract concepts and nonlinear context are not as quickly learned as are linear descriptions. Nonlinear concepts, however, are most easily absorbed by familiarity, which is relatively effortless.

For convenience, some material from previous works and lectures has been re-presented as the reader may not have read or have had access to previously published works.

The overall thrust of this book is to clarify the difference between appearance/perception/illusion versus Reality/Truth/Essence. Confusion of these levels has been the basis of mankind's sufferings over the ages. This book will explain what is meant by the famous quotation from Ramana Maharshi: "There is no point in trying to save the world you think you see because such a world doesn't even exist."

Also to be clarified is the meaning of the Buddha's statement that "Man lives in a world of *maya* (illusion)" and is unable to discern reality from projected perceptions and imagination. As noted, Jesus also had said that man's dilemma is "ignorance." Thus, this book is written at consciousness level 740 to 760, which addresses these issues directly and brings about their resolution through explanation.

CHAPTER 1

Overview

The historical development of any area of critical human knowledge is always interesting and rewarding for it reveals how new knowledge originates and then gains momentum. Investigative research is energized by the innate characteristic of an insatiable curiosity that is intrinsic to biological and human evolution.

All living creatures are devoted to constant research, investigation, and the discovery, gathering, and storage of data. This is essential to the survival of animal life for animal life is born deficient of internal sources of energy that therefore have to be derived and obtained from the environment and external sources. This in turn demands constant exploration to identify and sample available energy sources. Thus, learning (intelligence) is an innate requisite of survival. The acquisition of information follows preset biological programs that are inherent to the structure and function (design) of the organism itself. This capacity escalates up the evolutionary tree along with the calibrated levels of consciousness.

Upon examination, the primordial carrier wave of evolution is located within the substrate of all awareness and intelligence, generically termed 'consciousness', which is a nonlinear, formless, infinite, timeless energy field that is universal and includes all aspects of creation and the universe (not to be confused with the psychoanalytical term of the 'unconscious' of Freud, Jung, et al.). One unique quality of consciousness is awareness by which arises the unique capacity to 'know'. Without awareness, one *is*, but, paradoxically, does not 'know' that one *is*.

It is curious that not until very recently was mankind really aware of the field of consciousness itself or its importance. Historically, it was only the great sages or avatars who even made reference to the underlying substrate of reality that is the ultimate context of all experience (e.g., the 'Self'; the 'Buddha Nature'). Although philosophy and psychology had explored the mental *content* of consciousness ('the mind'), it did not address the basic substrate of the mind itself (consciousness/awareness) by which mentalization could be subjectively discerned and experienced.

Because the energy field of consciousness is invisible and nonlinear, it was not recognized as important to study or even mention except by the enlightened sages over time. In recent decades, however, a major scientific breakthrough was represented by the emergence of the important Heisenberg Uncertainty Principle. It noted that merely *observing* an experiment changed the outcome (collapsed the wave function from potentiality to actuality), and thus, for the first time, the subject of consciousness itself, as well as intention, entered scientific theory and discussion. (See Stapp, 2007.)

Intelligence

Intelligence includes the capacity to abstract and organize class, definition, and hierarchy of essential meaning and operation. These are then further clarified by differentiating them via thought or mentalization (semantics). These latter terms refer to the content of intelligence, which is more closely aligned with and consequent to the presence of the broader field of consciousness. Note that both intelligence and consciousness are themselves innately without form. Intelligence includes the capacity to extract design, meaning, and significance in abstract implication. Intellectual capacity is identifiable along a range of capability as reflected by the intelligence quotient (IQ).

Unlike IQ, which is a lifelong, rather stationary capability, the individual level of consciousness, which is already calibratable at birth, is able to rise even to a major extent as a consequence of favorable factors, such as influence of spiritual/religious teachers, motivations, spiritual education, and early exposure to aesthetics. These factors biologically influence brain function and hemispheric dominance as well as neural-connectedness patterns and brain chemistry via its neural and humeral transmitters. Thus, while IQ may refer to intellectual capacity, its importance is overshadowed by advances in the level of consciousness itself, which in turn reflects inherited propensities, volitional intention, and choices.

As the Buddha proclaimed, fortunate it is to be born a human being for the human domain offers almost unlimited multiple opportunities to grow and develop one's level of consciousness and concordant spiritual awareness. The well-known principle of 'karma' (spiritual destiny) includes the awareness that the human domain offers the maximum opportunity to acquire good merit and to undo negative debts.

While it is not necessary to believe in 'karma' as a

doctrine, all humanity throughout all time has been aware of the destiny of the soul as the spiritual substrate to life and existence. The fate of the soul has been a primary focus of all the great civilizations, such as that of ancient Egypt, long before the births of the Buddha, Krishna, Zoroaster, or Jesus Christ.

By even 10,000 B.C., in ancient Egypt the 'Ka', or soul, was depicted as leaving the body at the moment of physical death. Osiris, god of the Underworld, then weighed one's heart on the Scale of Truth. If it weighed in favor of truth, its destiny was heavenly, but if it fell on the side of falsehood, it went to the lower regions of hells. Mankind's collective spiritual inheritance (karma) and destiny were also enunciated in the Book of Genesis as the result of the lapse from the primordial, nonlinear, heavenly paradise (the Garden of Eden) to the descent into proclivity for falsity consequent to falling into the consciousness realm of duality and the linear domain (the dichotomy of good and evil).

It can readily be documented and illustrated that the overall consciousness level of life has slowly progressed over the archeological ages as represented by the evolution of the animal kingdom (see Chapter 4). Similarly, the consciousness level of human evolution shows the same type of progression over time.

At the time of the birth of the Buddha, mankind collectively calibrated at 90. The collective consciousness level had reached 100 by the time of the birth of Jesus Christ and climbed slowly to level 190, where it remained for many centuries. It was only in the late 1980s that it suddenly jumped from 190 to above the critical level of 200, to 204, and later to 207. It then went back down in the year 2007 to the level of 204.

Currently, approximately eighty-five percent of mankind calibrates below the critical consciousness level of 200. In the United States, fifty-five percent of the population is below 200, which is significant because it had been only forty-nine percent in 2005. The collective negativity of the population below level 200 is counterbalanced by the minority of people who calibrate well above 200 and whose positive power is far greater than the negative pull of the masses below 200. The increase in power is exponential; therefore, actually only a very few people with extremely advanced levels of consciousness are necessary to counterbalance the negativity of the rest of mankind.

Distribution of the Levels of Consciousness of Mankind

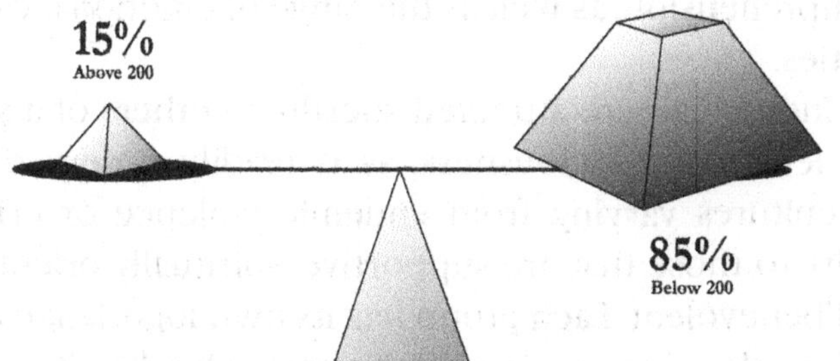

Of interest and great importance is that the distribution of the levels of consciousness of people on the planet is quite uneven. There is great disparity between different cultures and populations; this underlies the constancy of human conflict as reflected in interracial and international tensions and warfare termed "the clash of civilizations" (e.g., Washington, DC calibrates at

424; in contrast, Baghdad calibrates at 160).

Levels of Consciousness as the Source of Human Conflict

Each level of consciousness represents an energy field of dominance as a consequence of its concordant 'attractor field,' which acts similarly to magnetic or gravitational fields. These fields are of progressive power and dominance and reflect a polarity. Energy fields above consciousness level 200 attract and radiate that which is positive (true, loving, and life sustaining) and repel the negative, whereas levels below 200 attract the negative, false, and destructive (e.g., hate) and repel that which is positive. These previously undetected, unidentified prevailing invisible fields profoundly dominate and influence *all* human decisions, behavior, perception, culture, religion, and capacity for comprehension, as well as the range of emotional capabilities.

Individuals are attracted socially to others of a similar level of consciousness, as is readily observed by subcultures varying from endemic violence or criminality to those that are supportive, spiritually oriented, and benevolent. Each group has its own logo, language, and mode of mentation. Each group also has its own political strata and concepts of morality and social conduct. As readily observed, these frequently oppose each other and result in the endless parade of cultural and military wars.

At the lowest levels of consciousness, life is devalued, and murder, suicide, mass slaughter, killing of children, dog fighting, and genocide are characteristic since hate is endemic (e.g., "We worship death" calibrates at consciousness level 20). In contrast, at consciousness levels above 200, life is considered to be precious, and therefore killing the innocent is unthinkable for life is seen as a Divine gift. (That life actually is a Divine gift calibrates at 1,000.)

As is obvious, each level of human consciousness therefore has its own innate 'reality', and conflict is inevitable between people and cultures that are diametrically opposed to each other. What brings praise in one subgroup would result in ridicule in another. For example, is honesty a virtue, or is it a sign of absurd stupidity and weakness? Are women to be devalued and stoned to death or honored? Should people who have different beliefs be demolished and killed, or should they be understood? Is cruelty to be condoned or condemned? Are honesty and morality reality-based bulwarks of stability in society or merely 'politically repressive semantic constructs'? Is truth an absolute (essence), or is it arbitrary and merely a relative reflection of transitory public opinion (appearance, perception) that solely reflects social bias?

The most serious dichotomy arises from the reversal of truth and falsehood within consciousness levels below 200. Thus, in today's world, there is the dramatic confrontation between these polarized extremes in which cultures based on beliefs that calibrate as low as 20 (Primitivism, Jihadism) now threaten the entire world via nuclear technology. In civilized people and countries, rationality and restraint are an endemic expectation, but these qualities are ridiculed as weaknesses by the lowest levels of consciousness, which are themselves prone to animalistic xenophobia, paranoia, delusions, and rampant violence motivated by hatred.

Throughout history, the same patterns recur not only between individuals but also between classes, countries, cultures, and religions that demonize alternate viewpoints. Thus, there are actually two very different, diametrically opposed and polarized human cultures: those above and those below consciousness level 200, and each side sees the other as the enemy.

As will be described later, the conflict between these two opposing civilizations is rooted not only in ideology but also in the actual biology of different brain functioning in which the brain physiology is dominated by different hemispheres and neurotransmitters (see Chapter 4). The resultant disparity is thus not only social, religious, political, and cultural but also biological, hormonal, and neurochemical. The basic source of this dichotomy is evolutionary in origin and, thus far in history, endemic to the human race. It is therefore indigenous and innate to the hominid species/genus *Homo sapiens*.

Resolution

Acceptance of the above-described disparity between classes of hominids allows for the discarding of denial and idealistic wishful thinking as well as the ideologies of social/political naïveté. None of these alternatives has brought about resolution but only temporary lulls in human history during which the two sides retrench in order to prevail at the next major encounter. To 'be nice' seems normal to people who calibrate above 200, but below 200, it is considered to be a contemptible weakness as well as an insult and therefore not effective communication. The same internecine clashes occur within religious as well as secular subcultures.

Only through wisdom, acceptance, and compassion can understanding come about that brings forbearance and makes realistic allowances for widely disparate worldviews and values. Offense and insult result from the noncomprehension of these predominant conflictual worldviews, modes of thinking, and reality.

An obstacle to effective communication is the expectation of changing the other's viewpoint to be in accord with one's own by war, intimidation, 're-education', legalization, idealistic proselytization, indoctrination, propaganda, or 'tolerance' via 'reprogramming'. The defect of wishful thinking is that it fails to appreciate the major limitation of comprehension that is consequent to the lower levels of consciousness, much as it is difficult, if not impossible, to teach the physics of advanced theoretical quantum mechanics to persons who are educationally and intellectually limited. The difficulty with confronting propositions to promote idealistic social goals by 'cultural transformation' is that each level of consciousness has a different view of what is 'real' or of primary importance or value. Thus, one culture sees peace and accord as a sign of weakness rather than as a desirable goal.

By research, it is now possible to quickly identify the level of consciousness represented by specific subpopulations, cultures, persons, and countries as well as political, religious, and governmental structures. Thus, only then does it become possible for a science of diplomacy to provide a meaningful basis for effective dialog to ensue (see "Science of Diplomacy" in *Truth vs. Falsehood*). The above takes into consideration the nature of the ego itself whose primary characteristic is solely its desire for gain. Each level of consciousness has its own values that include what it considers to be desirable or a gain and thus material for negotiation. 'Peace' is a popular political slogan, but it has been said that it is really oil money that is persuasive in the world of socio-economic/political reality, e.g., "Money trumps peace" (cal. 365; Bush, 2007).

The ego clings to gain as the primary motivator of all intentions, goals, and actions. With spiritual evolution, these are relinquished, but only for a perceived higher good. Even with strong intention and dedication, human progress is slow and difficult. Thus, patience is the prerequisite to compassionate understanding, as the pace of human evolution fluctuates (e.g., a decrease in the consciousness level of mankind from 207 to 204 in recent years).

The acceptance that conflict and disparity are innate to the human condition (e.g., Cain vs. Abel) paradoxically brings a sense of inner relief from guilt. Human life offers the maximum opportunity for spiritual evolution. Perception, however, sees personal as well as social/political/ideational conflicts as obstacles to peace and happiness. In contrast, the spiritual Self sees perfection in the very same world.

Whether human life is frightening or dismaying, or exciting and challenging, is an option that characterizes the fulcrum of spiritual evolution. To 'take the high road' is an invitation from the spiritual Self to the ego/self. Human conflict, both within and without, however, serves as equally serviceable material by which to evolve. For example, without perceived 'enemies', who would there be to forgive?

Faith in the ego and its promises eventually brings dismay and disillusionment, which can then, however, paradoxically subserve spiritual evolution by intensifying motivation. Upon examination, it will be found that earthly human life is the optimal environment for the advancement of consciousness and the discovery of spiritual reality by which all life is transformed in order to reveal the innate perfection of existence itself (cal. 1,000). With patience and persistence, the Divinity of the Essence of All Creation shines forth and replaces the ego's misperceptions and projected values.

While some of the preceding statements may seem initially ambiguous, the purpose of the information that follows in subsequent chapters is to clarify and make obvious the full meaning. Comprehension is a consequence of context, and consciousness itself offers the ultimate context by which the seemingly obscure becomes self-evident.

Whereas falsehood and the ego instincts rely on force and the assumption of 'causation', in contrast, truth reflects effortless power. It does not overcome falsehood but merely replaces it by the realization consequent to the contextualization whereby 'meaning' takes on greater dimension by the expansion of paradigm. There is actually no conflict because the lesser is replaced and dissolved into the greater, just as light replaces darkness rather than opposing it. The ego/self is absorbed into the greater Self so they are no longer seemingly oppositional, nor are there seeming disparities as a source of conflict.

CHAPTER 2

The Human Dilemma

Introduction

This has been called the Information Age in that new discoveries are constantly and rapidly being made in almost every area of human endeavor. Science and technology are the catalytic agencies of rapid advancement in practical applications. They facilitate the emergence of an endless series of expansions that require the development of new conceptual schemes and intellectual constructs. These result in new, correlated literature that supports further research and development, which again spawns another cycle of discovery.

Evolutionary Stress

The evolution of human intelligence is a continuous expression of the emergence of potentiality that then facilitates the emergence of yet another level of increased capacity. The inherent faculty of intelligence is the consequence of the inner light of consciousness itself. This capacity to progressively evolve is unique to the species *Homo sapiens* in contrast to other life forms that evolve only to stationary expressions of their biological destinies and potentialities.

The consequence of constant evolutionary progression is that humankind is both gifted and simultaneously stressed by constant change and the resulting foment of social turbulence. Thus, disharmony, discord, and conflict are endemic to the human species, demonstrated by the fact that mankind has been at war during ninety-three percent of recorded history.

Evolutionary change results in the ubiquitous human characteristics of 'existential angst' and uncertainty due to a major hereditary defect in that the human mind, unaided, is intrinsically incapable of discerning truth from falsehood. This limitation is of such magnitude that the collective human mind is oblivious to the elephant in the room (further explored in *Truth vs. Falsehood*). This limitation is due to an innate naïve 'ignorance' as well as to the vanity of the ego's narcissistic core. In desperation, the ego clings to beliefs in order to arrive at some sense of certainty and a basis for rationalized decision making and action.

The wise realize that all human knowledge is at best tentative, suppositional, and subject to later correction. Even so-called 'facts' are also only provisional statements in that interpretation of data is dependent on context and therefore subject to later reinterpretation. The constant accretion of new data changes the proximate field of influence and results in the requirement for constant change and reevaluation of meaning and significance so that survival is both an art as well as a science.

Development of Consciousness Research

A new branch of human knowledge emerged from the evolutionary tree with the discovery of the pragmatic clinical methodology of consciousness research (cal. 605), which clarified for the first time both the capabilities and the limitations of the basic human condition. The emergence of this discovery was fortuitous when it was accidentally found that negative stimuli, which make 'normal' people go weak, had no such physically weakening effect on people who were spiritually evolved, and that the physiological responses of integrous people were also in accord with the level of truth or consciousness of a stimulus. This was first reported in the 1995 book, *Qualitative and Quantitative Analysis and Calibration of the Levels of Human Consciousness* and later in the book, *Power vs. Force,* which became widely known as a result of very positive reviews (e.g., *Brain-Mind Bulletin*), as well as affirmation by Nobelists and notables in diverse fields, such as marketing, business, and engineering design, and confirmation by spiritual teachers and institutions that incorporated the teachings within their own programs. The rapid spread and application of the information in diverse fields were indicative of the readiness and responsiveness of human consciousness to evolve as a consequence of the quality of innate intelligence itself.

Information derived from consciousness research was also incorporated in clinical medicine in what became the largest psychiatric practice in the United States in order to help diagnose and treat patients who were refractory to treatment and considered to be hopeless (Hawkins and Pauling 1973). From psychology, philosophy, psychoanalytical theory, and the classic "chain of being" (Lovejoy 1936), a scale of levels of consciousness was derived that was also in accord with man's history and the perennial philosophy (Huxley 1945; Wilber 1997). From this scale of 1 to 1,000, it was then possible to survey the entire human domain from which evolved a more comprehensive understanding of the human condition and its evolution.

Research confirmed that the dilemma of modern man is two-fold. First, the human mind, by virtue of its innate design and construction, is unable to discern truth from falsehood (opinion from facts), illusion from reality, or perception/appearance from essence. Second, the modern, scientifically educated mind is often unable to comprehend nonlinear spiritual realities or the teachings of religion and therefore accepts only a portion as plausible or probable truth.

Thus, in modern man, faith and reason become compartmentalized in order to avoid the conflicts so eminently displayed by the 1925 Scopes trial. The questions that arose out of that conflict have remained relatively unanswered. The reason for the lack of resolution is that the issues are actually not resolvable as presented for they can only be transcended from a greater context that represents a more expansive and inclusive paradigm of reality encompassing both the linear and nonlinear domains.

The political expression of the conflict, such as interpreting "a high wall between Church and State," represents the contentious battlefield on which both sides offer no compromise. One side proclaims faith in faith itself, whereas the other side paradoxically proclaims faith in secular nonfaith.

The Science of Context

As will become apparent with further explanation, science, reason, and social discourse operate primarily on the level of content (linear), whereas meaning is abstract and a consequence of context via comprehension (nonlinear). Although innate to consciousness itself, context is usually not stated, identified, or defined. Therefore, there has previously been no actual science of truth itself, much less a means of verification or confirmation. It is therefore inevitable that humanity flounders and repetitively falls into endless disasters (e.g., repeats the same mistake over and over, hoping for a different result).

Resolution of conflict, as will be explained further in the next chapter, is facilitated by expansion of context. As an example, the physical world is describable as mountainous, oceanic, volcanic, forested, or arid with deserts of sand. It is also hot at the equator and covered with ice at the poles. These terms, by virtue of their disparity, do not thereby describe different or separate worlds, as they are only descriptive terms denoting selective locations of observation. From a much greater altitude, such as that of a satellite, all the characteristics of the earth's surface are observable simultaneously. We do not separate them and declare that they therefore represent a 'conflict'. Thus, we see that descriptive terms only refer to limited regions and viewpoints but not to the totality.

The resolution of ambiguities is the automatic consequence of expansion of context from limited positionality to inclusive totality. In times past, such heated controversies emerged over whether the earth was round or flat, or whether it went around the sun or vice versa. The same type of pseudodilemma is now repeated by science/reason versus religious/spiritual truth and faith. By expansion of context, however, it will be easily observed that no actual conflict is possible in reality, and seeming conflict is only an artificial consequence of mentation from an arbitrary and limited point of view and observation (an 'artifact'). Thus, limitation of paradigm is a consequence of the dominance of the narcissistic core of the ego, which sacrifices truth and integrity in order to see itself as victorious. (Science is limited to the consciousness levels of the 400s; nonlinear context, or spiritual reality, calibrates at 500 and above.) Such limitation of vision is detrimental to human peace and progress, as well as being an impediment to wisdom and happiness.

The desire to win also results in relinquishment of integrity as we can see in the artificially contrived and staged Scopes trial itself during which Clarence Darrow lapsed into the *ad hominem* attack on William Jennings Bryan instead of directly addressing the core issues that were purportedly discussed (Sears and Osten 2005). In reality, as we shall see, evolution and creation are one and the same thing (cal. 1,000). The only difference is the viewpoint of their descriptions, which are themselves merely limitations of paradigm.

Deviations from truth repeatedly have catastrophic consequences and therefore are not to be dismissed as mere intellectual curiosities. Intrinsic to the conflicts of the Scopes trial are the very elements that are the cause of mankind's suffering throughout the ages. Propagated falsehood results in massive wars, death, and destruction; therefore, an understanding of paradigm and context is imperative as the world is again poised on the very brink of a war of nuclear dimensions.

The vanity of the narcissistic core of the human ego is infinite and boundless, even to the point of mass genocidal destruction or suicide. Despite the ego's illusions to the contrary, the source of suffering stems from within this blind core of the narcissistic ego itself, which is the locus of the ticking time bomb that periodically explodes and decimates the populations of entire continents. If 'ignorance' is, as described by Jesus, the Buddha, and the great sages, the basis of sin and suffering, then the ability to identify and confirm truth is not only the key to man's salvation but also his most imperative challenge.

The human psyche is impaired by reliance on its core of narcissism. This defect is denied, repressed, and kept politely out of awareness. However, the defect becomes grossly exhibited and overt in the condition referred to as 'messianic narcissistic megalomania', which calibrates at consciousness level 30 (see *Truth vs. Falsehood*, Chapter 15).

Fallacy as a Pied Piper

The world is enamored of theatrically displayed 'causes' that are actually based on falsity. This trend is exemplified by the charismatic attraction of the world's dictators, all of whom, historically as well as currently, calibrate at consciousness levels 80 to 180 (which is also the level of criminality and prison populations). Thus, dictatorship is actually political criminality, as clearly expressed by wanton killings of all those in opposition, even if they are family members. The rationale offered is flimsy at best, such as 'enemy of the State', 'apostate', 'nonbeliever', or suspected allegiance to an oppositional political party or belief system. The 'great leader' replaces God and becomes worshiped in a cult-like manner even as he massacres the starving population and brings the downfall and mass destruction of his own nation. Thus, to be unable to tell truth from falsehood is operationally suicidal on a massive national and international level.

The Ego's Proclivity for Error

Because of existential angst, the human mind frantically and indiscriminately grasps at any scrap of contentious information (e.g., blog sites collectively calibrate at level 180). All that is necessary is for the idea or slogan ('meme'), no matter how inane, bizarre or fallacious, to be formulated and then spread about by any form of communication. The rate of spread is increased by the addition of emotionalism and sensationalism, as well as hyperbole and purposeful distortion (McGowan 2001). Without context, the significance or meaning is left up to the observer so that routinely, the same information will be interpreted in very opposite ways.

The injurious effect of falsehood is further promulgated by the Internet and media exploitation of the fashionable, inflated dictum of 'free speech' as 'fair and equal' reporting by which, paradoxically, falsity and hate are given equal credibility and validity (relativism) with truth. This results in the 'dumbing down' of society (Mosly, 2000; Lasch, 1991). Discernment is left up to the individual listener or viewer (a capacity, however, that is lacking in fifty-five percent of the population in the United States and eighty-five percent in the world).

The mind is frantic for survival, so it is highly prone to grasp at straws rather than admit that all opinion is merely provisional, tentative, and transitory. By repetition, memes spread rapidly like an infection, and these serious deviations from truth take on a self-propagating, destructive life of their own (McGrath, 2006). Very severe falsehood often propagates relentlessly down through the centuries and tends to reappear merely in new clothes.

One of the most prominent examples is that of the history of *The Protocols of the Learned Elders of Zion* (Nilus 1897; cal. 90) by which very severe falsehood resulted in widespread anti-Semitism and became the basis of Nazi propaganda. It reappeared as false teachings in various countries, contaminating even Henry Ford. What is amazing is that the whole book was based on a French fictional satire; however, the very same false teachings are now being taught as actual 'truth' to school children throughout the Arab world (e.g., Hamas television) and continue to be a current source of hatred and war (Shea and Hoffman, 2006; "Obsession," *Fox News*, November 2006).

A parallel demonstration is afforded by the recurrent reemergence of (Marxian) dialectical materialism in new philosophical, rhetorical disguise (e.g., 'secular progressive', 'New Left'), which then captivates educational institutions that desert the minimum basic requirements of logic or reason in order to appear fashionably 'postmodern' and relativistic (Goshgarian, 2007; Horowitz, 2006). Horowitz was denied free speech at Emory University by "Leftist Fascists" (*Fox News*, October 2007). There is repressive prohibition of free speech (e.g., conservative student groups) on the campus, which is consequent to the philosophical theories of Marcuse and his "Critical Theory" (cal. 150). Bizarre as it may seem, in the case of time-honored ideologies that calibrate in the high 400s, prestigious universities invite visiting professors who characteristically calibrate at consciousness level 90 and preach hatred, intolerance, and paranoid delusions wrapped up in conspiracy theories that calibrate at consciousness level 90 and sometimes even lower (e.g., 'the United States orchestrated 9/11', and 'the Holocaust is a myth'). Thus, at Yale, a visiting choir was physically attacked for singing "God Bless America," and the National Anthem is prohibited in academia (which, itself, is now down to consciousness level 190). Emory University teaches that "all whites are racists and therefore in need of re-education indoctrination" (Horowitz, 2007).

While falsehood can seemingly be rationalized when it appears as conspiracy theory ideologies (cal. 160), in reality, none of its vociferous proponents would be willing to accept counterfeit money (false) in place of legitimate currency (truth). On the contrary, delusional, 'nutty professors' play the financial game (e.g., a salary of $100,000 per year) the same as any greedy entrepreneur (Horowitz 2006, 2007).

Respect for integrous truth, plus the capacity to recognize and identify falsehood, is the cutting edge of the evolution of consciousness as well as for spiritual evolution itself. Major discoveries have resulted in great improvements in human life. Just in this lifetime, the infectious diseases and plagues that killed millions of people in the past have disappeared altogether due to the discovery of antibiotics and immunization.

Grandiose psychoses and paranoid delusions were formerly recognized as characteristic of psychosis, cerebral syphilis, or severe mental illness, but now they are combined in a rampant disease of the human ego and the media itself, which feeds on the germs of propagated falsehood. The consequences of the new disease are as serious as that of the old ones in that it results in the fatalities of large numbers of innocent people who themselves are unable to differentiate truth from falsehood and therefore blindly follow false leaders. In all wars, it is the civilian population that is most decimated by the war itself; falsehood results in mass starvation, devastation, agony, suffering, genocide, and massive fatalities.

The naïve ego is also easily duped by platitudes (cal. 185) and wishful fantasies as to what are really serious problems, such as warfare. The world naïvely relies on ideological fictions and pseudosolutions, such as the United Nations (cal. 180), as well as platitudes so that an ideologically hyped 'world body' cannot even bring itself to condemn open warfare or overt genocide. Another downside of pseudosolutions is that they forestall and preclude the search for realistic solutions based on verifiable truth. By the sophistry of 'moral equivalency' (cal. 170), any action can be justified and promoted by some fallacious distortion of not only facts but, more importantly, of context.

Hypnotic Effect of Image

All the world's current dictators as well as heads of rogue nations calibrate in the same approximate range of 80 to 180. All that is detrimental to society, culturally damaging, and degenerative calibrates below level 200. Such trends gain impetus as the result of the glamorized images that increase momentum by popularization via celebrity figures who fatuously run to be photographed while fawningly embracing dictators.

Without consciousness calibration, it is difficult to differentiate freedom and liberty from seduction by simple licentiousness. Any and all indulgence in sensory pleasure, no matter how gross, e.g., Boulder, Colorado's Colorado's student lecture (cal. 180) on "Do drugs and have unprotected sex" (June 2007) can be rationalized by popularization or judicial caprice (Flynn, 2004).

Unaided, the human mind is unable to differentiate truth from falsehood because it is so easily fooled by well-crafted sheep's clothing in the dazzling glamour of image and presentation. (Interestingly, the 'wolf in sheep's clothing' calibrates at an ominous 120.) Various leaders develop a public image (perception) and reputation that obscure recognition of the underlying reality (essence). Also, to complicate the situation further, many such public figures start out as integrous but then later succumb to popularity and megalomania consequent to a fallen level of consciousness that occurs unbeknownst to the public.

That 'power corrupts' is a verifiable truism, and many of the world's seemingly great personages declined very severely. From Napoleon to Hitler to current dictators and supposed 'emancipators', along with current 'liberators' and purported leaders, all have turned into their opposites. Historically, *today's liberator is tomorrow's dictator*. Characteristically, many of them calibrated as high as 400 early in their careers but then later fell to far below 200. The same phenomenon occurred in ancient as well as recent cultures that degenerated to endless public scandals.

There are entire cultures within which the imitation of spiritual erudition and advancement has been perfected to the degree that it requires expertise in consciousness calibration techniques to detect the difference. The Internet also displays endless solicitations for a variety of purportedly spiritual programs that make wild promises of instant enlightenment. Note that these are all done for a sizeable fee, with very special 'blessings' or 'powers' for sale for five thousand dollars and up. That such solicitations cater to the narcissism of the spiritual ego is quite obvious and would thereby actually be self-defeating.

To the impressionable, naïve ego, the mere fact that someone or some avenue of thought is prominent or in the spotlight or the news confers a mystical, magical, glamorized aura of credibility, which is perhaps further reinforced by some important-sounding title.

Safeguards

By inner humility plus wisdom, the seeker of truth takes serious note of the inherent limitations of the human psyche itself and no longer relies on the impressionable personal ego as its sole arbiter of truth. That this attitude is based on confirmable reality is evidenced by the realization that, as mentioned previously, approximately eighty-five percent of the world's population calibrates below level 200. This collectively constitutes ninety-two percent of human problems overall. In America, the percentage of people below 200 is fifty-five percent and has the same negative consequences to society overall.

Collectively, subpopulations tend to stratify in society, and the subculture that calibrates below level 200 has been defined as living in an "alternate reality" (Pitts, 2004) of the "reality impaired" (Marzeles, 2007).

Even integrous institutions may include nonintegrous individuals and defective areas of functioning. However, truly responsible, integrous organizations tend to self-correct over time; thus, it is not necessary to always be perfect but to be responsive. Honesty admits to error and mistakes and takes on the responsibility of their rectification. All humanity and its institutions are on a learning curve so that tolerance for human error is more appropriate than denunciation. (In Christian theology, 'sin' is technically actually error.)

Resolution

While the seeds of self-deception are hidden within the recesses of the human mind, hidden also are the seeds for salvation that are innate to the field of consciousness itself. By utilization of the methodology of consciousness research, it is now possible to bypass the mind's inherent limitations and differentiate essence from appearance. This then provides the means to resolving the enigma of the human mind that was so accurately and classically stated by Socrates and Descartes and exhibited by the Scopes trial. The Information Age, despite its proclivity to spreading disinformation, surprisingly also provided a means of differentiation of truth (essence) from appearance (falsity), which has obvious and profound implications with potential benefit for every aspect of human life, including personal happiness.

Many advances in human knowledge throughout time have elicited initial skepticism or even ridicule. Thus, the human psyche is ambivalent about any new discovery for it requires a change of viewpoint and challenges cherished opinions.

CHAPTER 3

Paradigms of Reality

It is a general observation that expansion of context brings about the resolution of conflict between seemingly disparate viewpoints. This applies to reason/science versus faith/religion as well. The word 'paradigm' implies domain, region, area, territory, expanse, or realm, which, in everyday life, is referred to by the utilization of abstract concepts as, for example, the classic stratification of levels of existence as implied by the terms 'kingdom, phylum, class, order, family, genus, and species'. Thus paradigm implies an overall domain or realm of comprehension, reference, and viewpoint.

Paradigm Blindness

Each person perceives, experiences, and interprets the world and its events in accord with their own predominant level of consciousness. This is further reinforced by the mind's proclivity to explanation via mentalization and rationalized interpretation of perceived data. Thus, each level tends to be self-reinforcing by the circuitry of reification. This process results in what is best described as "paradigm allegiance" (Hawkins, 2006) or the presumption that one's own personal perceived/experienced world represents 'reality' (Protagoras's error as pointed out by Plato).

Because the mind, by virtue of its innate structure, is unable to differentiate perception from essence or *res cogitans (interna)* from *res externa (extensa)*, as noted by René Descartes, it makes the naïve assumption that it experiences and thereby 'knows reality', and that other viewpoints therefore must be 'wrong'. This phenomenon constitutes illusion, which is the automatic consequence of the limitation resulting from the ego's structuring of mental processes whereby it misidentifies opinion as truth and actual reality (e.g., solipsism).

For comfort and mental reinforcement, people seek for agreement and thus tend to congregate with others who share the same paradigm or worldview (e.g., blog site). Paradigm is also alluded to as 'dimension' and more distinctly as 'context' or 'overall field'. The problem is addressed philosophically by metaphysics, which literally means 'beyond the physical', by which the mind derives levels and categories of abstraction and meaning, or even basic common characteristics, such as living versus inert and organic versus inorganic.

Context determines parameters with implied or stated qualifications or limits, as well as requirements and specifics that identify the levels of abstraction, which in turn modify or even determine meaning (hermeneutics) that is concordant with appraisals of value, significance, or worth.

Paradigm is aligned with orientation, expectation, and also intention, as represented by the Internet's search engines that preselect the range of possible discoveries by the introduction of the initial key word or phrase. Paradigm thus predetermines the range of possible experiences or discoveries and is a factor about which ordinary consciousness is unaware. Paradigm is infrequently defined directly and is most often just ignored or naïvely presumed.

The perceived reality of science is discrete, definable,

provable, factual, and linear as well as limited to the dimensions of time, space, and place (measurement). Its mechanisms are assumed to operate via the Newtonian concepts of causality and presumptions of cause and effect (force).

In contrast, the realities of love, faith, inspiration, and the basic invisible premises of abstract truth, spirituality, and religion are nonlinear and operate via principles of power by means of cascading levels of strata of dominance by the influential fields of consciousness energy. These are orchestrated and even determined by "attentional set" (Medina, 2006), which is in turn the result of intention, choice, and decision.

Science deals with content (facts), whereas abstract and spiritual realities refer to context (truth). The paradigms of reality of science are quite different from those of spiritual realities. Facts are linear, observable, and provable. Truth, however, is nonlinear but confirmable. Facts deal with limitation, whereas truth includes meaning, significance, value, and worth.

Resolution of the Problem of the Limitation of Paradigm

The linear and the nonlinear are entirely different levels of reference and paradigms. They do not share common terminology or conceptual constructions. Science is limited to the linear, observable, definable, and primarily structured and mechanistic Newtonian dimension (with later expansions to subparticle physics and quantum mechanics) and its associated dialectic of logic, reason, and provable hypotheses ('facts'). Thus, by virtue of its innate inherent limitation, science has been unable to bridge the gap between Descartes' *res interna (cogitans)* and *res externa* (existential reality as it is in nature).

The mind stretches itself via metaphysics, epistemology, theology, ontology, and intellection in futile attempts to cross an unrecognized barrier (e.g., Hayakawa's famous quote, "The map is not the territory"). Thus, the intense intellectual effort is analogous to looking for one's lost keys only under the street lamp because 'the light is better there'. This limitation is also demonstrated in very apparent fashion by the intellectual dissertations and presentations in such publications as *Zygon, Science and Religion, Science and Theology, Science and Consciousness Review, the Journal of Consciousness Studies*, and others, all of which calibrate in the 300s to 400s. These represent studious, valiant attempts to cross the Rubicon but fail to achieve the proposed goal by virtue of the limitation of paradigm blindness. Simply restated, the nonlinear is not understandable, describable, or subject to the logic of the linear. They are different paradigms with different languaging and requirements for comprehension.

The linear is definable, limited, conceptual, purportedly 'objective', and locatable in time and space. In contrast, the nonlinear is nonlocal, diffuse, beyond dimensions, and is influential, subjective, and experiential. Realization and comprehension of the nonlinear spiritual realities are the province of the mystic. The spiritual realm is one of context, whereas that of the linear is content. The spiritual field is all-inclusive yet beyond delineation in terms of merely time or space.

Transcending the Limitation of Paradigm

From the calibrated scale of the levels of consciousness, it is apparent that the scientific domain calibrates in the 400s, whereas spiritual realities begin to emerge in the high 400s but are only prevalent at the levels of 500 and above. The science of consciousness research (cal. 605) enables discernment of these levels by utilizing the distinctive energies inherent as the essence of each evolutionary level. To repeat, on the scale of 1 to 1,000, the levels below 200 indicate falsity, and from 200 and above, truth. Levels of Enlightenment are from 600 to 1,000, with 1,000 being the maximum level of consciousness possible in the human domain.

Whereas science and logic are described as 'provable', 'definable', and 'objective', spiritual realities are by necessity subjective (experiential). It is therefore impossible to 'prove' spiritual truth via linear logic or science, just as it has been pointed out that it is not possible to 'prove' love, significance, happiness, meaning, worth, inspiration, and other qualitative abstractions. Thus, it is not possible to either 'prove' or 'disprove' the reality of Divinity or the nonlinear dimension, including even the characteristics of consciousness itself (e.g., the pitfall of the skeptic).

Notable in publications, organizations, and endeavors addressed to 'science and religion' is the dominance of the entire field by academic intellectuals. Lacking are enlightened (cal. above 600), advanced scholars. Characteristically, the mystic autonomously realizes, comprehends, and 'becomes', whereas the scientist reasons and 'thinks about'. Thus, by virtue of the limitations and constraints of academic science (the consciousness level of the 400s), the entire world's greatest spiritual geniuses and enlightened teachings of all time (cal. 500 to 1,000) are excluded by the intellectual block of doubting the authenticity of the 'first-person subjective'. How then could there be a conference on 'science and spirituality' (all calibrate in the 400s) that completely eliminates the only source of actual spiritual information, which is primarily via report and testimony of the first-person subjective? (See *I: Reality and Subjectivity*.) The paradox is that *all* intellection is itself merely a 'first-person account' of subjective mentalization.

The linear dimension is the province of the objectively provable, whereas, in contrast, the nonlinear is affirmable, demonstrable, and confirmable but primarily intrinsic and subjective. The nonlinear is neither subject to nor definable nor describable by the linear because of the major differences between the two paradigms.

These contrasts of paradigm are classically noted, for example, by the differentiation between 'academic' (cal. 440) and 'clinical' (cal. 445) science. Whereas the former is constrained to statistical intellectual processes, the latter is inclusive of numerous influences of context, such as intention, integrity of purpose, and calibration level of participants. Thus, in medicine, the seasoned clinician utilizes not just the science but also the art of medicine and all appropriate modalities which experience has shown to be beneficial, including the introduction of so-called nontraditional modalities that are frequently essential to a positive outcome ("Paradigm Blindness," Hawkins, 2006). Thus, the author's life-threatening perforating duodenal ulcer that was impervious to all medical treatment was permanently cured after only three 'unscientific' acupuncture treatments (as reported in the lecture "Illness and Self-Healing," Hawkins, 1986).

The area of academics deals with predictables and statistics. The clinician deals with outcomes and results. Thus, to 'have a heart' is a requisite for the successful clinician, but not a measurable factor in academics. Paradoxically, the clinical success and experience of seasoned clinicians is often primarily with people who have not been responsive to scientific academia. This factor was a core discovery of the largest psychiatric practice in the United States over a twenty-five-year period (Hawkins and Pauling, 1973).

While academic science fails to recognize the validity of 'unscientific' ideology or methods, or even denigrates them, the clinician is more versatile, intellectually humble, and therefore interested in what actually works. Perhaps the best-known and universally recognized example is that of Alcoholics Anonymous, by which literally millions of the most hopeless have dramatically recovered, including many high-profile persons and celebrities. Also included in these spiritually based recoveries are many thousands of doctors and other professionals. The only requirement for recovery from hopeless and devastating addictive illnesses is the spiritual attitude of humility and the surrender to a higher power (Tiebout, 1999). Thus, the power and efficacy of spiritual premises is overwhelmingly and impressively demonstrable (the calibration level of twelve-step groups is 540).

The value of consciousness calibration research (which itself calibrates at level 605) is that it is inclusive of both the linear and the nonlinear domains and their respective paradigms of reality. It provides a continuum with verifiable crossovers of the two paradigms. This is most notable in the range of the calibration levels of the high 400s and then continues up through the 500s and into higher levels that include the saints (cal. 570-700), and then the great avatars, such as Jesus Christ, Zoroaster, Buddha, and Krishna (all at cal. level 1,000), all of whom have contextualized human life for many centuries.

The power of the consciousness levels of the 400s is exemplified by the great giants of science, such as Steinmetz, Edison, Galileo, Kepler, Newton, Einstein, Heisenberg, and Freud (see Chapter 5). As one can see by contrasting calibration levels of famous scientists with those of famous spiritual teachers, the level of the 400s indicates a crossover, showing that spiritual reality as such formally starts at level 500 and above.

Each level of consciousness above 200 contributes to the progress and fulfillment of the human potential. The great pyramids in Egypt built by the pharaohs were fashioned by human labor and linear engineering but were actually the result of the nonlinear factors of inspiration and intention, as were the great cathedrals of Europe (which calibrate at 700 and above).

It is notable that a consistently best-selling book in America in recent years has been *The Purpose-Driven Life* by evangelical minister Rick Warren. Its wide popularity is demonstrated by its availability at every truck stop in America. Its goal as well as appeal is to give meaning, spiritual value, and significance to life, and thus, like science, to make a major contribution to society and the value of human life.

Without science, millions of people die of diseases, but without adherence to spiritual values, they also die by the millions from scientifically developed explosives and nuclear weapons. Thus, it is said that science without faith is hollow and reckless, yet faith without good works is of limited social value. Wisdom combines both, for man lives simultaneously in both the linear and nonlinear domains.

While faith is confirmable, truth has untold benefits to humanity. Faith in falsehood is the greatest danger of all, as can be seen by history's calamitous wars and even today's eschatological Islamic terrorism, the concepts of which 'worship death', not life (as per bin Laden), and calibrate at an ominous 20. Verifiable truth in both science and faith is essential to human survival as well as happiness and fulfillment.

Content and Context

Context refers to an overall field that is inclusive of content. Content deals with specifics, whereas context refers to prevailing conditions, just as vegetation fluctuates with the seasons of the year. Often context is not specified, not known, or even suspected. Thus, biological phenomena (such as fertilization of an ovum by a sperm) have been recently discovered to be quite different in a zero-gravity condition, such as a space shuttle. This was previously unsuspected. Not uncommonly, healings and even miraculous events occur within a high-energy spiritual field (e.g., the saints).

Some therapists are simultaneously healers and have high recovery rates. The dominant influence of a contextual field is also demonstrated by migratory patterns or moon-phase-related biological activity of crustaceans that live deep in the sea (as so beautifully illustrated in the television documentary *Blue Planet* (cal. 480), which also reveals the exquisite aesthetics of evolution as creation).

Intention is thus a hidden but often crucial factor in determining outcome (the 'Heisenberg effect'). As was noted, even the simple muscle test for levels of consciousness/truth does not work unless done in an overall field that is at 200 or above. Thus, faith plus intention facilitate spiritual comprehension and discovery. Dedication to truth instead of the opinions of the ego facilitates the revelation of truth. Thus arises the saying, "Virtue is its own reward" in that it precipitates more beneficial outcomes with much less effort. "What is held in mind tends to manifest" is also a manifestation of the contextual field.

Manifestation via emergence is thus a function of not just linear causality, but also probability, depending on overall as well as local conditions, including human consciousness. Inasmuch as the power of Divinity is infinite, all of Creation is the ongoing manifestation of potentiality emerging into the actuality of existence itself. What is a possibility in a weak field becomes a probability in a stronger field and a certainty in a field of Infinite Power (e.g., Divinity).

In the human dimension, likelihood is an expression also of 'will', which is an expression of intention. Ordinary limitation is frequently overcome by intensity of volition which is exhibited even in major disasters that have widely divergent outcomes due to preexistent predisposing (karmic) propensities that are also operative as unseen factors.

Events that may serve the high Self do not always coincide with the wishes of the ego/self but serve the unseen higher purpose of the real Self. Human events represent the outcome of a multiplicity of unknown factors as though they are the final outcome of a series of fields of influence similar to banks of step-down transformers. Thus, without Divine Grace, life would come to a total standstill (calibrates as true at cal. 1,000).

Quantum Reality: Consciousness Research

As explained elsewhere, beyond the Newtonian dimension is an infinite field of consciousness itself in which there is no 'here' versus 'there', nor 'then' versus 'now', nor linear sequence of events. It is omniscient and includes all that has ever had existence.The instant a question is posed, the answer instantly arises simultaneously. Only that which actually exists is subject to the question, but it does not exist until the question is asked.

In the mathematics of the Heisenberg Uncertainty Principle, the energy of a real question facilitates the transition from possibility to its appearance as an actuality. This is analogous to the precipitation of dew as the temperature decreases and passes the 'dew point', which is dependent on humidity.

The higher the level of consciousness of the questioner/observer, the more likely is the 'collapse of the wave function' (potentiality) to manifestation as actuality. This is the basic mechanism of consciousness calibration methodology in which accuracy increases concordant with the level of consciousness of the questioner (Jeffrey and Colyer, 2007).

CHAPTER 4

Is Reality Subjective or Objective?

Introduction - Personal Identity: The 'self'

The mind is certain only in that it knows "I am me." Yet, what does 'me' indicate? The self is ostensibly unique, separate, and the focal point of attention yet also presumably similar to the 'self' of other people. People presume that the primary difference between themselves and others is physical or situational. Differences seem to arise from personal likes and dislikes, plus presumptions or even dichotomies, such as Descartes' "I think; therefore, I am," or should it be the other way around: "I am; therefore, I think" (Sturme, 2007)?

The sequence of internal and external events and experiences builds up data in the brain's memory banks so that the sense of 'I-ness' now includes serial internal as well as external events along a time-and-space track that is also owned as 'me' and 'my mind'. The mind thus progressively comes into possession of enormous amounts of data from multiple sources with multiple levels of meanings and significance. With progressive maturity, there arises the awareness of responsibility and accountability as well as degrees of freedom of action. Out of all these factors arises the image of subjective self as a primary, intentional, volitional agent in the execution of options and choices and the locus of experiencing. It is then also the decider, the chooser, and, therefore, the will.

From the inner self also arise instinctual needs, intentions, aversions, and attractions, the primary focus of which is in that phenomenon called 'experiencing'. The sense of self then shifts progressively as the sequential data processing compounds, and finally the mind concludes that *it is the experiencer* of events both past and present, within and without, as well as in the anticipated future. Thus, the mind concludes that it is primordial, causal, unique, individual, and separate from others, yet presumptively similar.

Out of this complexity arise the images of a personal as well as a social self (e.g., 'personhood'), and a personal identity as well as presumptions about the nature of human existence itself. This integrated singularity of self as 'me' has a history and a name and thereby becomes a personhood that is linked with a discrete body and its numerous animal instinctual functions, but it also has an innate sense of autonomy, with the self as a primary causal agent.

The totality of experiencing is denoted by the abstract term 'life'. The matrix of existence is affirmably biological, transient, and mortal, out of which arises the existential conundrum, "Whence did I arise? How do I know? How do I know that I know?" Thus, the individual faces the question of consciousness itself and its more abstract denotation as 'spirit'.

Evolution of the Self/Ego

As described, by utilization of the simple technique of consciousness research, the truth or falsehood of any statement can be quickly ascertained, as can the specific degree of certitude by means of a progressive, exponential scale of consciousness calibrated from 1 to 1,000, which includes all possibilities within and even beyond the human domain. The calibrated number is obtained by means of a blind, impersonal technique resulting in biologically based physiological responses that occur (like litmus paper) independently of personal opinion. It is comparable to taking a person's temperature or any other clinical laboratory data. (See Appendix C for methodology.) This capacity is merely an inherent responsive quality innate to biological life. The historical development of consciousness itself over great periods of time has been mapped and previously described elsewhere (Hawkins, 1995, 2006) and reprinted here for convenience.

Calibrated Levels of Consciousness

Animal Kingdom

Bacteria	1	Dolphins	95
Protozoa	2	Migratory birds	105
Crustaceans	3	Birds of prey	105
Insects	6	Rodents	105
Arachnids	7	Rhinoceros	105
Amphibians	17	Baboons	105
Fish	20	Song birds	125
Octopus	20	Doves	145
Sharks	24	Polar bear	160
Vipers	35	Grizzly bear	160
Komodo dragon	40	Water buffalo	175
Reptiles	40	Black bear	180
Predatory mammals		Jackal, foxes	185
(hyena, lion, tiger)	40	Wolves	190
Snakes	45	Hippopotamus	190
Alligators	45	Javelina	195
Dinosaurs	60	Grazers	
Whales	85	(zebra, gazelle, giraffe)	200

Deer	205	Dogs	245
Bison	205	Family dog	250
Domestic pig	205	Family pig	250
Elk	210	Black crow	250
Dairy cow	210	Oscar, famous cat	250
Sheep	210	Gorilla	275
Range cattle	210	Chimpanzees	305
Elephants	210	**Exceptions:**	
Monkeys	210	Alex, trained African gray	401
Farm horse	240	Koko (trained gorilla)	405
Cats	240	Song bird's song	500
Parrot, African gray	240	Cat's purr	500
Family cat	245	Dog's wagging tail	500
Race horse	245		

The consciousness-research muscle-response ('Truth Reflex') technique can be utilized by approximately one-third of the people in America (if they are integrous of intention). They have to calibrate over 200 and be more interested in arriving at the truth than at bulwarking a preferential viewpoint. The higher the level of consciousness of the participants (as pristine intention), the greater the accuracy (Jeffrey and Colyer, 2007).

By utilization of the simple technique, the qualities of consciousness expressed as thought, feeling, or knowingness can be analyzed and described along a progressive scale by which it is possible to obtain the specific degree of truth revealed by a set of questions and answers. (The muscle-strength test is the simplest, but there are others, such as pupillary response (Davis, 2007) or changes in brain function displayed by magnetic imaging. The physiological responses to truth versus falsehood are the current focus of extensive multimillion-dollar research by United States government security agencies (Applebaum, 2007), as well as current Transportation Security Administration 'Spot Security' systems in airports to detect possible terrorists.

By reflective self-inquiry, it will be discovered that thoughts and mentalizations are discrete, unique, separate, and different from each other and are therefore described as 'linear', which means they are definable as well as locatable in space, time, and relationship. In contrast, the capacity to become aware of that which is held in mind is consequent to the overall nonlinear field of awareness/consciousness itself. Thus, the field of consciousness is like the blank screen of the television set. The linear content is the program that can then be viewed. All experience is thus simultaneously that of content (perception, images, thoughts, feelings, etc.) illuminated by the nonlinear field of context (the light of consciousness/awareness).

The failure to make this distinction is why prevailing, supposedly scientific discussion and argument about the nature of consciousness is so limited and unproductive; it calibrates at 400 or commonly even lower. It is critical to differentiate the substrate infinite energy field of consciousness/awareness itself (cal. 600 and above) from its limited linear mental content (e.g., thoughts, images, feelings, and memories).

Consciousness is thus an impersonal 'given', but its content consists of linear definitions in time and space that are also a consequence of programming, which can be either deliberate or accidental. The mind of man is thus both subjective/experiential and selective as well as impersonal, nonselective, and unintentional.

Therefore, the mind is uncertain whether the screen or the program is really 'real'. Upon simple observation, it becomes apparent that the quality of consciousness/awareness is the primordial impersonal capacity intrinsic to the condition of life itself, but that its specific content is of personal historical development.

Is reality subjective or objective? At some point, the introspective mind ponders the truth of its qualities, that is, "How do I know? How do I know that I know? How do I know that which I presume to be truth is actually true?" In addition, "Whence arose life, and what is its source?" This subjective state is nonlinear, primordial, and a priori. Out of this impersonal field arises the very personal sense of 'I-ness' as a primary quality of content. This basic subjective sense of 'I' is capable of reflexive *self-knowing*, whereas, in contrast, the mind merely *thinks*.

As mentioned previously, René Descartes made the seminal observation that there is the mind itself *(res interna/cogitans)*, and then there is external reality (*res externa*—the world or nature as it is). The principle could be seen as a way of stating the difference between perception and essence. That there is often great disparity between the two conditions is the dilemma of humankind, as has been noted by the sages of history, such as in Socrates' dictum that man always chooses what appears to be the 'good', but his difficulty is that he cannot tell the 'real' good from that which is illusory (i.e., differentiate appearance from essence). Note that 'do-gooders' (cal. 190) frequently bring about long-term social disasters (Charen, 2004).

In all spiritual traditions and teachings, the recognition of this disparity is basic and fundamental, and recognition of man's primary defect is technically termed 'ignorance'. In consciousness research, the difficulty is seen to arise from the limitation of the degree of the evolution of consciousness itself (both personal and collective). Thus arise the problems of culpability versus responsibility and the consequences of one's choices and actions.

Construction of the Human Mind

In previous works and studies (Hawkins, 1995-2006), the structure of the human mind has been likened to a computer in that the mind's basic structure is akin to the hardware and its content to the software. The mind has limited control over the content of the programming; thus, the human is simultaneously accountable and responsible yet innocent.

In this information age, the mind's programming is incessant and constant, yet the mind is lacking in protective mechanisms; therefore, it can be made to believe anything by mere repetition no matter how outrageous or absurd, as was noted by Joseph Goebbels, the propaganda minister of Hitler's Third Reich. Such programming is likened to indoctrination that is outside of awareness. The human mind is actually unwittingly subject to constant indoctrination (see Horowitz, 2007).

The above is, of course, now common knowledge. Research of prison-guard/prisoner experiments (Milgram, 1974; Zimbardo, 2007) indicates that even normal people can be turned into cruel victimizers. This is also exemplified by the famous movie and book, *Lord of the Flies.*

Under appropriate conditions, primitivism that arises from deep within Freud's 'Id' can be activated, brought to the surface ('going postal'), and expressed via destructive activity as was shown by the slaughtering of thirty-two innocents by Virginia Tech University student Cho Seung-Hui (cal. 5!) in April 2007. This same primitivism has been demonstrated by school or workplace spree killers and in rampant criminality such as occurred in the aftermath of the Hurricane Katrina disaster, which was followed by genuine social anarchy. (One wonders at the sanity of purported anarchists when one views the catastrophe of actual real-life anarchy in contrast to its philosophical promulgation as social theory.)

In summary, the mind is so constructed via biological evolution that its capacity to discern even an operational reality from illusion and emotionalized misperception is not only impaired but also greatly limited. This limitation becomes most marked at calibration levels below 200, so the consciousness substrate of both personal and politicized violence can calibrate as low as 10 to 20 (e.g., terrorist indoctrination).

The brain's physiology itself is reflective of the level of consciousness as represented by the following very critical diagram of brain physiology.

BRAIN FUNCTION AND PHYSIOLOGY

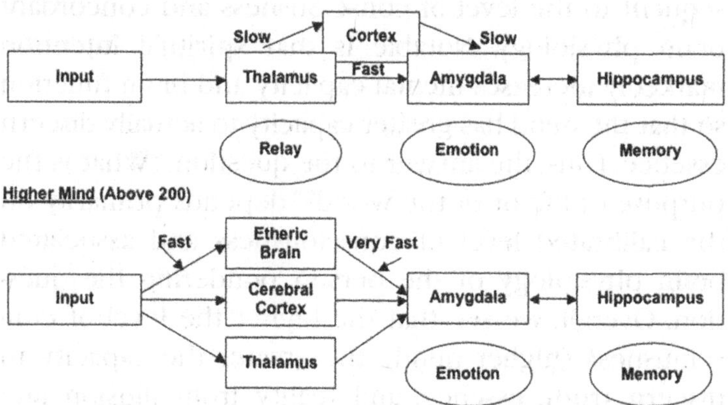

Below 200	Above 200
Left-brain dominance	Right-brain dominance
Linear	Non-linear
Stress—Adrenaline	Peace—Endorphins
Fight or flight	Positive emotion
Alarm—Resistance—Exhaustion (Selye—Cannon: Fight/Flight)	Support thymus
▼Killer cells and immunity	▲Killer cells
Thymus stress	▲Immunity
Disrupt acupuncture meridian	Healing
Disease	Balanced acupuncture system
Negative muscle response	Positive muscle response
▼Neurotransmitters—Serotonin	
Track to emotions twice as fast as through prefrontal cortex to emotions	Track to emotions slower than from prefrontal and etheric cortexes
Pupil dilates	Pupil constricts

Importance:

Spiritual endeavor and intention change the brain function and the body's physiology and establish a specific area for spiritual information in the right-brain prefrontal cortex and its concordant etheric (energy) brain.

The individual's capacity to recognize reality is consequent to the level of consciousness and concordant brain physiology. Notable is that spiritual intention markedly increases mental capacity and brain function so that the mind has greater capacity to actually discern essence. Thus, the answer to the question, "What is the purpose of life or of the world?" depends primarily on the calibrated level of consciousness and associated brain physiology of the person pondering the question. Overall, we see that the higher the level of consciousness (higher mind), the greater the capacity to discern truth, essence, and reality from illusion and emotionalized misperception (lower mind).

The Sense of Reality

The mind automatically assumes that it is continuously aware of reality, and it is unaware that what it considers to be reality is actually only its own presumptive inner processing function that has been termed 'the experiencer' (Hawkins, 2000-2006). Thus the data has already been automatically processed and edited via ego mechanisms within 1/10,000th of a second that have thereby added or subtracted value, meaning, and importance as well as emotional tone and shadings of memory and significance. What the ordinary mind presumes to be 'truth' is actually a processed composite of thousands of variables of differing degrees with superimposed editing, selection, distortion, and emotionalized, preferential evaluation. This editing is done unconsciously in 1/10,000th of a second and is not eliminated or bypassed until one reaches Enlightenment (cal. 600 and above).

Faith and Science

The term 'science' implies detached observation of data and the presumption of selfless objectivity via the dialectics of reason, rationality, and logic. The processing of data is considered 'objective' yet, at the same time, its value, significance, and meaning are all simultaneously the result of subjective colorations. While abstract fields of science are within the levels of the 400s (see Map of Consciousness), individual scientific experiments often fall far below the necessary level of Truth at 200 (e.g., 'junk science'). In fact, the same scientist can, at different times of life, perform research experiments that vary quite widely, from as high as 460 down to 170, due to the interference of intention.

An example of this is a recent study on the efficacy of prayer in promoting healing, which appeared in the *American Journal of Cardiology* (April 2006) and reported negative results. This, of course, is contrary to the wealth of literature that has arisen over the years affirming the opposite conclusion, along with the millions of recoveries in faith/prayer self-help groups. The research design of the years-long million-dollar study calibrates at only 170. (Oddly enough, this study was financed by the Templeton Foundation, which itself calibrates at 500.)

A similar example is Crick's research that resulted in the discovery of the DNA helix. That research calibrated at 440, while his last research project, which was designed to show that consciousness is solely the result of neural activity, calibrated at only 170. (He was an atheist.)

The deviation of science from authenticated truth

is rampant due to the favoritism of funding sources for politicized positionalities and promoted causes by which faith in science becomes 'scientism', with associated faith and blind enthusiasm. Thus, 'environmentalism' results in earth-warming panic as purportedly being due to human causes (greenhouse gases, etc.), which calibrates as false (cal. 190). Deep polar-ice drillings and other data indicate that earth-warming cycles are the consequence of the magnetic activity of the sun's surface (Lehr and Bennett, 2003; also Mehlman, 1997). Those studies calibrate at 455, which is the level of scientific validity. Note that while the mass of Arctic ice has diminished, the volume of Antarctic ice has increased even more than the Arctic loss.

The *Journal of the American Medical Association* (June 2005) reports that one-third of research reports are later proven to be in error. The collective research of the supposed dangers of secondhand smoke calibrates at 190 and was declared invalid by a federal court (Meier, 1998). Even the studies linking obesity to later-life diseases turned out to have been overstated by two hundred percent.

Another source of misleading scientific research reports is the misinterpretation of statistical correlation as causality. (The fact that ninety percent of people who develop tuberculosis wear brown shoes does not mean that brown shoes cause tuberculosis.) That statistical correlation is not causation was also reported by Austin in *The Economist* (February 2007). Paradoxically, the more prestigious the reporting institution, the greater is the likelihood of reporting error.

This is apparently due to the media's advantage of capturing a big name as a purported sponsor. Note that, historically, nearly all the great discoveries that have benefited mankind originated from very humble beginnings (e.g., Fleming's discovery that eventually led to the development of penicillin).

Due to the inherent defects and vagaries of the human mind, without consciousness calibration, it is not possible to actually ascertain the level of truth, even when it is expressed as intended. While the likelihood of bias may be suspected or intuited, it can only be conclusively detected and proven by consciousness research itself. It will then be discovered that profound falsehoods can be uncovered in almost any human endeavor. However, most people are influenced by the commonality of social beliefs (e.g., the earth is flat; the sun circles the earth) as well as those documented in the famous book, *Extraordinary Popular Delusions and the Madness of Crowds* (Mackay, [1841] 2003).

Dominance of Subjectivity

The sense of 'real' is the consequence of subjective processing, and thus all supposed 'objectivity' is itself a purely subjective presumption and conclusion. Intrinsic subjectivity is therefore the a priori premise of all mental processing, and it operates as a dominant premise. To be precise and specific, it can be said that 'objectivity' is itself a purely subjective presumption.

The sense of being 'real', however, also accompanies altered states of consciousness, such as dreams, hypnotic and 'oneric' (fugue) states, as well as hallucinations, delusions, and induced suggestions; UFO abductions (cal. 170); and out-of-body experiences of other realms and 'visions', such as astral trance.

In contrast are amnesic states that may be brief and transitory or may last for hours, days, or even longer. Long-lasting conditions are seen in compartmentalized split-personality disorders. Such 'Jekyll and Hyde' personalities do indeed exist, and the two personalities actually calibrate quite differently. Some of these cases played critically important roles in very serious security breaches, including atomic energy projects where the defection of high-profile double agents resulted in the current world's atomic bomb hazard (e.g., Robert Hansson, Klaus Fuchs, and the Rosenbergs).

Unsuspected compartmentalized personalities currently continue to pose a grave risk to security in the United States. They can be detected only by consciousness calibration techniques by which identification occurs quickly and easily. This would seem to be important in that in today's nuclear world, the lives of millions of innocent people are at risk.

CHAPTER 5

Science and Religion: Levels of Truth

Introduction

Conflict between science and religion is endemic to American society and has been the focus of even judicial issues over the decades, such as the arguments over eugenics in the 1930s, and now similar conflicts over stem-cell research or Darwinian theories. Valuable classification of the essence of the issues can be derived from application of consciousness research to their various elements.

The levels of consciousness are intrinsically impersonal and denote what have been called (in the field of nonlinear dynamics) energy 'attractor' fields (Hawkins, 1995), which dominate and are expressive of the infinite nonlinear source energy of all life. For convenience of investigation, the levels fall into general ranges for purposes of classification and description.

As we have noted, the major demarcation of Truth is at level 200. The 300s denote positive influence, and the 400s denote logic, reason, and the general realm of science, including chemistry, medicine, physics, astronomy, mathematics, astrophysics, and other areas. It is also interesting that the great geniuses of science over the centuries have calibrated in the high 400s, as do the authors of *The Great Books of the Western World* (with the exceptions of Marx and Engels), reprinted from Truth vs. Falsehood, for convenience.

Calibrations of The Great Books of the Western World

Aeschylus	425	Fourier	405	Mill, J. S.	465
Apollonius	420	Freud	499	Milton	470
Aquinas, Thomas	460	Galen	450	Montaigne	440
Archimedes	455	Galileo	485	Montesquieu	435
Aristophanes	445	Gibbon	445	Newton	499
Aristotle	498	Gilbert	450	Nicomachus	435
Augustine	503	Goethe	465	Pascal	465
Aurelius, Marcus	445	Harvey	470	Plato	485
Bacon, Francis	485	Hegel	470	Plotinus	503
Berkeley	470	Herodotus	440	Plutarch	460
Boswell	460	Hippocrates	485	Ptolemy	435
Cervantes	430	Hobbes	435	Rabelais	435
Chaucer	480	Homer	455	Rousseau	465
Copernicus	455	Hume	445	Shakespeare	465
Dante	505	Huygens	465	Smith, Adam	455
Darwin	450	James, William	490	Sophocles	465
Descartes	490	Kant	460	Spinoza	480
Dostoevsky	465	Kepler	470	Sterne	430
Engels	200	Lavoisier	425	Swift	445
Epictetus	430	Locke	470	Tacitus	420
Euclid	440	Lucretius	420	Thucydides	420
Euripides	470	Machiavelli	440	Tolstoy	420
Faraday	415	Marx	130	Virgil	445
Fielding	440	Melville	460		

The 400s express reliable, integrous, confirmative intellectual analysis of the linear domain and include the best efforts of the human intellect. This is the paradigm of reason, logic, and linear realities, which are characteristic of the scientific/rational/logical paradigm of human intelligence and comprehension. In this realm, the rules and dialectic of logic apply, as do the Kantian categories of abstraction. Affirmation of the characteristics of the level of the 400s is apparent from the chart of the calibrations of the greatest scientists over great expanses of time.

Reason: Great Scientists

Bernard, Claude	450	Jenner, Edward	450
Bohm, David	505	Kekule, Friedrich	440
Bohr, Neils	450	Kelvin, Lord (Wm. Thompson)	450
Burbank, Luther	450	Kepler, Johannes	465
Byrd, Adm. Richard	420	Mach, Ernst	460
Eddington, Arthur	460	Malthus, Thomas	480
Edison, Thomas	490	Maxwell, James	460
Einstein, Albert	499	Newton, Sir Isaac	499
Fleming, Sir Alexander	460	Pasteur, Louis	465
Freud, Sigmund	499	Plank, Max	460
Galvani, Luigi	450	Poincaré, Henri	430
Hawking, Stephen	499	Semmelweiss, Ignaz, Dr.	460
Heisenberg, Werner	460	Steinmetz, Charles	460
Helmnoltz, Hermann von	460	Teilhard de Chardin, Pierre	450
Huxley, Thomas	460		

Science is valid within its own linear paradigm, as was documented by the calibration levels of scientists over the centuries. In addition to affirming the level of truth of scientists, the calibrations of scientific theories themselves also document the degree of validity of reason, logic, and the paradigm of the linear realities of the 400s. Thus, the basis for Clarence Darrow's position has a solid but limited basis as was documented in the previous chapter.

Science—Theory

Theory	Calibration
Attractor Fields (Nonlinear Dynamics)	460
"Big Bang" Source-of-Universe Theory	False
Biofield	460
Black Hole Theory rev. 2004	455
Bootstrap Theory	455
Chaos Theory	455
Collective Unconscious (Jung)	455
Consciousness as consequence of neuronal Activity	140
Consciousness Calibration	605
Darwinian Theory of Evolution	450
Dinosaur Extinction Theory	200
Dirac Equations	455
Discovery of Double Helix of DNA	460
"Distant Healing"	False
Divinity as Source of Universe	Infinite
Drake Equation	350
Earth's magnetic field weakening	True
Earth slowly reversing magnetic poles	460
Earth warming due to pollution	False
Earth warming due to solar magnetic surface cycles	455
$E=mc^2$	455
Entanglement (Quantum Theory)	False
Frame Dragging	460
"Gaia" (planetary theory)	False
"God" gene	False
"Greenhouse" gas earth-warming theory	False
HeartMath	460
Heisenberg Uncertainty Principle	460
Hormesis	180
"Holographic Universe"	395
Inflation Theory (post-Big Bang)	450
Intelligent Design	480
Microbe Organisms on Mars	True
Mind Fields entangled with Divinity	True
Mind Fields entangled with others	False
Morphic Resonance	460
Morphogenetic Fields (Sheldrake)	460
M-Theory (formerly String Theory)	460
Multiple Universes	True
Newtonian Causality Principle	460
Nonlinear Dynamics	460
Prayer increases healing	True
Nuclear Fission reaction (actuality)	200
Nuclear Fission Theory	455

Organisms on Mars	True	"Steady State" Theory of on-going expansion of the universe	405
"Parallel Universe" Theory	False	Stem Cell research	245
Quantum coherence	460	Subparticle Physics	455
Quantum gravity	460	Telekinesis	True
Quantum Mechanics	460	Teleportation of quantum states (electrons in ions)	400
Schrödinger Equations	455	United States space program	400
Singularities	455	von Neumann Process	450
S-Matrix Theory	455		
Consciousness caused by Neuronal Activity	125		

Of interest is the recent report from the University of California at Santa Cruz that the floods reported in the Bible and other religious histories occurred in 2807 B.C. as the result of a huge comet that landed in the Indian Ocean (calibrates as true).

The benefits of science to human civilization are obviously enormous and touch every aspect of modern life. Clarence Darrow's faith in reason and logic was well founded on demonstrable reality. The error of his presentation, however, was his naïve presumption that religion belonged to the same paradigm of reality and should therefore meet the same criteria of logical scientific proof. Darrow thus represented the paradigm blindness of 'that's all there is,' which prevails in society as the political viewpoint of secularism (cal. 165) or skeptical scientism (cal. 190) and is a product of Lower Mind's limitation to pedestrian reductive materialism.

The science-versus-faith debate continues unabated as described in a major article in *Time* magazine (13 Nov. 2006) and recurrent public debates (Birmingham, Alabama, October 2007, et al.). Darrow's position is now argued by the polemics of Richard Dawkins, avowed atheist and author of *The God Delusion* (2006). The book is at calibration level 190. The religionist position is represented by Francis Collins, head of the Genome Project and author of *The Language of God: A Scientist Presents Evidence for Belief* (2006) at calibration level 400.

Of interest is that the Darwinian Theory of Evolution calibrates at 450, Intelligent Design at 480, Creation*ism* at 245, and Genesis (Bible) at 600. Divinity as the Source of life and the universe calibrates at the level of Infinity, and the great Avatars of history calibrate at 1,000.

Thus, from all the above recurrent discourse emerges the obvious conclusion as stated throughout this current study that the nonlinear is neither provable nor disputable from the linear paradigm of the reductionistic linear level of intellectualization. The linear describes only mechanisms and ignores context. All scientific viewpoints represent Descartes' *res cogitans*, or appearances, whereas spiritual reality represents *res externa*, or essence (Reality).

The realization of Divinity as the Source of life and creation emerges at calibration level 600 and is radically subjective and beyond mentalization. It is experienced by virtue of the field of consciousness itself and is devoid of all thought (as described in *Transcending the Levels of Consciousness* and *Discovery of the Presence of God*, along with autobiographical summaries in other books in this series [Hawkins, 1995-2007].)

An indication of the limitation of truth by polemics is revealed by attempts of persuasion by emotionalism (e.g., scientists 'outraged' at any credence given to religion and faith [Van Biema, 2006]). The truly integrous pursuit of truth is not characterized by polemics or emotion. (Antireligionism calibrates at 180.) Truth is not revealed by coercion or promotional proselytization. Its acceptance is the consequence of purity of intention and the level of consciousness of the inquirer. Marco Polo's discovery of the Far East was scoffed at by skeptics but held as provisional and worthy of investigation by objective investigators.

Proselytization is an expression of the vanity of the ego that seeks status through agreement or dominance. Truth is complete and total within itself and is therefore without needs. Thus, $E=mc^2$ is just a fact that is not in need of personal opinion nor hostile *ad hominem* attacks on Einstein's private life. The skeptical attack is often merely an expression of jealousy-based ill will, and envy is an indication of stinginess of spirit, which feels diminished by greatness. Thus, the Grinch hates Christmas, and the ego of the atheist secretly hates the Infinite Glory of God. In miserly fashion, the ego seeks to discredit the Absolute by which all of Creation's energy from the potentiality of the Godhead emerges into manifestation as never-ending Creation.

Evolutionary psychology (cal. 210) supports Darwinian theories via the mechanism of cognition as represented by the work of Daniel Dennett (2006) at calibration level 250. These arguments represent the efforts of cognition itself to try to comprehend realities that are, however, of a much higher dimension. Importantly, they confuse the linear content of consciousness with the nonlinear field of consciousness itself, which is like confusing the planets with the cosmos, or the clouds with the sky.

Atheism (cal. 165) is currently academically popular, very 'in the know', 'Hollywood', fashionable, chic, hip, cool, savvy, and 'modern'. Among elitists, God is passé, old hat, and fuddy-duddy. Absolutism and Reality are ridiculed by relativism's narcissistic positionality that all viewpoints are equally valid (as in Lewis Carroll's *Alice in Wonderland*). Relativism is the voice that actually represents the child's petulant, egocentric wishful thinking and fantasy (e.g., "A thing is only just what I say it is.").

While the reductionist arguments for 'bottom-up' seem learned to the unsophisticated, they sound very pedestrian and prosaic to the educated mind that, via a true liberal education, is accustomed to the erudition of the great classics of Western civilization which clearly define levels of abstraction and categorization of thought. In general, the greater cannot be disproved by the lesser. When transposed into levels of consciousness, those that are below level 200 are unable to comprehend higher paradigms. Thus, for analogous example, there are arithmetic, geometry, trigonometry, and then differential equations, quantum mechanics (the Heisenberg Uncertainty Principle), etc. There are *different levels*. Thus, mechanistic reductionism ('bottom-up' theories that calibrate at 185) does not even reach the realms it purports to disclaim. Even 'causality' itself pertains only to calibration levels of the mid-400s. The Realities of Creation, Divinity, and spiritual truths calibrate from 600 and above and cannot be refuted from the caliber of the positionalities of the levels of 190-250.

This nonintegrous bias is seen in the expressions of current antireligionists who are 'angry', 'upset', 'outraged', etc., by creationism. In contrast, a true seeker of truth is objective, nonpositional, and concerned with confirmable certainty, which means experiential confirmation and not emotionality.

The vanity of the ego (at 190) is endless and vainglorious in its grandiose delusion that it can disprove the existence of God. Cognition is only linguistic supposition confined to linear symbols, the limited content of mentation. That it has any actual objective reality at all is a purely subjective presumption.

Language is only descriptive appearance at best and not in the same category as essence. Experience is of a different level from symbols. Thus, the musical score of the opera or symphony does not create aesthetic delight, but only the music itself results in delight because it is of a different and higher paradigm level than the written score of musical symbols.

Why does the mind even struggle so valiantly to try to supplant Divinity? The answer is that it really refutes and secretly hates any sovereignty other than its own. That is the self-perpetuating core of narcissism. The mind can create opinions about the universe, but it cannot create the universe or even life, much less consciousness itself, which was the 'Light' of Creation as per Genesis (statement calibrates at Infinity). Critics of God do not address the Light (Godhead) itself, which is very far from the limited domain of simplistic mentation.

In contrast to the descriptively objective linear paradigm of reality represented by the levels of the 400s, nonlinear spiritual realities begin to express in the high 400s and then become dominant at level 500 (Love) on up to 1,000, which is the maximum power of energy possible in the human domain.

A chart of the world's religions, teachers, and teachings demonstrates a different paradigm in which the predominant reality is subjective and experiential rather than objective and provable, which characterizes the limitations of the 400s. (The following is reprinted from *Truth vs. Falsehood* for convenience.)

Spiritual Teachers

Abhinavagupta	655	Gandhi, Mahatma	760
Acharya	480	Gangaji	475
Allen, James	505	Goldsmith, Joel	480
Aquinas, Saint Thomas	570	Gupta, Mahendranath	505
Augustine, Saint	550	Gyalpo, Lamchen Rinpoche	460
Aurobindo, Sri	605	Hall, G. Manley	485
Bertalanffy, Ludwig van	485	Holmes, Ernest	485
Besant, Annie	530	Hopkins, Emma Curtis	485
Black Elk, Wallace	499	Howard, Vernon	480
Bodhidharma	795	Huang, Chungliang Al	485
Bohm, Jakob	500	Huxley, Aldous	485
Bucke, Richard M.	505	John, Saint, of the Cross	605
Buddhananda, Swami	485	Karmapa	630
Butterworth, Eric	495	Kasyapa	695
Calvin, John	580	Khantsa, Jamyung	495
Chandra, Ram	540	Kline, Jean	510
Confucius	590	Krishna, Gopi	545
Dalai Lama (Tenzin Gyatso)	570	Lawrence, Brother	575
de Chardin, Teilhard	500	Leadbeater, C. W.	485
Dilgo Khyentse Rinpoche	575	Linpa, Kusum	475
Dionysius, the Areopagite	490	Luther, Martin	580
Dogen	740	Madhva Charya, Sri	520
Druckchen Rinpoche	495	Magdeburg, Mechthild von	640
Dzogchen Rinpoche	510	Maharaj, Nisargadatta	720
Eckhart, Meister	705	Maharshi, Ramana	720
Eddy, Mary Baker	495	Maezumi, Hakuyu Taizan	505
Erasmus	500	Merton, Thomas	515
Fillmore, Charles	515	Moses de Leon of Granada, Rabbi	720
Fillmore, Myrtle	505	Mukerjee, Radhakamal	475
Fox, Emmett	470	Muktananda	655
Gaden Shartse	470	Nanak	495

Naranjo, Claudio	465	Rumi	550
Nityananda, Bhagavan	500	Sai Baba, Shirdi (not Sathya)	485
Origen	515	Sannella, Lee	505
Otto, Rudolph	485	Satchidananda, Swami	605
Padmasambhava	595	Shankara (Sankara Charya)	710
Pak Chung-Bih, Sotaesan	510	Smith, Joseph	510
Palmo, Tenzin	510	Socrates	540
Paramahansa, Yogananda	540	Steiner, Rudolf	475
Patanjali	715	Suzuki, Master Roshi	565
Patrick, Saint	590	Swedenborg, Emanuel	480
Paul, Pope John II	570	Tagore, Rabindranath	475
Phuntsok, Khempo	510	Tauler, Johann	640
Pio, Father	585	Teresa, Mother	710
Plotinus	730	Teresa, Saint, of Avila	715
Po, Huang	960	Tillich, Paul	480
Poonjai-Ji	520	Tzu, Chuang	595
Powell, Robert	525	Tzu, Lao	610
Prabhavananda, Swami	550	Underhill, Evelyn	460
Prejnehpad, Swami	505	Vivekananda	610
Pulku, Gantey Rinpoche	499	Watts, Alan	485
Ramakrishna	620	White Brotherhood	560
Ramdas, Swami	570	White Plum Asanga	505
Ramanuja Charya, Sri	530	Yukteswar, Sri	535

Interestingly, although the Scopes ("monkey") trial itself was artificially contrived, the primary contestants were themselves authentically representative of their respective positionalities. William Jennings Bryan's presentation calibrated at 505 and that of Clarence Darrow at 450; thus, there was an irresolvable conflict because each side represented a different paradigm of reality. In addition, Darrow intellectually was a secularist while Bryan was a man of religious and spiritual faith.

By contrasting the paradigms of science (the 400s) with that of spiritual faith and religious realities (500 and above), it is apparent that the issues could not be resolved solely on their own levels but only by recognition that they represented the viewpoints of different paradigms of reality. "Science and religion exist in different boxes" (Gould, 2002).

The linear is temporal, circumscribed, logical, provable, and objective. The nonlinear is influential, subjective, experiential, unrestricted, and contextual rather than provable. Levels below 200 are actually destructive, but levels in the 400s are constructive. From the 500s and above, they are uplifting, inspirational, and empowering. It would therefore seem that the most beneficial combination would be that of love and faith, plus reason, in which logic and reason are instituted in the service of love for self and others as well as Divinity (as per St. Thomas Aquinas). The hallmark of this combination is seen as compassion, which takes into consideration mankind's naïveté, limitation, and Achilles' heel of blind ignorance of even the nature of its very own mind.

The overall consciousness of humanity only crossed over the level of 200 in the late 1980s. A primary difficulty of human life is, and has been, that the subpopulations of different levels of consciousness are thrown in together so that conflict is inevitable, as demonstrated by the previously cited fact that man has been overtly at war during ninety-three percent of recorded time. One might postulate that during the other seven percent of the time, the lack of war was probably due to some other catastrophe (e.g., the Black Plague, famine, etc.).

As is apparent from the above, explanations of the source and nature of the universe represent conceptualizations from different levels of consciousness as well as progressive paradigms from the literal pedestrian to the advanced consciousness levels of Enlightenment and the revelations taught by the great spiritual teachers of history.

An innate quality of creation is evolutionary progress, as demonstrated by the organic expressions of life. Whether the source of life is considered to be a random chemical accident (bottom-up theory), or Divinity (top-down theory), the fact that it is evolutionary is certainly documentable and strikingly obvious.

The term 'creation' is an abstraction that implies emergence, appearance, and progressive existence of increasing complexity and efficacy. Every field of human inquiry has been progressive; simultaneously, the universe has been expanding in infinite directions at the speed of light. With a little reflection, it would appear that there really is no conflict between Evolution and Creation for they are intrinsically one and the same process (e.g., Creation is progressive, ongoing, continuous, unfolding, and emerging as Evolution).

Darrow's arguments tended to focus on Biblical passages that were inclusive of primitive myths and legends which were allegorical and of cultural moral value rather than provable scientific statements. By faith, these could be believed to be literally historical facts even though they appear to be fallacious to logic and reason. Actually, the realization of Divinity as the Source of Creation does not depend on literal belief in associated folklore that is primarily allegorical, just as the truth of Buddhism does not rest upon believing whether the Buddha actually sat under a bodhi tree.

Scientific validity was not yet born at the time of the assemblage of ancient scriptures. To a sophisticated mind, whether the Red Sea actually parted or Jonah lived for three days in the stomach of a whale is irrelevant to the basic truths presented. Their appeal is to the mind's attraction to the presumably miraculous nature of the described ancient events.

The naïve mind is attracted to mystification and the seeming magic and sensationalism of the miraculous for it cannot discern essence. Thus, average people are impressed by stories of the miraculous, which are perceived as a major physical demonstration and validation of the power and presence of unseen Divinity.

The Miraculous

The average person is impressed by (or alternatively, dubious of) descriptions of the miraculous because the phenomena are rarely recognized as such below consciousness level 570, which itself is a level that is reached by only a small fraction of the world's population (less than 0.1%). Because the great majority of miraculous events falls outside the range of ordinary perceptual experience, they are generally unrecognized, and even when perceived, they are dismissed as merely being 'lucky', 'fortuitous', or 'accidental'. In contrast, truly scientifically verified miracles do actually occur as documented by the thorough investigations of the many miracles of Lourdes and other faith-based miraculous phenomena, such as religious stigmata or the long-term incorruptibility of the bodies of dead saints (calibrates as true).

Although ordinary people may experience the miraculous on occasion, they have no adequate context within which to comprehend the actual reality of the event. As a possible rational explanation, the famous psychiatrist Dr. Carl Jung had proposed the concept of 'synchronicity'. Reports of the miraculous, however, are not infrequent among survivors of major disasters and are reported in first-person accounts relatively often in such documentaries as *Storm Stories* on television's Weather Channel. Almost all survivors report that they prayed intensely or were even lifted up by a tornado into a state of Infinite Peace and Stillness (cal. 600). Thus, it can be noted that deep faith and surrender tend to favor the occurrence of the miraculous.

To provide a context for understanding the miraculous, the following excerpts, with added explanation, are from *Transcending the Levels of Consciousness*, Chapter 6, reprinted for convenience:

Spiritual Phenomena and the Siddhis

From consciousness level 540 and up into the higher 500s, phenomena occur spontaneously that are inexplicable by reason, the customary conceptualization of logic, or by cause and effect. They are an accompaniment to the progressive dominance of the spiritual energy (kundalini) and occur as a consequence of the contextual field rather than by volition. They are witnessed and seen to occur autonomously. These have been classically termed siddhis (Sanskrit) and denote seemingly 'supranatural' or 'miraculous/mystical powers', as they are not explicable by logic.

These begin to appear at approximately consciousness level 540 and become prominent by level 570. "While the early stages of their appearance they may be sporadic, as consciousness advances, they become frequent and sometimes continuous. They are autonomous, unintended, and arise nonvolitionally of their own accord. These phenomena include faculties such as distant viewing, precognition, clairvoyance, clairaudience, extrasensory perception, psychometry, bilocation, and the occurrence of the truly miraculous, including spontaneous healings and transformations as well as unique facilitations that are beyond expectation or possible explanation.

The capacities or phenomena are not within personal control; they are not the consequence of 'cause and effect'. Therefore, when they occur, students are cautioned not to claim them as personal as they occur independently of the person's 'I', or self. Thus, as said previously, no 'person' performs miracles for they are solely a consequence of the Spirit. Inflation of the spiritual ego is precluded by honesty and humility as well as by rejecting the temptation of exploitation for gain.

In the author's personal experience, the phenomena tend to emerge and become strong for variable durations of years. Some then seem to fade away and become sporadic and less predominant, while others continue permanently.

The spiritual kundalini energy flow is itself extraordinary in that subjectively, the sensation can only be described as exquisite as it flows up the back and into the brain. It may then emerge through the heart chakra and then go on out into the world where its presence facilitates the unfoldment of the truly wondrous. The occurrences are witnessed as happening without intention. It is as though Divine qualities are brought into manifestation via higher realms that transcend the mundane physical world.

In previous research, it was substantiated that Jesus' famous thirty-three miracles were indeed actual phenomena, and that they were observed by others. They are major demonstrations that "In God, all things are possible," and the historic examples subserved as teaching instruments that substantiated and confirmed the Divine incarnation of Jesus (cal. 1,000). Advanced spiritual devotees often witness very numerous but less dramatic unfolding of miracles. Such occurrences tend to become more numerous and frequent and may also be witnessed and confirmed by other observers.

The 'miraculous' represents the emergence of potentiality into physical actuality by virtue of the influence of the power of context (when local conditions are also favorable). Events represent manifestation of the influence of nonlinear power, including intention, which activates linear potential (e.g., the Heisenberg Uncertainty Principle). It is this unseen 'Higher Power' (nonlinear contextual field) that facilitates the recoveries of millions of people in faith-based recovery groups such as Alcoholics Anonymous and A Course in Miracles, plus the healings that occur in proximity to saints, highly evolved devotees, Lourdes, and spiritual Teachers. These have been reported throughout history and are documented as well as witnessed by observers.

Thus, by consciousness calibration research, the miraculous is confirmable as a reality. Such phenomena have historically profoundly impacted human experience as have the numerous reports of the near-death experience (cal. 625), which have often been dramatically life changing and transformative (Siegel, 1986).

As history attests, the occurrence of the miraculous has had profound consequences and changed not only the personal lives of thousands but also world history when it occurred to world leaders who became converts (e.g., Saul of Tarsis who became St. Paul).

Ancient Rome worshipped the pagan Roman gods, but in the year 312, the emperor Constantine had a miraculous vision in the sky of a sign from God of the Divinity of Christ. His consciousness jumped from level 200 to 350. He had the sign put on the shields of the Roman warriors who were thenceforth always victorious. Constantine then proclaimed Christianity as the religion of the Roman Empire and thus eventually for all of Europe.

From an historical viewpoint, it can be seen that the basic overall context and primary structure of Western civilization was the consequence of the miraculous in its emergence through Jesus Christ, St. Paul, and Emperor Constantine. While these major examples may seem to be remote in recent times, the miraculous experience of Bill W. (Wilson), the famous founder of Alcoholics Anonymous, spawned the twelve-step recovery movement through which millions of people have recovered from not only alcoholism but also many other grave and incurable human conditions. All the self-help programs came out of Bill W.'s revelation, which calibrates at 575 (sainthood).

The dissolution of the dominance of the ego

precedes the emergence of the miraculous. Intense prayer and surrender to God can be consequent to crisis ('hitting bottom') and despair, but it can also be the result of integrous intention and dedication. A Course in Miracles, which emerged in recent decades, provides an orderly progression of practices that lead to the ego's dissolution via insight and by means of following the recovery steps (the workbook calibrates at 600, the textbook at 550). The lives of many people have been transformed, and recovery from serious ailments has also occurred, thus attesting to the validity of the name of the yearlong course.

Eventually, the seemingly 'extraordinary' becomes a new reality as though one now lives in a different dimension in which the ostensibly impossible manifests effortlessly as though orchestrated. The power of the field autonomously facilitates the emergence of karmic potentiality into a manifested actuality in a harmonious unfoldment. The dynamics are nonlinear and therefore incomprehensible to the intellect, which presumes the limitations of the linear Newtonian model of causality and is unable to conceptualize emergence, Divine Order, or Harmony.

While reason and logic are powerful tools, they have their limitations, and Nature still holds many inexplicable mysteries. Thus, although the chances of being struck by lightning are approximately one in one hundred million, a still-living forestry worker was struck by lightning on five different occasions. Also provocative is the story presented by *Fox News* in July, 2007, of the now famous cat "Oscar" (cal. 250) that consecutively correctly identified twenty-six patients who died within four hours of his cuddling next to them in a nursing home. Thus, as the common saying goes, "Truth is stranger than fiction."

CHAPTER 6

Social Reality and Levels of Truth

While calibrating the levels of consciousness and their expressions may seem to be academic and abstract, the consequences of their actual social impact are profound, concrete, and extensive. Each level reveals possibilities as well as limitations of awareness and concordant brain-function capacity for comprehension. These then reflect a presumptive worldview of 'reality' and therefore presumptive 'truth'. They also result in characteristic political, intellectual, and even geographical social groupings with very different expectations, requirements, and styles of expression. These social constellations also include different communication styles as well as moral standards and ethical premises that in turn influence presumptions about relationships and social roles.

Choices and options often reflect subtleties and nuances of projected symbols and values that are in themselves implicit signals of group and cultural identifications. The different levels also have their own characteristic ideals as well as their symbols of worth. These complexities interact and are then reflected back to society via the politicized media, which superimpose yet another layer of influence and interpretation. This editorial influence further compounds the process of perception so that essence or verifiable truth becomes progressively more obscure and frustratingly difficult or even impossible to discern.

In today's world, the Scopes' dilemma persists in its expressions as materialistic secularism versus traditional religions and their respective ethics and morality. Paradoxically, both science and religion are equally based on faith, trust, and belief and are bulwarked by the authority of impressive literature and historical documentation (see McGrath, 2005). As seen by even brief analysis, each paradigm draws from a different realm of presumptive reality with no means of crossover except for the useful methodology of consciousness calibration research itself.

The term 'secular' falls below the critical level of truth at 200 when it becomes an 'ism' ('ism' calibrates at 180), which implies that it is a limited, positionalized viewpoint. There is actually no inherent conflict between religious or secular viewpoints until they are converted to ideological 'isms' and thus imply a claim to emotionalized exclusivity.

Conflict exists in the mind of the observer and not in that which is observed. William Jennings Bryan's views of religious truth (cal. 505) were not confirmable by the laws of science, nor were Darrow's restricted views of mundane reason and logic (cal. 450) applicable to the realms depicted by religion.

The levels of consciousness of spiritual realities denote nonlinear dimensions, which are related primarily to *context*, essence, and realm rather than to provable, factual specifics of linear *content*. The Bible utilizes parables, myths, legends, allegories, and metaphors to illustrate principles rather than the use of specifics so that the literal factuality of Biblical stories is operationally irrelevant. Meaning is an abstract category of nonlinear thought and reason (e.g., Kantian levels) and its symbolism is not compatible, concrete, literal terminology.

We see the same principle illustrated by the wisdoms that are revealed solely by humor. A joke is not a factual statement but instead utilizes paradox or hyperbole to clarify reality by the use of ambiguity. Like the fable, humor is a means of crossing over parameters of paradigm. The same principles are illustrated by fiction and fairy tales as well as poetry and all forms of art. The mechanism is often one of contrast or purposeful distortion in order to highlight significance, implication, and meaning.

It is a mistake to confuse the abstract and the literal. Thus, we could summarize the Scopes' conflict as being incompatibility of the literal versus the abstract levels of comprehension and presentation. Truth can be obscured or rejected but it cannot be disproved.

Conflict in Today's Social Dialogue

The human ego is an evolutionary development that originated in the instinctual realm of the animal (the hominids), and it is still invested in the desire to 'win' and thus gain status via rivalry, contention, and control of turf (e.g., hegemony). This endemic social style is thus primarily contentious and made to order for gain and media attention. The downside is the exploitation of the principle of freedom of speech and its extrapolation to unbridled extremes of expression, the boundaries of which are under constant attack via relativism and social anarchists whose dream is a society with no rules or restrictions, where all forms of expression are of equal value and validity, and where even overt falsehood has equal value and credibility with Truth.

The distorted presumptions and promotional idealizations of the 'post-modern' world are consequent to fallacious intellectual/sociological/philosophical theories of recent decades; all of them primarily boil down to Marxist dialectic elaborations of 'relativism' (ethical, moral, social, cultural, etc.). Their inherent defects are demonstrated by consciousness calibration levels of recent influential philosophies (excerpted from *Truth vs. Falsehood* for convenience).

Problematic Philosophies

'Academic Left'	180	Multiculturalism	180
Afrocentrism (Racism)	180	Nihilism	120
Anarchism	100	Pacifism	185
Atheism	165	**Philosophical Theories:**	
Authoritarianism	180	Baudrillard, Jean	175
Conspiracy Theories	135	Caputo, John	185
'Critical Theory' (Marcuse)	150	Derrida, Jacques	170
Deconstructionism	190	Foucault, Michel	190
Demonize	80	Husserl, Edmund	195
Dialectical Materialism	135	Irigaray, Luce	155
'End Justifies the Means'	120	Kristeva, Julia	150
Epistemological Relativism	190	Kuhn, Fritz	195
Eugenics	105	Lacan, Jacques	180
Fascism (Secular)	80	Lyotard, Jean-Francois	185
Fascism (Theocratic)	50	Menchu, Rigoberta	180
Fascism (Islamic/Militant)	50	Marcuse, Herbert	150
Feminist Politics (Sexism)	185	Marx, Karl	135
Hate	70	Moral Equivalence	170
Hedonism	180	Olsen, Karl	160
Iconoclasm	175	Popper, Karl	185
Irresponsibility	195	Sartre, Jean-Paul	200
'ism' (suffix)	180	Singer, Peter	195
Libertarianism	180	Vidal, Gore	180
Misanthropy	180	Zinn, Howard	200

Political:		Rhetoric	180
Far Left	135-195	Ruthlessness	180
Far Right	135-195	Skepticism	160
Far-Right Radical	80	Slander	75
Far-Left Radical	80	'Social Justice' doctrine	190
Revolutionary	100	Social Relativism	185
Relativism	185	Sophistry	180
Reactionary	155	Syncretism	195
Pop Sociology	165-210	Theocratic Totalitarianism	50
Populism	200	Vituperation	75
Racism	110	Xenophobia	185

Notable is that the calibration of current 'free speech' in the United States is at level 180, whereas free speech during the World War II era calibrates at 255.

As can be seen by their low calibration levels, these popularized relativistic philosophies all guarantee serious negative social consequences and are therefore primarily destructive in social impact, as historically demonstrated by the Marxist regimes of Pol Pot, Stalin, Chairman Mao, Fidel Castro, and other totalitarian 'liberator' regimes.The impact is also seen in the serious decline of the consciousness calibration of current academia in which writings of fallacious relativistic philosophies calibrating at level 180 or lower are substituted for the intellectual integrity of classical philosophy (cal. 450) as represented by *The Great Books* (with the exception of Marx at 130 and Engels at 200).

While academia collectively calibrated at 440 in 1955, it has now fallen (in 2007) to the current level of 180, intellectual anarchy. (See Goshgarian, 2005; Horowitz, 2007.) In response to this major tragedy, the Intercollegiate Studies Institute of Wilmington, Delaware, has published a list of traditional colleges that collectively happen to calibrate at level 440 (*ISI Guide to All-American Colleges*, 2006). For example, Texas A&M calibrates at 440.

Social conflict, including the international 'conflict of civilizations', can be readily characterized as the clash of paradigms between the levels below 200 and those above 200. For example, Hugo Chavez, the Venezuelan dictator (cal. 90), waved a book by Noam Chomsky (*Hegemony or Survival*) in the air at his public appearance (September 2006). He was embraced later on by American political 'activists' (who calibrate at 170) even as he closed down public television and freedom of speech. Extremist Hollywood activists routinely run to be seen hugging draconian mass-murderer dictators, such as Castro, Saddam Hussein, or Che Guevara. One could postulate that the only reason they do not flock to salute and kiss bin Laden is that they cannot find him.

Hegemony means "dominant influence, especially of one nation over others" *(Webster's Dictionary)*. From an evolutionary viewpoint, this is the predominant pattern of nature both between as well as within species (e.g., the alpha male of animal packs). This is also innate to Homo sapiens and human organizations, countries, and cultures. It is also innate to economics and corporate/financial/political realities that now emerge and reflect the hegemony of the competition of the media for dominant ratings. (All the above is demonstrated in the popular, humorous Animal Planet channel television series, *Meerkat Manor*.)

"May the best man win" is a biological/evolutionary social principle of survival that is innate to all forms of life and well represented in human history by the shifting dominance of various empires (e.g., Mongol, Ottoman, Goths, Huns, Roman, British, etc.). It is easy by means of sophistry to demonize dominance as 'wrong', which characterizes relativism by which the majority is always blamed for the limitations and misfortunes of the minority. Thus, dominance of a culture or enterprise becomes demonized and the target of vituperation (e.g., America, classic philosophy and reason, morality, ethics, religion, Wal-Mart, the Boy Scouts, and the founders of America as 'Dead White Men'). Interestingly, the 'liberators' from a revolutionized culture themselves then personally take on all the very same characteristics (e.g., Castro, Chairman Mao, Hitler, and 'presidents for life'). Thus, the cure is worse than the disorder. Paradoxically, relativism seeks dominance (e.g., hegemony) of the culture by resort to even the most extreme means, including blatant, gross falsehoods such as the teachings of Joseph Goebbels.

The new promise is that the hegemony of relativistic secularism will free the populace from the 'oppression' of ethics, morality, verifiable truth, and personal responsibility. The academic sophists purport to free the population from the 'oppression' of reason and logic and usher in the new hegemony of postmodernism as atheistic anarchy and chaos. By this supposedly Utopian transition, YouTube.com will ostensibly replace the Holy Grail, and America will transform into all the Islamic characterizations of the

'Great Satan' with a religion of narcissistic hedonism (cal. 160). (In contrast, traditional *God in America* [Gingrich, 2006] calibrates at 480.) Even business Web sites are the target of endless pornographic solicitations and overly offensive vulgarity.

In the United States, this conflict of civilizations is represented by the examples of the America Civil Liberties Union in contrast to the Alliance Defense Fund (ADF, cal. 480), or the American Civil Rights Union (ACRU, cal. 460). This conflict is not surprising in that the ACLU was founded by Roger Baldwin, and the ADF was founded by a group of Christian ministers. It was Baldwin who engineered the Scopes trial. His motivation was not to establish liberty but to destroy religion altogether and attract publicity. He was a communist sympathizer and follower of Karl Marx (Sears and Osten, 2005).

Relativism

Despite the warnings of Pope Benedict (the deleterious impact of Islam and Relativism), Western civilization is still primarily oblivious to the realization of its decline (calibrates as true; see *Truth vs. Falsehood*, Chapter 12), and that its basic structure and very underpinnings have been sabotaged and weakened to a major degree by pervasive, deleterious philosophical indoctrination. This originates from the ideological culture of intellectuals whose fallacious premises became popularized and gained political fervor primarily in the 1960s. Even its most fervent proponents were and still are generally unaware of its origins. Because of hyped popularity, the basic premises escaped examination and were naïvely accepted at face value as though they had some intrinsic validity.

The actual vulnerability of society was the fact that fifty-five percent of people in the United States are intrinsically unable to discern truth from falsehood, or perception from essence. It was via this large segment that the rhetoric of relativism gained favor, aided and abetted by the media and the celebrity culture. This phenomenon is a contemporary popular example of *Extraordinary Popular Delusions and the Madness of Crowds* (Mackay).

The impact of relativism on Western civilization is the exact opposite to that which ensued from the era of enlightenment that superseded the Dark Ages and replaced ignorance with reason, logic, and rationality and an education based on truth, morality, and integrity. The intellectual core of the Age of Enlightenment was the erudition of the great minds of history, from the Golden Age of ancient Greece to great intellects represented collectively in *The Great Books*. Classic erudition calibrates (as does *The Great Books*) from level 440 on up to 499 and is the intellectual basis for free speech via the United States Constitution and the Bill of Rights. In contrast, relativism calibrates from 180 to 190 or even lower in many of its expressions as per the following chart:

RELATIVISM VS. REALITY (A)

Reality/Truth/Essence		Relativism/Appearance/Illusion	
Absolutism	650	Relativism	125-190
Earth temperature due to Sun	455	*Inconvenient Truth*	180
Academia (1955)	440	Academia, U.S. (2007)	180
Professors, U.S. (1955)	440	Professors, U.S. (2007)	180
Logical Integrity	400-499	Sophistry, rhetoric	180-190
Traditional Morality	490	Hedonism	180
Hollywood (1955)	265	Hollywood (2007)	180
Hays Movie Code (1955)	430	Sundance Film Festival (2007)	165
Boy Scouts, Girl Scouts	450	NAMBLA	140
Classic Philosophy	440-485	Frankfurt School	130-180
Aristotle	498	Marcuse, H. (Critical Theory)	150
Sophocles	465	Relativistic Philosophy	130-190
Huang Po	960	Atheism	190
People of the Lie (Peck)	450	Conspiracy Theories, paranoia	90-110
Modernism	400	Postmodernism	180
Intellectual Morons (Flynn)	440	Ethical, moral, social relativism	180
U.S. Society (in 2007)	421	World overall (2007)	205
Cable News	410-440	Huffington Post, MySpace, YouTube	140
Prefrontal cortex (human)	200	Limbic/amygdala (animal)	120
Discretion	375	Vilification, desecration	120
Statue of Liberty	500	Flying Imam's plane setup	180
Abstract thought	450	Concrete thinking	190
Meaning	450	Definition	200
'Higher Mind'	275	'Lower Mind'	155
Friendly	255	Hostile	125
Stand up for the truth	500	Tolerance	190
World as karmic expression	575	World unfair	200
World as karmic opportunity	600	World exploitive	180
Traditional religion (U.S. impact)	450	Secularism	190

Destruction of society by iteration	510
"Money Trumps Peace"	355
Call a spade a spade	490

The infiltration of relativism was accelerated by celebrity popularization as the antiestablishment 'cause' of the 1960s, which politicized and glamorized adolescent rebellion and hedonism via memes and slogans, e.g., Timothy Leary, "Turn On, Tune In, and Drop Out" (cal. 180), etc. Anti-tradition meant dropping allegiance to rationality, ethics, morality, and personal responsibility, resulting in refutation of religion as the historical source and basis of morality and law. This was facilitated by the pseudointellectualists of the Far Left in the 1950s and 1960s via the flirtation of Hollywood celebrities' with communism and its sympathizers, during which the McCarthy Hearings added fuel to the fire. From the viewpoint of the social protesters of the Vietnam War era (cal. 170), the "Great Generation" of the World War II era (cal. 470 to 480) seemed staid and unexciting in comparison to the carnival of 'hippiedom', drugs, sex, and rock-and-roll.

While the ideological revolution was presumed to be the consequence and reaction to world events, in actuality, it was based on a new, revolutionary, radical interpretation of basic Marxism but couched in purposely non-Marxist terminology.

The actual philosophical premises of the relativistic 'leftist' revolution were derived from the Frankfurt School of philosophies and social activists of whom Herbert Marcuse was a primary literary protagonist and standard-bearer. His basic teachings (cal. 150) were that truth is falsehood and falsehood is actually truth. How such an absurdity could arise and even gain ground is beyond comprehension. The basic irrationality of this rhetorical system of thought is addressed in some detail in Truth vs. Falsehood (see "Relativism" in Chapter 12). Its social presentations are obvious as illustrated by the following chart.

RELATIVISM VS. REALITY (B)

Reality/Truth/Essence		Relativism/Appearance/Illusion	
Absolutism	650	Relativism	125-190
Discern essence from appearance	600	"Perception is reality"	190
Descartes (res interna vs. externa)	490	Marx (victim/perpetrator)	130
Plato	485	Protagoras	190
Jesus, Buddha, Krishna	1,000	Atheism	165
The Apostles	990	Skepticism	130-160
Socrates	570	Chomsky, N. (writings)	135-185
Great Books of the Western World	465	"Dead white man"	130
Science	440-499	"Science is oppressive"	160
Plotinus	503	Marcuse, H. (writings)	130-150
1984 (Orwell)	425	"Newspeak"	180
Freud	499	Victimology/blame	160-180
Patriotism, love of country, honor	520	Hate America	130
U.S. Nat'l Anthem, Pledge, Flag	510	Treason	80
Honest dissent, disagree	495	Sedition	105
Balance	205	Extremism	140
Chivalry	465	"Honor killing"	90
Personal responsibility	475	Narcissism	140
Free speech (1955)	255	Free speech (2007)	180
U. S. Philanthropists	455	United Nations	180-190
Amish forgiveness of murder	540	Blame	180
Emergence	600	Materialism	180
Consciousness calibration	605	Narcissism/opinion	140
Honesty	475	Apologist	190
Social equality (U.S. Constitution)	550	Wolf in sheep's clothing	120
Transparency	425	Sexism	180-190
Truth	475	Deception	160
U. S. Jurisprudence	525	Slander, false witness	60-75
U. S. Constitution	710	Social Justice	180
U. S. Bill of Rights	485	Sharia	190
Einstein, A.	499	Critics of Einstein	190

Heisenberg uncertainty principle	460	Mechanistic reductionism	160
New Testament (minus Revelation)	880	Secularism	165
American Civil Rights Union	460	Reverse Discrimination	180

Many vociferous extremist organizations that are constantly in the news via activism calibrate extremely low. The collapse of the reign of reason, truth, and logic into their opposites then results in the reversal of good and evil as well as right and wrong, and thus, all ethics or morality (Bruce, 2003). It then results in the dictum that substitution of falsehood for truth is 'elite' and 'superior', which gains great enthusiasm and energy from the narcissistic core of the ego that values self-centered opinion and perception over validity and essence.

This fall of integrity was predicted by Socrates as the inevitable downfall of free-speech democracy. America, however, has continued to be the primary source of philanthropy and major advancements and discoveries, including science, medicine, technology, and engineering. Of interest is that Marxism ridicules not only religion ('the opiate of the people') but also even science itself as being 'oppressive'. Paradoxically, many of the libertine philosophers and writers of the Frankfurt School led dissolute personal lives and suffered or even died from combinations of perverse addictions for which, paradoxically, American science has developed life-saving treatments.

All the above is included in the social/political/philosophical expressions of 'postmodernism' (cal. 180) by which academia has fallen so drastically (see Horowitz, 2006, 2007). Indoctrination (as recommended by Marcuse) has now replaced education as a goal. This is represented by 'radical math' now used to indoctrinate grade-school children via 'social justice' (cal. 180) doctrines (Stern, 2007).An excellent description of the phenomenon is presented by Flynn (2004) in *Intellectual Morons* (cal. 450) in which he states that (true to the title's name) most of the professors who indoctrinate students with the false philosophies of Marcuse have never even read his works although he is the most often cited reference in a decade of sociological texts.

Catastrophic to American and Western civilization is the severe drop of academia from its prior calibrated level of 440 to its current level of 180 (2007). Even a famous law school dropped from 440 to the current level of 175. The purpose of education has now declined to become 'sensitivity training' via political indoctrination (e.g., race, gender, class, and 'social justice'). Interestingly, small community colleges now calibrate much higher (at 440) than the big-name, prestigious Eastern universities.

The above confirms Pope Benedict's observation that the greatest threat to Western civilization is the combination of relativism (the apologist) and Islamic triumphalism of which the events of 9/11 were merely the warning shot across the bow (calibrates as true). Thus, relativism is the Trojan Horse by which the enemies of freedom hide under the sheep's clothing of apologists (termed "useful fools" by Lenin). To avoid being labeled as anti-Marxist, the Frankfurt School distanced itself from communism by removing the name of Marx. The school was originally named Marxist

Sociology but chose to hide under another nominalization to avoid political attack. Thus, under subterfuge, it was hoped the ideological essence of Marxism (atheistic dialectic materialism at cal. 130) would survive political attack.

Marcuse and fashionable French philosophers politicized almost all aspects of life so that adherence became cleverly termed 'correct' or 'elite'. This grandiosity of being 'superior' was, of course, immensely seductive to the narcissistic core of the ego. Thus, celebrities whose lives were primarily narcissistically based, via glamorization by the media, were very attracted to the egocentricity of Marcuse's premises and became proponents of a new 'cause', just as some of them had done earlier with Marxism itself. Revolution was glamorous and emotionally seductively exciting, and 'noble causes' attracted celebrity spokespersons, just as they do today. Any 'anti' parade or demonstration attracts crowds, accompanied by the requisite stoning of the police and the routine storming of the barricades. The Communists had already perfected the techniques of staging 'spontaneous' demonstrations and did so during and after the Vietnam War with increasing skill. With the help of a few dollars, the routine crowd of protesting rabble-rousers can be produced almost anywhere in the United States or Europe (e.g., every international 'summit' meeting).

Traditional wisdom and its intellectual foundation were now considered 'old hat' and passé, and the ideological, pseudointellectual, ambitious leftist academics quickly went on the bandwagon to show their 'superior' intellectual 'postmodern' savvy. Even the presidents of formerly prestigious, elite universities now routinely calibrate at consciousness level 190, and the level of truth of the curriculum has fallen drastically. The professor holds an authoritarian position and thus is seen as an authority. Via the dictum of 'tolerance', 'social justice', 'multiculturalism', 'accommodation', etc. (Goshgarian, 2005), major universities then began stylishly inviting even overtly psychotic (cal. 90 to 160) visiting trendy 'professors' to lecture on delusional subjects (e.g., 9/11 conspiracy, or, the Holocaust "never happened"). The intellectual descent of academia was orchestrated by the combined impact of a group of touted postmodern professors, all of whom calibrate below the critical level of 200.

All the above examples display intellectual narcissism and the mental inability to discern nominalized perception from essence. The victims of this disorder are currently termed 'ideologues' and, as such, have been responsible for much of the current political damage to the United States and Europe. They have also been responsible for the destructive effects on the overall caliber of true equality and justice by virtue of preferential promulgation of pet programs and fallacious concepts that result in actual mental damage to naïve citizens. Thus, eighty-eight university faculty members cosigned a condemning statement (cal. 180) against innocent sports team members who were falsely accused because of maudlin sympathy for a supposed victim due to race and sex of the accuser (proven later to be false). Notable is the important fact that after the accused were proven innocent by DNA testing, the faculty did not retract the fallacious condemnation. Very belatedly, the president did apologize. This is illustrative of why the collective faculty of United States academia has fallen to below consciousness level 200. While community colleges and Texas A&M University still calibrate at 440, the Ivy League universities generally calibrate at only level 220.

When 'far left' ideology is applied to the structure of a university, the result is collapse of the institution itself (Allen, 2007, in a major article in *The Weekly Standard*, November 12, 2007). The actual closing of the formerly traditional Antioch College is described in pathetic detail.

The degree of absurdity of Marcuse and similar pseudophilosophers is best demonstrated by merely quoting some basic dictums that form the core of concepts constituting those with which students and the politicized public are to be 'indoctrinated' (e.g., a 'holy cause'). The basic dictums are quoted here:

1. Freedom is totalitarianism.
2. Fiction is truth.
3. Lying is legitimate. ("It's for their own good.")
4. Indoctrination is the purpose of education.
5. Tolerance is intolerance.
6. Conservatism should be banned and attacked.
7. All minorities are victims.
8. The purpose of human life is sexualization.
9. The enemies of freedom are family, religion, patriotism, work, capitalism, science, conservative rationality, morality, and more.

The above indoctrination of the minds of naïve students is more damaging in that it leaves the victims crippled with impaired reality–testing capacity, and their naïve innocence savaged by true corruption. Of historical interest is that the universities' teaching of Nietzsche was held by Clarence Darrow to be partially responsible for the acts of murderers Leopold and Loeb, and therefore their death sentences were commuted (Brookhiser, 2007).

Illustrative of all the above is that college-level schools of social work are now required, for accreditation, to include political indoctrination (e.g., "all minorities are oppressed," "all whites are racist," etc.). Thus, they fail to actually identify the real underlying facts and social evolutionary patterns (as detailed in *Indoctrination U*, Horowitz, 2007).

As can be readily intuited, the underlying source is a primordial malevolence that stems from energies classically referred to over the ages as both Satanic and Luciferic. Inasmuch as these are the prime characteristics of evil, it is apparent why Pope Benedict (cal. 565) warned the Western world about relativism, which had become the apologist for terrorism's hiding beneath the sheep's clothing of religion and ostentatious theatrical piety.

Another consequence of relativistic dogma is the pervasive hypersexualization of society via the media, including even the indoctrination of sexuality in young children, encompassing all varieties of polymorphous perverse sexuality to the degree that grade-school sex or teacher-student sex is becoming commonplace (e.g., the sex-and-drugs indoctrination of Boulder, Colorado, high school students in 2007 calibrates at 160). These phenomena are seized upon by the enemies of America who view it as decadent and therefore deserving of destruction. America gives away the moral high ground to its avowed enemies via much publicized violence (girl gang beatings), sexually provocative celebrities, school shootings, and politically supported decline of ethics or honesty. The Internet is bombarded by endless vulgar sexualization and gross obscenities, even at commercial work sites.

Constitutional Impasse

Minimal recognition is given to the fact that the Constitution (cal. 700), the Declaration of Independence (cal. 705), and the Bill of Rights (cal. 485) of the United States (cal. 700) were formulated by Freemasons who were deists and theists (cal. 515) and not religionists. Thus, there is the guarantee of freedom ***from*** government imposition of religion (theocracy) as well as freedom ***of*** expression of religion. The original pilgrims who founded America sought freedom from prosecution and religious liberty of expression (Napolitano, 2006). The historic decline of interpretation of the Bill of Rights and the United States Constitution is described in detail in *Men in Black* (Levin, 2005).

The weakness of interpretations comes down to the lack of clarity about what the phrase, "to establish a religion," means. Obviously, the mere mention of the word 'God' does not in itself 'establish a religion'. The United States government actually spells out in detail the requirements for legally establishing a religion, and the Internal Revenue Service gives rather lengthy descriptions of the necessary components (fourteen major categories) for the recognition of a religion. If just affirming belief in the reality of God or putting up holiday decorations were sufficient to 'establish a religion', then ninety-two percent of Americans could thus become tax-exempt.

The Fuel of Social Conflict: 'Creationism vs. Secularism'

The Scopes impasse is still with us in new clothes as 'Intelligent Design vs. Darwinism.' Although Intelligent Design would seem relatively innocuous as a compromise in that it does not presume a deity, it is nevertheless seen as a threat by secularism on the shaky premise that it could be a 'slippery slope' by which God might surreptitiously come in through a crack in the back door. By the same reasoning, science itself should be condemned because its secularism as a political premise might also slip in through the back door. Paradoxically, science is itself the epitome of the study and description of the details of design but is apparently unable to recognize the intrinsic innate intelligence of biological evolution. (Darwinian theories are critically examined with humor in David Stove's *Darwinian Fairytales* [2006].)

Briefly stated, science has noted that what works survives, and that which does not work fails to propagate. As yet, science has failed to appreciate the fundamental premise of consciousness itself and is therefore unable to ascertain the energy field in which intelligence evolves. Even if nature evolved via randomness, design is represented by the very structure of DNA. It could be postulated that the random learning of curiosity/searching is the most basic level of intelligence in that useful data is compiled in a progressively organized and beneficial, linear biological substratum.

As noted, science is itself a product and an example of Intelligent Design via the accumulated ordering of data (intelligence) to identify intrinsic order. If only 'blind luck' were involved in scientific discovery, it would still take intelligence to recognize the value of that discovery. Even so-called artificial-intelligence computer systems operate via design to discover new designs, which is intrinsic to the process of research.

Propagation of the Scopes Conflict

From previous research on the basic nature of the human ego itself (see Hawkins, 2005), it is clear that the instinctual origins of the ego mechanisms are based on satisfaction and gratification of survival needs and desires. From animal origins, instinctual drives still dominate the consciousness levels of approximately eighty-five percent of the world's population. As a consequence, the primary motivation of large segments of society is that of gaining and winning rather than identifying affirmable truth. For example, seventy-five percent of the current political speech in the public media calibrates below 200 (November 2007).

Although resolution of conflicts is often readily available to either side in a debate, it is refused because of vested interests and the egoist gain of media-inflated contention. Thus, politicized positionalities are commonly transparent and use obtuse arguments by which each side misrepresents the views of the other (the 'straw man' fallacy). Fallacious viewpoints gain attention (e.g., "The Holocaust never happened," and

"America engineered 9/11") and media recognition. The prize winner in this type of fallacious hype is the now-famous MoveOn.org's General Petraeus/"General Betray Us" ad in the *New York Times* (September 2007) by which the originating political organization shot itself in the foot and also substantiated the premise that the *New York Times* had indeed become a supporter of left-wing causes (also a huge discount to the favored advertiser). The ad itself calibrates at level 90.

The operations of the human ego could also be pessimistically termed 'unintelligent lack of design' in that those who fail to learn from history are doomed to repeat it. As noted previously, man has been at war for ninety-three percent of recorded time, and it can readily be seen that conciliation or compromise is misinterpreted as defeat and therefore resisted at all costs. Malignant dictators are repeatedly initially hailed as great liberators and deified as leaders who then proceed to massacre their own countrymen. Belatedly, they are recognized as mad men (Cohen, 2007).

Compromise and Resolution

In view of the guarantees of the United States Constitution and the Bill of Rights, it could be assumed that because of free speech, public education would include descriptions of creation as well as evolution as alternate plausible hypotheses. For example, a lack of education about the impact of religious colonies and their place in American history would prevent an educated comprehension of the very bedrock of American society (e.g., the Pilgrims' search for religious freedom). Likewise, neglect of scientific education would result in widespread ignorance, as represented by Islamic totalitarian theocracy where education is limited solely to the memorization of a single scripture (the Koran) and nothing else, except hatred via *The Protocols of the Learned Elders of Zion* (cal. 90) or falsified Mickey Mouse cartoons.

Freedom is represented by presentations of alternate options rather than the suppression of other viewpoints, which is characteristic of current academia (e.g., university riots). Thus, secularism is repressive, as indicated by its low calibration of only 165. Repression is historically demonstrated by book burning and historical revisionism as exhibited by totalitarian regimes and academic politicized ideologies (racial and gender language police, etc. [Ravitch, 2003]). Freedom and integrity are served by mutual respect aided by forbearance.

Political/Sociological Polarization

Within the hidden substrate of social dialogue is the Yin/Yang polarization by unconscious gender-archetypal paradigms of the male and female principles. Meritocracy is a male principle by which performance is rewarded, as it has been earned through endeavor and self-discipline plus hard work and pragmatic application. This represents the structure of capitalism (Smith's *Wealth of Nations*, cal. 440), free enterprise, and personal responsibility. Thus, rewards have to be earned by effort that produces results. This is the archetypal pattern of patriarchy.

In contrast to the above is the archetypal feminine/matriarchal principle by which all children are treated as equals just by virtue of their very existence. Thus, the maternal principle implies obligation to provide for the needs of all, irrespective of performance. From the maternal principle, needs can then be escalated and conceptualized as basic rights to be supplied with the necessities for survival. Thus socialism, the welfare state, and varieties of collectivism represent political expression of the feminine/matriarchal archetype and function. In contrast, free-enterprise capitalism represents the masculine pattern.

From the polarized masculine viewpoint, the feminine principle is seen as potentially weakening, leading to dependency (the welfare state), loss of autonomy, and loss of drive and ambition. It points to the failure of collectivist societies and their widespread poverty and starvation. (Chairman Mao's China resulted in the starvation of thirty million people, which is replicated in today's North Korea.) The downside of a strict meritocracy, however, is often economic and social disparity between the strata of society. The wide discrepancy results in the problem of defining exactly what is the moral responsibility of society to the various segments.

In America, both principles operate strongly. A highly productive capitalistic economy produces enough wealth to support everyone at least at a subsistence level. Business produces great wealth that, via taxation, provides vast government resources to support the basics of life and survival for the whole population. Thus, the practical resolution is for judicious experience and implementation of both the masculine/patriarchal and the feminine/matriarchal principles.

Political discussion and negotiation realistically address the problems of how to ascertain the correct moral balance in the pragmatic application of fairness and legality. Each has its contrasting, prevailing ethical/moral standards and principles. The 'male' pattern becomes criticized for its proneness to dominance and hegemony, and the 'feminine' is seen as indulgent and overly permissive. The social dialogue reflects the interaction of the two principles (Yin and Yang) as each strives for dominance.

Truth vs. Falsehood

As has been demonstrated by consciousness research and previously stated, the human mind, unaided, is intrinsically incapable of discerning essence (truth) from appearance (perception or illusion). Thus, deception is a primary tool by which to mislead the public via the traditional sheep's clothing ruse. This is often done simply via false labels or descriptive titles. We can see that secular 'progressive' is in reality 'regressive' in that it postulates replacing a 'conservative' society that calibrates in the high 400s (e.g., Gingrich's *Traditional America*) with liberalism, which calibrates at 160 to 180 (atheistic hedonism), so as to recapitulate the fall of Rome via the teachings of Marcuse rather than Caligula. ('Mainstream' America calibrates primarily in the 300s—fairness, good will, and honesty.) Similarly, Islamic terrorist triumphalism (cal. 90) hides behind the slogan that Islam is a "religion of peace," whereas, in actuality, it has been continuously at war since the seventh century and is at war even now in numerous countries around the world; it is a constant threat to everyone on the planet. (Visit the nearest airport for confirmation.)

While it is currently unfashionable to 'call a spade a spade' (which calibrates at 490), the discernment of reality from illusion or truth from falsehood is an essential requirement of even basic physical survival as well as spiritual integrity. The repeatedly demonstrated basic pattern of destruction in human history is a result of the classic ('Luciferic') reversal of truth and falsehood. (The 'wolf in sheep's clothing' calibrates at an ominous 120). The touted 'Liberator' conceals the hidden totalitarian, malignant, narcissistic dictator who then enslaves the people. Similarly, the 'liberation' from the restraints of ethics, morality, or reason leads to anarchy and the enslavement of hedonism, Hollywood 'hotties', debauchery, dog fighting (cal. 50) and addiction via the unbridled lust for sensory pleasure (e.g., the fall of Rome). To throw off the Ten Commandments and simultaneously indulge in the Seven Deadly Sins has devastating consequences. The seduction by the serpent of the Garden of Eden is ever present.

There is nothing more surreptitiously destructive than dismissing good and evil as 'just labels', for the differentiation is quickly revealed by the simple technique of consciousness calibration, which distinguishes appearance or nominalization from essence and truth. That the human mind, unaided, is unable to make this distinction is what gives relativism its seductive veneer. This is basically the crux of the human dilemma by which being deluded is the prevailing norm. This inherent limitation is why man needs spiritual truth as a savior via the great avatars and sages—Buddha,

Christ, Krishna, Zoroaster, Socrates, and many others previously listed together with their calibrated levels of truth.

As Samuel Adams wrote in a letter to James Warren on February 12, 1779:

> A general Dissolution of Principles & Manners will more surely overthrow the Liberties of America than the whole Force of the Common Enemy. While the People are virtuous they cannot be subdued; but when once they lose their Virtue they will be ready to surrender their Liberties to the first external or internal Invader.
>
> (Samuel Adams Papers, Lenox Library, Lenox, MA)

Counterbalance

Since the year 2004, the overall consciousness level of mankind has decreased from 207 to 204. America has decreased from 426 to 421, and Western civilization is currently at 270. People ask what they can do. From research, it appears that what people become rather than what they 'say', 'do', or 'have' is most profoundly influential, for what people say and do is merely a reflection of what they believe, have become, and therefore *are*. Because the levels of consciousness are exponential, a rise of even a few points has a powerful influence. Thus, what people can 'do' is become as spiritually advanced as they can by alignment with spiritual principles and the highest Truth. As said previously, by raising the level of the sea, all the ships afloat are raised effortlessly. Prayer, worship, and lovingness plus prayer are of great unseen value to all humankind.

CHAPTER 7

What is Real?

As first described by Protagoras of ancient Greece, everyone naïvely presumes that their own perception, opinions, and comprehension of life and its events are 'real, true, factual', and therefore 'right'. Hence, if other people have a different viewpoint, they are considered to be 'wrong, misinformed, prejudiced, politically incorrect, or ignorant'. The innate vanity of the narcissistic core of the ego has a vested interest in being 'right', which carries with it an associated sense of importance. This in turn adds the subtle flavor and quality of empowerment, even when its basis is completely illusory. Thus, being 'right' is associated with pride and self-esteem that then has to be defended as per the constant national and international contentious political struggle for the moral high ground.

Inasmuch as the consequences of belief systems and their resulting emotional behaviors are critical to happiness as well as success and even survival, it is obviously beneficial to analyze the underlying processes involved. Because they are very basic, understanding the mechanisms is of considerable importance.

An easily observable fact to be discovered is that the mind functions on the basis of presumptions that are simultaneously emotionalized and ranked as to priorities. These provide provisional models for belief and action as well as agreement or disagreement. Subsequent processing can then result in either doubt or certainty and thereby weaken or reinforce personal as well as group identifications with their alignments of loyalties and commitments.

The sense of reality is an experiential, subjective

focal point of interactive complexity that arises from a multiplicity of factors, both identifiable and subtle. When examined and enumerated, any moment of subjective awareness involves literally millions of contributory elements with internal ranking of importance and dominance. Some of the most obvious that influence opinion, belief, faith, and other mental processes are age, gender, education, brain physiology, prior experience, training, language skills, IQ, and psychological and intellectual expertise and capacity. These factors are dominated by the overall evolutionary level of consciousness, which is influenced by intention, commitment, internalized goals, and "attention set" (Medina, 2006). All these factors are further influenced by politicized cultural and societal presumptions and axioms that are accepted as 'reality' and intrinsic to social structure.

Reality as an Interpretation

From the foregoing, it is obvious that a sense of reality is a truly subjective presumption that is operationally useful but not 'provable' as are, for example, the linear descriptions and dimensions of material objects. All the mind's statements are provisional at best, and an awareness of that limitation is an intrinsic quality of wisdom. Wisdom denotes a degree of humility as well as flexibility. It also implies a conservative, cautious attitude which is aware that further information will accrue over time and experience. Thus, wisdom considers all knowledge to be provisional and subject to change, not only in meaning but also in significance and value. The definition of 'real' also implies verifiable truth that, until recent times, was not available; thus, verifiable reality/truth/veracity have emerged only very recently in human consciousness.

Capacity to Discern Reality

The human mind automatically presumes the validity of its own subjective experience, and therefore its operations are based on an innate characteristic called 'faith'. The quality of faith itself has been under attack in recent times by professional skeptics who paradoxically exhibit extreme faith in their own skepticism (cal. 160) and associated narcissistic sophistry. Thus, skeptics fail to be skeptical of their own skepticism and therefore display a naïve belief system that operationally results in rejection of the higher levels of consciousness and an inability to comprehend meaning, abstraction, or context (field) from linear content (appearance) as per the Brain Physiology chart in Chapter 4.

Intrinsic to the very basic construction of the human ego is an innate innocence in that it believes in the reality or truth of its own programs and is unaware that it lacks an intrinsic capacity for self-correction. The reason for the ego's inherent lack of capacity for verification is that its data is limited to only internal processing systems. The internal mechanisms of the ego lack any external, independent source of reference for verification.

The human mind is like a ship at sea that is unable to correct its direction without a compass or an external source of reference, such as the stars. It is important to realize that a system is only correctible when it has access to an external point of reference (e.g., a global positioning system) that therefore serves as the absolute by which all other data are compared.

(Absolutism calibrates at 650, and the Absolute itself calibrates at 1,000.)

As described in all prior books (Hawkins, 1995-2007), there is now a reference scale of verifiable truth by which levels below 200 are false, levels above 200 are progressively true, and the level 1,000 represents an absolute fixed point of reference to which all other calibrations are relative. Note that relativism (via post-modernism) denies the reality of the Absolute as it believes that all supposed truth is only social, linguistically constructed opinion (perception/definition), e.g., 'just rhetoric'. Therefore, relativism sees only perception and is blind to essence as well as context. Paradoxically, relativism considers its own premises to be absolute (as well as superior and elite). If all statements are hypothetically only semantic constructs, then obviously that very statement itself has no inherent reality and is also just a value-laden linguistic construct. Thus, by its own criteria, postmodernism is fallacious (as demonstrated historically by Plato's defeat of Protagoras's self-defeating arguments).

Content vs. Context

It is apparent that all statements of purported truth or claims to reality are dependent on prevailing conditions of both identifiable as well as unknown factors. Interpretation of data depends on overall situational factors, as has been described by the prior analysis. To the observer, what an event seems to mean or 'look like' depends on the point of observation and prevailing circumstances.

The capacity for observation and its correct interpretation is actually a function consequent to the level of consciousness and concordant brain function. These factors in turn are affected by intention and motivation. These can range from detached, refined, trained perspicacity and expertise to identify essence to emotionalized, distorted bias and politicized, deliberate falsification (perception) and rhetoric (cal. 180).

Reality as a Social Product

Discernment of reality and truth has always been problematic to the human mind, whether it was aware of it or not (i.e., the subject of epistemology). The process is now made even more difficult by the overall impact of the media, the effect of which is both subtle and unconscious as well as visible and apparent. The most obvious influence of the media is by virtue of the selection itself, as well as the time devoted to its reporting, all of which are enhanced on television by visual as well as musical pictorial additions. Emotional and political distortions and dramatizations add to the editing impact reinforced by the sequence and style of presentation. The material presented by the media can calibrate from as low as 10 to as high as 570, but the mind of the observer witnesses the presentations with the same presumptions of reality despite the very wide differences in the levels of truth presented. The overall impact of the media is the production of a 'virtual reality' that includes distorted values.

While the modern, sophisticated viewer is subliminally aware of the foregoing, persons of lower levels of consciousness are not so aware and, like children, they tend to believe fiction is truth and live in an "alternate reality" (Pitts, 2007; Marzeles, 2007). Fifty percent of blogs calibrate below level 200 (as of October 2007). In

America, fifty-five percent of the population calibrates below 200 and is thus innately prone to distortion and misinterpretation. Worldwide, the percentage of the population below 200 is eighty-five percent, and in some subcultures and countries, it is close to one hundred percent. Thus, falsehood dominates the thinking and reality testing of the majority of people in today's world. As the Nazi propaganda minister Joseph Goebbels observed, if a lie is told frequently enough, it is eventually believed to be factual (a virtual reality) because the population lacks the capacity to discern truth from falsehood.

The Progressive Nature of Truth and Reality

Information processing is evolutionary and revealed in a progressive fashion along a developmental timeline. Confirmation of supposed facts may take decades or even centuries and requires editing as more information is obtained and analyzed. With the emergence of greater knowledge, meaning and significance change as do criteria for validation. All fields of human knowledge change over time, and even the reporting of history itself is subject to revision based on new discoveries and methodologies. Thus, all beliefs and information are tentative in that even if the facts do not change, their significance or meaning is subject to change over time.

Comprehension of reality/truth is subjective and changeable because of individual variation in the style of processing of information, such as "I know/think/feel/sense/believe/have faith in...," etc. There is also an unstated allegiance to an unspecified paradigm of reality; thus, people 'intuit', 'realize', 'become aware of', 'understand', 'comprehend', etc. These are influenced by factors of education, specialization, talent, innate capacity, IQ, projected value, opinion, emotionality, and bias, as well as geographical, cultural, family, ethical, and moral training.

It could be said that truth and reality represent an equivalence, and the validity of that equivalence can now be verified by reference to a calibrated scale of levels of truth that are objective, impersonal, and independent of the opinion of the observer. Again, it is important to realize that *a statement of an alleged truth requires specification of context.*

Is the Spiritual 'Real'?

Until the advent of quantum mechanics, it was presumed that Newtonian descriptions of the physical universe were complete and final. The emergence of subparticle physics, nonlinear dynamics, quantum theory, and other advances of science indicated that previous presumptions had to be reexamined. Although there was a change in understanding, the basic reality of scientific data had seldom come into question. Not so, however, with spiritual realities, which dealt with the nonphysical paradigms.

Spiritual realities are not concrete or discrete, nor are they linear or adequately describable as they relate to context rather than content. The spiritual realms are experientially subjective, conceptually contextual, and nonlinear. Thus, they are described as ineffable, religious, etheric, primordial, celestial, eternal, timeless, omnipotent, omniscient, omnipresent, and Divine (as per James in *The Varieties of Religious Experience*). This is also the province of unknown karmic propensities as well as celestial realms and Divinity.

The nonlinear greater Reality has been described over the millennia by the great avatars, saints, illumined sages, and spiritual geniuses who collectively agree upon an experiential, confirmable Reality. These realities begin to emerge at the calibrated consciousness level of the 200s and then progress to more powerful subjective states that calibrate in the 500s on up to the levels of 600 to 1,000—the levels of Enlightenment.

The great spiritual teachers over time have taught the processes by which spiritual realities can be subjectively and experientially confirmed. These realities can be verified by the clinical methodology of consciousness calibration research, which allows for a new dimension of validation and investigation.

Spiritual Reality vs. Spiritual Illusions

Because, historically, there has not been a means of discerning truth from falsehood, the spiritual realm includes a great deal of misinformation as well as belief in what can only be described as spiritual fiction and fantasy. The chart below illustrates this. The following calibrate as false and are below level 200.

Fictions and Myths

Alien abduction	(The New Testament)
A Million Little Pieces	Channeling
Apocalypse prophecies	Crop circles
Aquarian cults	Crystal Children
Area 51 conspiracy theories	*Da Vinci Code, The*
Astrological religions	*Da Vinci Code Decoded*
Babaji	Divination
Bible Code, The	DNA Code
Book of Revelation	End-times prophecies

Extraterrestrials
Ghosts
God gene
Incoming fifth dimension
Judas Gospel, The
Maitreya
Mayan calendar predictions
Natural Healing
Neg. Prayer-Healing Study (*Amer. Heart Journal*, 4/06)
New Ageism
Opus Dei Code
Protocols of the Learned Elders of Zion, The
Raelians
Reincarnate as lesser species
Reincarnation of Buddha as Ram Bahadur Banjan
Shroud of Turin
Snake Pit, The (Book)
Solar Temple, Order of the
Starseed Children
Transmediumship
UFOs from extraterrestrials
UFO Religions
Urantia Book, The

Historical Analysis

It will be discovered that the realm termed 'spiritual' covers a wide spectrum that includes a range from high levels of confirmable truth over great periods of time in contrast to fallacious spiritual fantasies, fictions, myths, and misinterpretations. Myths, allegories, fables, stories, parables, and legends, however, can serve a teaching function to allegorically illustrate abstract concepts of truths in simplistic format. Comparably, humor, poetry, and art use similar metaphorical communicative styles along with paradox to highlight abstract principles.

Historic religious texts, such as the Old Testament, thus include cultural myths and stories that are not literally confirmably factual but are inclusive of cultural folklore. They are comparable to the symbolism of Santa Claus who does not literally fly onto the roof with reindeer or go down the chimney, yet the legend represents the spirit of Christmas in a concrete style that is comprehensible to even the mind of a child.

In the Scopes trial, the allegorical stories in the

Bible were the focus of specific attack by Clarence Darrow in a manner that is comparable to attacking the difference between the letter and the spirit of the law, which is typical of current political debate over freedom of religious expression versus imposition of religion.

As previously cited, the United States Constitution and the Bill of Rights establish freedom *from* imposition of religion by government (theocracy), yet simultaneously, freedom *of* religious expression (e.g., Christmas trees, Santa Claus, the Menorah) is a fine distinction conveniently ignored by positionalized secularists, including even the judiciary. A fact overlooked by 'legislators from the bench' is that the constitutions of *all fifty states* include reference to God as the ultimate source of human existence (G. Williams, 2007); thus, there is uniform allegiance to the 'natural law'.

Reality and Meaning

Significance and meaning are clarified as a consequence of utilization of concrete examples to illustrate abstract concepts. Spiritual truths and realities are consequent to nonlinear context, which then poses the problem of exposition in language that is linear in form.

Meaning is not a 'provable' because the impact is subjective, much like art is a form of expression that bypasses linguistic constraint. Thus, what may not be provably 'real' *objectively* can be very strongly 'real' *subjectively*, despite difficulties of expression.

The distinction between literal and abstract truth is a subtlety and capability consequent to the evolution to higher levels of consciousness, often referred to as the degree of sophistication. Allegory is expressed in poetic license, which utilizes symbolic images and concepts to communicate contextual coloration, and thus significance and meaning. For example, although a dragon may not be a literal reality, its symbolism is universally recognized and understood at the archetypal level.

The failure or inability to discern the distinction between symbols and their abstract significance or meaning is termed being 'literal', 'facetious', or 'pedestrian', which implies a limitation of capacity for full comprehension. Purposeful distortion between literal and abstract levels of truth (e.g., the spirit and the letter of the law) is a basic mechanism of much political and legal, as well as ecclesiastical, debate. Thus, the basis for argument and conflict is often a self-serving artifact (error) of focused misinterpretation. This is often purposeful, resulting in undue exaggeration of the supposed importance of what are actually irrelevant details.

The study of meaning, termed 'hermeneutics', reflects subtleties, references, and shades of classification of levels of abstract thought that are consequent to definition and identification of context. That all men are created equal by virtue of their Divine origin is an abstract truth of high level but not literally demonstrable or scientifically provable. In what sense is everyone 'equal' despite extremely wide variation in talents, physical endowments, and circumstances of birth from rich to poor?

If human rights are the consequence of the Divinity of man's creation, then they are inherent and consequently inviolate. On the other hand, if they are merely consequent to the caprice of secular definition, then all rights are only tentative, arbitrary and therefore transitory, vulnerable, and merely subject to political and legal negotiation (e.g., 'big money').

To be 'real' implies that a proposition relates to what is actual, existent, manifest, and measurable in space/time and confirmable by the sciences. Thus, it represents a conclusion about a specific state of being and existence as 'factual'. Therefore, 'realness' is a subjective statement confirmable by sense-derived information and description. As a communication, a statement of factual reality implies the capability for consensual validation and confirmation by others, which is not actually possible with purely personal realities. The degree of reality is also reflective of conviction and continuity, which are also, however, subject to interpretation, doubt, or bias.

All suppositions about reality are again at a higher level subject to personal limitation as, quoting Protagoras in Plato's *Theaetus*, "Each and every event is for me as it appears to me, and is for you as it appears for you." Thus, statements about reality are testimonial. The above argument, however, is further limited by its reference to appearance/perception rather than essence. So, although opinion is subjective, essence itself is not subject to opinion, even though the observer may not be capable of making such a distinction. Therefore, calibrating the level of truth of Essence is the only known method thus far discovered to transcend the potential errors of perception, observation, and interpretative conclusion. Consequently, reality is identity rather than description.

There are purely subjective realities that cannot be

confirmed experientially by others, such as dreams, imaginations, images, memories, etc. Even when data is confirmable, its meaning, significance, value, or importance is then superimposed as contributory to the overall context.

The inference from consciousness research is that in the United States, for instance, approximately fifty-five percent of the population is actually not capable of discernment of the truly 'real'. In evidence of this is the court experience that approximately fifty percent of the identifications of crime suspects are misidentified by photos or suspect line-up procedures. Thus, even a single statement, such as, "Yes, that is the person I actually saw commit the crime" is fallacious fifty percent of the time. (Note also that approximately fifty percent of the information on the Internet calibrates below level 200.)

Data is subject to extensive processing by the human mind itself. For example, some people are 'diminishers' and others are 'expanders', so that even exaggeration of importance or dismissal of significance influences the capacity for reality testing. To a delusional mind, all sorts of beliefs become 'real' while actual facts are denied to be true. Thus, fiction becomes 'real' because of underlying intention to make it subserve narcissistic intention (e.g., right versus wrong).

The mature mind is thus aware of the possibility of error from which it sees the value of humility. As with the classic dictum, "I think, therefore I am," all other statements about reality are provisional.

Summation

In the final analysis, what is considered to be 'real' is a subjective, presumptive conclusion that is a consequence of multilevel processing of content within a given context, which in turn is dependent on the level of consciousness. The level of consciousness is correlated with the capacity and style of brain function and the presence or absence of spiritual energy in which intention plays a dominant role. Thus, pride or self-servingness limits the capacity for the recognition of truth/reality, whereas humility and respect for integrous truth diminish error and increase the capacity to differentiate appearance from essence. The processing of meaning, significance, truth, and reality involves recognizing the distinction of abstract levels of truth and not mixing levels, which commonly leads to misinterpretation.

Because of the complexity of the above process, an enormous amount of literature has evolved over the centuries that is devoted to philosophy, theology, and ontology and to the branches of philosophy termed metaphysics and epistemology. For example, how do we know, and how do we know that we know?

For many centuries, the majority of mankind has relied on authority to provide the answers to what seemed to be endlessly ambiguous complexities. The question in current society is, "Wherein lies true moral authority?" True authority is a consequence of the level of truth discerned as a consequence of the level of the evolution of consciousness. Many ambiguities that have persisted over time can now be resolved by calibrating levels of consciousness/truth against a common point of reference, such as an impersonal calibratable scale that represents the Absolute, just as does a thermometer, a barometer, or an altimeter.

The calibration level is a consequence of the reality

level of essence and is thus in direct refutation of post-modern deconstructionism and relativism, which presumes that only perception and its nominalization by language represent reality. By such sleight-of-hand conjecture, comprehension of reality via reason is progressively obliterated and descends to levels below 200 (primitivism).

It is important to reemphasize that discernment of reality from philosophical distortion and fallacy is not just an intellectual politicized problem but instead is vital to survival itself. Millions of people have died over the centuries for lack of the capacity to discern truth from propagandized fallacy, and they do so daily in today's world as well. In an atomic age, the inability to identify militant fallacy may well cost the lives of tens of millions of people.

Malignant messianic narcissism (cal. 30) remains a primary source of potential disaster due to the failure to recognize the disorder because of relativistic sophistry and rhetoric (e.g., Neville Chamberlain prior to World War II; see Chapter 15, *Truth vs. Falsehood*.) While it is currently politically fashionable to be 'tolerant' of falsehood or socially destructive regressive trends, the cost is the loss of strength and the capacity to recognize the real 'wolf in sheep's clothing.' It could be said that it is better to be a live realist than a dead relativist.

Derailment of Reason and Truth: Passion

Although modern man has the most well-developed prefrontal cortex of any mammal (cal. 200), logic, reason, and rationality are quickly and routinely eclipsed by emotionality. Below consciousness level

200, the emotions are based on animal instincts (the limbic system calibrates at 120), and their negativity blocks the effective utilization of reason and rationality. Thus, 'feelings' can obliterate the hard-won capacity for intellectual discernment of reality. Passion can be attached to any attraction, which then becomes hypervalued.

If passion itself is valued (and even promoted) for its own sake, then why is that so, especially in view of the gross disasters of mankind that were consequent to inflamed passion (e.g., Nazi era, Ku Klux Klan, and terrorists)? 'Passion' is exhibited by the animal world in its struggles for existence and survival. Thus, it has a pragmatic value in select circumstances but becomes a negative if not dominated by intelligence. 'Passion' often merely signifies unbridled narcissistic emotionality and is thus quantitative rather than qualitative. *'Free speech' means the freedom of ideas and expression of viewpoints, not excess of emotionality and infantile actions.*

In the search for Enlightenment, detachment becomes a necessity that requires relinquishment of attachments and emotional excesses. Thus arises the necessity for the dictum, "Be passionate only for God" (Hawkins, 2006).

Reality Testing and Brain Function: Mental Disorders

Scientific studies and professional experience indicate that both personality disorders and even severe mental illness are prevalent in society due to genetic biochemical disorders of brain function. The incidence has risen most rapidly since the closure of the public/state mental hospital system that had previously offered protection for both patient and society. The closures were due to false depictions of the mental hospital system in such movies as *The Snake Pit* and *One Flew Over the Cuckoo's Nest*. These gave emotional energy to the emergence of the application of the Marxian dialectic (victim versus perpetrator) to political ideologies as mental illness was even termed a "myth of nominalization and labeling." The 'grand cause' resulted in the closing of the entire mental hospital system and was heralded as a 'great forward stride' by ideologists.

In reality, the result was a widespread social disaster. Psychotics roamed the streets and added to crime, poverty, homelessness, prostitution, and bizarre crimes, including the frequent killing of classmates (one such killer calibrated at level 5), torturing and sexually assaulting children, and even burying them alive.

Less dramatic consequences, but also indescribably destructive, were the outpouring of severely distorted stories, viewpoints, and falsified 'facts' onto the Internet and into the media, which indoctrinated the public with an endless barrage of fallacy and misinterpretation of events and their significance. The public was caught up in 'grand causes' that calibrated below 200. Under the sheep's clothing of 'free speech', disinformation became progressively dominant, resulting in the fall of the level of consciousness of mankind overall, including Western civilization and America.

Another consequence of the foregoing is that personal and social life is less safe, and any innocent citizen can arbitrarily become the victim of targeted malice and gross falsehood. This is furthered by the loss of privacy and legal protection inasmuch as slander, libel, and gross prevarication have equal legal protection under the law. Although 'the price of freedom is vigilance', the citizen of today does not really know 'vigilance' about 'what'.

As tectonic plates of traditional ethics, morality and common decency are crumbling, society overall seems to be in a 'free fall' transition. This fluctuation is recurrent throughout human history and reflects the varieties of the overall learning curves of human evolution. Without a compass, human society cannot even differentiate political progress from social disaster.

CHAPTER 8

Cultural Premises and Truth

Introduction

Both individually and collectively, the decision of what is 'real' or 'true' and thereby 'important' dominates all levels of society and determines customs, morality, and ethics as well as politics and law. It defines obligations, freedoms, and responsibilities along with options and alternative choices. These beliefs then become indigenous to the prevailing culture and lead to expectations of behavior as both written and unwritten rules of conduct that reflect wide extremes of value systems. Cultural myths influence and often even define the relationships of the population as well as the structure and function of government itself.

The human mind presumes that the commonality of a belief system is evidence of truth, and, of course, history is full of obvious examples to the contrary (e.g., *Extraordinary Popular Delusions*, Mackay). Some centuries ago, everyone believed that the sun rotated around the earth and that the earth was flat. These examples merely demonstrate that all information is presumptive and not absolute because even the 'laws' of science are constantly changing (e.g., there are now only eight planets instead of nine as of August 2006).

The foundations of government and societies reflect a wide variation between reality-based altruistic belief systems resulting in governments that are benevolent, or their alternative, governments that are oppressive and exploitive. Historically, dominant cultures were established by force of conquest and militancy and were governed by sovereign caprice. In those days as well as now, religions were established and enforced by the sword and political alliances of rulers.

In every culture, the necessity arose to define the relationship between the ruler and the people, as well as between religion and the state, and to define parameters of authority. Conflicts of allegiance frequently arose between the state and the religion, and failure to resolve the conflicts often resulted in dire consequences, such as excommunication, beheading, or being burned at the stake. The Inquisition (cal. 35) was the extreme example of the conflict by which totalitarian theocracy brought extreme oppression that fueled subsequent distrust of ecclesiastical authority. This is specifically reflected in the United States Constitution, which grants freedom *from* government-enforced religion but also guarantees freedom *for* religion.

The importance of religion in the establishment of the United States government cannot be overlooked (Gingrich, 2006) because historically, the very purpose of the Pilgrim founders was to seek religious liberty and freedom of expression, which is therefore intrinsic to the very founding of democracy as expressed in the Constitution. The argument continues today over what it means to 'establish' a religion or 'prohibit' the free expression thereof.

Political structure therefore reflects the organization and expression of belief systems that are revealed to be the true seat of power. The government is merely the formal depository of ideas in a legalistic structure to facilitate enactment from the conceptual to their concrete application. The true source of power and authority, however, is the faith of the citizenry in the alleged truth of basic premises. Thus, government is the mechanism that transforms the reality of nonlinear truth or the illusions of falsity into pragmatic, operational expression in the linear domain.

The forms and expressions of politics represent the distillation of moral/spiritual/religious premises to their practical application via law in everyday life. Thus, there is no possible way to avoid that universal human requirement for discernment between 'right and wrong'; even the extreme iconoclast or criminal abides by this primordial distinction. Codes of right/wrong behavior are inviolate in criminal gangs and as well as in the animal world. Even the antimoralist is paradoxically caught in the dichotomy by making ethics and morality 'wrong' (e.g., 'politically incorrect').

As history has so aptly demonstrated, the processing of concepts in political dialog is often passionate to the degree that millions of people die in the heat of the fray. Political frenzy begets violence, fanaticism, and extremes of belief systems whereby worship of the state becomes a religion in and of itself, as exemplified by the worship of Chairman Mao, Kim Jong-il, the Ayatollah, Adolf Hitler, and many others over history as well as in today's world. Pathognomonic of fascist totalitarianism is the military goosestep at calibration level 90. (Note Iran's current military display.)

While such societies may still give lip service to God or religion, mass demonstrations are actually staged consequent to the malignant messianic narcissism of the God-substituted leader in whose presence the multitudes weep openly with extravagant overwhelms of emotion and awe.

As noted previously, the Constitution and the basic structure of the United States government were created by theists or deists who were not overtly political religionists. Thus, Divinity was given formal recognition as the sole source of equality and freedom ('common law') without establishing the primacy of any particular religion that could have resulted in the establishment of a theocracy.

Another source of the right to the expressions or displays of religions as a cultural/social reality is accorded by the basic dictum of 'free speech'. In some decisions, the courts have extended great latitude by which free speech has been expanded to even include behaviors or physical actions that are then regarded as 'symbolic speech'. Ironically, such extreme liberality is not afforded the free speech of mentioning the word 'God' in public places. This is again a paradox inasmuch as all high public officials, including the President and the Chief Justice of the Supreme Court, have for centuries traditionally taken their oaths of office with their hand placed on the Bible.

The juxtaposition of such divergent rulings brings into question the operationally prescriptive sovereignty of political slant, cant, and deviant rhetoric for the presumptive rewards of political gain. Such distortions occur as a consequence of the willful manipulating of interpretations that argue the letter of the law but, at the same time, obviously violate the spirit of the law, the intention of which is quite obvious to any person of integrity whose innocence has not been programmed by positionalities. One might naïvely presume that the high judiciary would be somewhat above catchy memes or the transient popularity of relativistic ideologies that calibrate at the consciousness level of only 160.

When people shrug their shoulders at recognizing the importance of sociopolitical fallacies, one could ask, "Would you like to have a surgeon who calibrates at 160 operate on you?" Or even an auto mechanic, or your legal representatives?

Historians have noted that democracies seldom last more than a few centuries for the same reasons that were initially pointed out by Socrates. He viewed that integrity would unlikely prevail as the voting masses would award themselves more and more benefits to the point of eventually losing their freedom. Notable in this regard, as previously mentioned, is that at the present time, approximately eighty-five percent of the world's population calibrates below 200 (in the United States, it is approximately fifty-five percent), which denotes a significantly narrow margin of safety.

The social expressions of spiritual reality as levels of consciousness were extensively documented in previous works (e.g., *Truth vs. Falsehood*, Chapter 9). Modern man is profoundly influenced by the media whose presentations of ostensible truth include even extreme falsehood, which is then given publicity as though it were of equal, integrous validity. Due to its importance, this subject will be discussed more fully in a later chapter. Because the mind is intrinsically unable to discern perception from essence or truth from falsehood (as detailed in *Truth vs. Falsehood*, Section 1), a common presumption of the naïve mind is that truth is established by popularity and commonality of agreement. Thus, the mind looks for confirmation and searches for reliable information.

In this regard, it is important to note that the *Encyclopedia Britannica* calibrates at 465, whereas fifty percent of the information on the Internet (as well as fifty percent of blog sites) calibrates below the critical level of 200. Thus, even the integrous search for truth leads to misinformation. The percentage of error overall in the *Britannica* is only approximately five percent. This is not surprising in that the *Britannica* has long-established, rigorous requirements.

That the media include fallacious material is a consequence of the illusion created by the catchy meme, "Fair and balanced." The implication, of course, is that, via relativism, falsehood is of equal value to truth, a rather absurd presumption just on face value. As an example, we can take that the earth is flat as a fair-and-balanced affirmative to the view that the earth is round. This can be further elaborated based on the fallacious meme, "There are two sides to any question." (This calibrates as false and was actually the comment of a public official caught red-handed on video while stealing cash and stashing it in tin cans in the basement of his house.)

Social validation is thus of little value in trying to discern truth. Even basic religious texts show extremely wide variation in levels of truth in various verses, some of which can calibrate as low as 70 (see Chapter 16, *Truth vs. Falsehood*) as do some popular belief systems noted (see Chapter 17). Cynically, it has been said that political/economic/social truths depend more on the price of oil than on any verifiable yardstick of validity. Consideration of drilling for oil within the United States has itself created an intense battle between ideologies where litigious environmentalism has blocked the drilling of any new wells or the construction of any new oil refineries. This has resulted in throwing enormous amounts of money to the regions of the world that are most vociferously hateful of America. The shift of power enables the terrorists to become even more aggressive, which enhances the overall tension of the clash of civilizations between Islamic triumphalism and the traditional values of Western civilization.

Whether cultural trends or belief systems are integrous actually depends on the multiple factors of both intention and context as well as on content itself. This is revealed by the fact that truth is often distorted and utilized to implement and paradoxically support falsehood. By this curious device, a provable fact is then reinterpreted in such a way as to appear to be supportive evidence of its exact opposite, which is then used to support the false accusations (e.g., the 'straw man' fallacy). Malice is often disguised as feigned innocence.

In contrast to the twisting of truth for surreptitious ends, open honesty is inclusive of both context and content. This is the basis for situational ethics, which recognizes that whether an act is to be judged as right or wrong and to what degree depends on the context, including contributing circumstances and, importantly, intention. This is exemplified by the everyday application of evidence in courtroom law in criminal cases to establish motive and also Federal laws to protect citizens in times of war.

Although commonality of belief is persuasive, it is not indicative of truth. As will be pointed out later, media play into this back-and-forth gaming of manipulation as politicized 'spin'. Threat of media attack is now used to intimidate via orchestrated 'blog' attack composed of well-crafted malevolent falsity (i.e., blogger blackmail). Under the banner of "free speech," plus propagation via the Internet, 'hate' Web-site malevolence has gained ground and facilitated the decline of Western civilization.

Independence from Social Programming

Safeguards against being programmed by society are (1) emotional detachment, in which all information is viewed as provisional, (2) awareness that ordinary mentalization is unable to discern perception from essence, and (3) knowing that the wolf often hides beneath sheep's clothing. This suspension of belief is the practical application of the basic dictum to "wear the world like a light garment." To "be in the world but not of it" is a mode of attention that nevertheless still allows spontaneous interaction and function in society.

To avoid entrapment by the world, many spiritually aligned people take advantage of retreats, and some even become renunciates and join religious communities. In this regard, it needs to be pointed out that true renunciation is actually an internal attitude and discipline where what is denied is not external appearance but the ego's attraction to its own projections. Traditionally, the Sabbath was a day of contemplation and detachment from ordinary activities whereby the overriding importance of the long-term life of the spirit was given formal recognition and implemented by devotion and withdrawal from worldly affairs and monetary concerns, such as business.

To what degree and in what style one wishes to continue to participate in the world are a consequence of one's prevailing level of consciousness and overall spiritual intention, as well as degree of dedication. The world offers maximal opportunity for spiritual growth and motivation, which is characterized as gaining spiritual merit and undoing the effects of prior negative choices and their spiritual consequences.

A traditional avenue has been through humanitarian efforts and selfless service (Karma Yoga). Major disasters often elicit significant outpourings of this inner spiritual awareness in which compassion and altruism are genuinely expressed by all levels of society, and even the government itself. Thus, under what appears to be society's veneer of cynicism, materialism, or sensationalism, there still resides the very active, influential heart of humanity.

Despite all the critics and naysayers, as mentioned previously, America is the most generous of all the world's nations, and its humanistic philanthropic aid is hundreds of times greater than that of any other country. This effort is the result of individuals (eighty-nine percent of the households in America), plus humanitarian organizations, corporate America, and philanthropies, including nonprofit organizations, churches, and the like (*Philanthropic Research*, 2006). This unique quality of United States' society was noted as long ago as 1835 by Alexis de Tocqueville in his famous book, *Democracy in America*. Note also that the United

States rebuilt all of war-torn Europe after World War II and still currently pays twenty-seven percent of the overall expenses of the United Nations.

In contrast to the above, the countries that are the most virulently hostile to the United States consistently give little or even nothing at all to the poor or to destitute regions of the world despite their enormous oil profits and accumulated wealth. Fortunately, generosity, benevolence, and philanthropy are not commonly labeled or viewed as 'spiritual' values or presumably they would also be under attack by radical secularists who might argue that by humanitarian programs, the federal government is illegally supporting religious/spiritual practices.

Wisdom versus Popularity

Government is the expression of the ideology associated with political systems that vary from the extremes of savage, oppressive, totalitarian regimes and monarchies to benign rulers who brought peace and prosperity. (The following is reprinted for convenience from *Truth vs. Falsehood*.)

Political Systems

Benevolent Sovereign	500	Tribal	200
Oligarchy	450	Theocracy	175
Democracy/Republic	410	Collectivism	175
Iroquois Nation	399	Communism	160
Coalition	345	Dictatorship	135
Socialism	305	Fascism	125
Monarchy	200	Anarchy	100
Feudal	145-200		

As can be seen, the most beneficial governments arise from benevolent rulers, such as those responsible for centuries of peace and prosperity in ancient China, where social accord and cooperation were the consequence of respect for integrous wisdom. Leadership by oligarchic counsel is also based on reliance on proven wisdom as was practiced by American Indian as well as other tribes for centuries. The Iroquois Nation served as a model for democracy and significantly influenced the foundation of the structure of the United States government. The Presidential cabinet is analogous to the oligarchic council. (The current United States cabinet calibrates at 455.)

As previously noted, despite populist critics, the value of the solid fruits of wisdom stand on their own and result in the United States being the most philanthropic of all nations via the generosity of private United States citizens, the American business community, the United States government, and the giant foundations. (Buffett, Carnegie, Gates, Ford, Rockefeller, and other foundations donate more than all the rest of the member countries of the United Nations combined.)

United States society collectively calibrates at 421 (November 2007). In contrast, the populist (e.g., Hollywood) critics collectively calibrate at 190. (The most recent Sundance Film Festival calibrates at 165). Thus, while populism appeals to narcissism, nobody, as pointed out before, wants a surgeon, an accountant, a lawyer, or even a bus driver who calibrates at 190. Interestingly, while the consciousness level of America is at 421, Singapore, which arose from an oligarchy, calibrates at 440, and crime is almost nonexistent.

The application of the basic principles of wisdom requires self-discipline, personal integrity, hard work, respect for self and others, and often self-sacrifice, meaning delaying immediate gratifications for long-term goals (the 'Protestant ethic').

The most destructive government leaders have characteristically been dictators whose effect on their countries has been that of devastation. This popularity reflects an inflation of value due to mass hysteria and promotion of a personality culture. Thus, Chairman Mao's collectivist regime calibrated at 175 and resulted in the starvation of thirty million peasants. China has now risen to calibration level 385, and oddly enough, represents the benefit of establishing pragmatic business principles (paradoxically as exemplified by Sam Walton). Thus, the old dictum proves that the way to success is to imitate it rather than to envy it or jealously demonize it.

Countermeasures to Cultural Illusion

A study of Western civilization indicates that its overall level of consciousness is currently in decline for the reasons that have been stated succinctly by Pope Benedict (relativism plus Islamic aggression and 'cultural Jihad'; see Burton and Stewart, 2007.) The decline is the result of social and intellectual influences via the media, academia, and politicalization from lower consciousness levels which have been heavily financed from sources that calibrate below the critical consciousness level of 200 ('power brokers'). The net result is the progressive dominance of narcissism, which is aggrandized as 'progressive', 'free speech', or human 'rights' and appeals to egocentricity. Thus, even formal education is no longer a safeguard against blatant nonintegrity and gross falsehood.

The most practical countermeasures are:

1. Spiritual alignment with truth (which facilitates a favorable shift in brain chemistry).
2. Intellectual sophistication via familiarity with the *Great Books of the Western World*.
3. Awareness of the Map of Consciousness.
4. Advancing one's own level of consciousness by following and practicing verified spiritual teachings and principles of discernment.

Limitations of Wisdom and Valid Social Truth

Although integrity and collective intelligence support happiness and survival, they do not guarantee omniscience or immunity from error or defect. Humankind overall is on an evolutionary path, and life on earth is not a celestial realm. The innate value of human life on earth is that it affords maximum opportunity for spiritual growth through the mechanism of freedom of the will via choice and option. Thus, human life represents the maximum opportunity for the transcendence of negative traits and the gain of positive merit. Acceptance of human limitation, both individually and collectively, allows for forbearance, forgiveness, and compassion rather than condemnation. Human progress is evolutionary, and, therefore, mistakes and errors are inevitable. The only real tragedy is to become older but not wiser.

CHAPTER 9

Faith

Human activities and actions are based on faith, belief, and trust because the qualities themselves are intrinsic to the very structure and function of the human mind by virtue of its evolutionary origin. As previously noted, everyone unconsciously presumes and has faith that their own mind is processing and reporting 'reality', and that their own viewpoint is therefore true, which means that other viewpoints are false or mistaken. With progressive education and wisdom, this basic presumption becomes tailored to more humble dimensions, but even then, it remains a bedrock of the ego's confidence in its capacity to know the truth and, therefore, 'reality'.

Everyone is basically vulnerable to error, as was pointed out by Jesus Christ, the Buddha, Socrates, and later philosophers, such as René Descartes and many others. With the recognition that the mental discernment of truth was actually quite difficult, there arose the great philosophical systems as are exhibited by the erudite *Great Books of the Western World*. Even Newtonian science was later superseded by the great discoveries of the theories of relativity, quantum mechanics, subparticle physics, and, importantly, the Heisenberg Uncertainty Principle, and more. Independent of science or academics, there have always been the great religions and mystical traditions as well as the teachings of the great sages.

As noted, the matrix of the mind is innocent by virtue of its innate structure. The mind is in a constant state of presumptive believingness. Even if it doubts, it does so out of the innocent reliance on seemingly logical argument. Although ridiculing faith and trust, skeptics themselves exhibit the same naïve confidence and faith in their own subjective intellectualizations and mentalized perceptions. The skeptic states that the mind is unable to know the truth, and then, paradoxically, uses that very mind to prove the validity of doubt and mistrust; thus, even the skeptic is basically motivated by naïve trust and faith.

Inasmuch as it is primarily by faith and trust that any human endeavor is possible, the most obvious necessity is for a means to ascertain truth and reality from a point of observation that is free of the distortions of mentalization or bias. Nor can emotions be substituted to fill the lack because they are instinctual responses to perception, without an inherent capacity to verify reality. Thus, current scientific/philosophical discourse includes such terminology as 'intuitive' versus 'counterintuitive', which is an argument about the validity of so-called 'first-person' subjective reporting. The current philosophical debate in science concerns the question of whether 'subjective' is more real than 'objective', or vice versa. Such discourse ends up as rambling conjecture and circuitous intellectualization, most of which is primarily addressed to other intellectualizers prone to similar limitation.

In the search for trustable, unimpeachable sources of verifiable truth, the human mind has relied on prophets, dreams, visions, shamans, ecclesiastical doctrines, religious authority, history, intuition, revelation, myth, intelligence, legends, oracles, divination, astronomy, astrology, transmediums, channelers, archeology, paleontology, political systems, philosophy, metaphysics, reason, logic, Newtonian science, quantum mechanics, relativity theory, advanced theoretical and subparticle physics, and now the realizations described by Peter Lynds (2003). He points out that the same limitations that have been discovered by consciousness research—even duration and time itself—are primarily projections of consciousness, with no actual physical existence. With no self-existent reality such as 'time', there is no real 'now' or moment, and therefore, no time-dependent relative position is possible in physical reality. Thus, Lynds solves the classic 'Xeno' paradox, which was originally stated in ancient Greece.

Consciousness research has made available a means of discerning truth from falsehood as well as the capacity to ascertain the degree of relative truth compared to an absolute (a scale of 1 to 1,000). The effect was comparable to the impact of the development of the telescope on astronomy, or the microscope on biology in that consciousness research provided a pragmatic instrument which facilitated the opening of an entirely new field of research containing an objective, practical tool for verification and validation of levels of truth. The simple methodology of consciousness research (cal. 605) is easily comprehensible and does not tax the intellect or require advanced degrees of formal education or belief systems because it is experiential, nonintellectual, and self-reifying. Simply stated, truth (reality) makes the body musculature go strong in people who calibrate over 200, and falsehood (nonreality) makes them go weak, just as litmus paper is pink to acid and blue to alkaline substances.

Basis of Consciousness Calibration

That truth makes the body musculature go strong and falsehood result in its weakening was an empirical clinical discovery (Hawkins, 1995). The phenomenon is due to the fact that truth exists as an actual reality, whereas falsehood merely has no substrate of reality. Thus, the muscle-testing response is either "yes" or "not yes" ("no"). The mechanisms are clarified by understanding basic principles of quantum physics by which the Heisenberg Uncertainty Principle itself is the 'litmus paper'. Phenomena are the consequence of the collapse of the 'wave state' of potentiality to the 'particle state' of manifestation and actuality. These are the result of intention and observation itself. The observer and the observed become an operational unit. Truth has actual existence and therefore collapses the wave function. Falsehood has no reality (nonexistent) and thus fails to get a response (the arm weakens). Thus, like electricity, the wire is either 'on' and carries current ("yes") or is 'not on' ("no"). Furthermore, detailed description is readily available through Henry Stapp via his personal Web site, and Scott Jeffrey (Jeffrey and Colyer, 2007).

Evolution of Faith

When the infinitely powerful, nonlinear energy field of consciousness (the Light of God) interacted with matter, life originated out of the resultant organic substrate (calibrates as true at the level of Infinity).

Early life forms lacked intrinsic sources of energy for survival and further growth; therefore, energy had to be sought and obtained from the local environment. The vegetable form of life, however, utilized chlorophyll to convert sunlight into energy, but animal life forms had to obtain necessary nutrients by contact and incorporation. Thus, animal life had to learn to distinguish usable life-sustaining substances from those that were antithetical to life and thus develop the capacity for intelligence.

Survival itself was based on the evolution of the capacity to develop reliable information gathering, interpretation, and organization of data (e.g., discern 'good' from 'bad'). This later became what is known as intelligence, with its innate capacity to sort, stratify, and store linear data via meaning (essence) and survival value. The reliance on correct information for survival then formed the matrix out of which faith (reliability) later evolved.

In the human, there evolved not only the capacity to process and interpret linear data, but there was also available the nonlinear energy of consciousness/awareness that was called 'spiritual' because the energy source was nonphysical and not definable by linear concepts. This, too, was evolutionary in its human development and was called the 'human spirit'. It was characterized by the emergence of a nonphysical ('etheric') energy body, the survival and evolution of which were independent of the physical body itself. Thus, spirit is related to essence, and reason to linear form and definition.

As can be seen from its evolutionary development,

faith was a biological necessity for survival that was built into a basic structure of the ego as the sense of self. The capacity to be aware of and experience the self was a quality of sentient awareness innate to the animal kingdom. Thus, humankind lived by faith. Naïvely, the ego placed its primary faith in the narcissistic core of the ego itself (e.g., perception/opinion), which therefore assumed autonomy and sovereignty as the arbiter of reality. The ego is, by virtue of its structure and origin, blind to its own limitations.

Faith versus Reason

This dichotomy could be more accurately depicted as reliance on the unseen, ultimate nonlinear contextual reality versus reliance for truth on the limited linear content of mentalization. Generally, linear intellectual constructs, such as science and philosophy, are viewed as presumptively objective, verifiable, and provable, while nonlinear reality is described as subjective, mystical, ineffable, and (prior to consciousness research) nonconfirmable.

The Scopes trial is the best-known example of the confrontation between the disparities of paradigms. Actually, as described previously, there is no real conflict anymore than there is a 'conflict' between organic and inorganic matter, or between living and nonliving entities. The limitation is merely an artifact of the limitation of viewpoint that occurs when a subject is addressed from different levels of consciousness (Van Biema, 2006).

On the calibrated scale of consciousness, as previously mentioned, the linear, provable dimension is represented by calibration levels up to 499, and the nonlinear levels of consciousness from 500 up are experiential, confirmable, and demonstrable but not 'provable' by the rules of reason or logic because they are beyond the paradigm of reality as defined by consciousness levels in the 400s. Intelligence is the capacity to discern basic patterns (principles) that can then be creatively utilized in problem solving.

The change in brain physiology (as per the Brain Function chart, Chapter 4) at level 200 indicates a shift of neurotransmitters. This major shift in the basic physiology of the brain itself is confirmatory of the importance of reliance on spiritual values and their contribution, significance, and meaning. Thus, man's higher development is expressed by the use of intelligence in the service of spiritualized intention.

Curiosity: The Mental Engine of Survival

For life to survive, organisms had to constantly search for external sources of energy as well as to locate water and favorable physical and environmental conditions. This required development of the capacity to sample and identify data and eventually discern basic principles. The pattern of 'search and sample' is the process identified as curiosity and exploration whereby information is subsequently stored, processed, and categorized for the sake of efficiency. This capacity emerged as intelligence, and its linear symbolic products were reason and mentalization.

Reason is the capacity to categorize and manipulate symbols and images that originate as extractions of principles from the physical world so that experience can be amplified and elaborated by the faculty of mentation, independent of actual physical contact or experience. Thus, experimentation could be freed from actual physical location, and explanation could result in the excitement of adventure and pleasure from the 'new', as well as reconfirmation of the familiar. The amoeba's exploration for survival has become the 'research and development' of today's world as an important major activity of all business, industry, and commerce.

Scientific theories evolved over the centuries via often-contentious debate and refinement, and they are still currently evolving, especially regarding quantum theory (Rosenblum, 2006). The benefits of faith in science were not only intellectual but also included the production of technology and other means of verifying and demonstrating the reliability of linear processing. In contrast, processing of information in the nonlinear spiritual domain historically has been purely subjective and experiential and therefore reliant on first-person testimony. The benefits of nonlinear spiritual realizations are observable and verifiable but not provable in the same way as is linear documentable data. Spiritual experience is the consequence of high-frequency energies beyond the consciousness range of the provable. Their expressions are observable, much as friendliness is recognizable in contrast to impersonality. By virtue of its impact on brain physiology and hormonal processes, spiritual context impacts the biological level as demonstrated by worldwide faith-based recovery groups in which the previously impossible becomes possible.

Spiritual intention, commitment, and alignment alter context within which content is influenced and modified. By analogy, when applying the Heisenberg Uncertainty Principle, spiritual intention collapses the wave function of potentiality into actuality. Spiritual intention also has a notable effect on perception itself so that life events and human interaction are experienced, witnessed, and comprehended from a higher perspective (e.g., 'miraculous'). This also results in a major shift of emotions consequent to the more favorable shift of brain function and its information-processing pathways as well as neural hormones and transmitters.

With spiritual progress, there is a transformation of subjective experiential witnessing accompanied by a concordant positive change in the appearance of the world and its events. It is discovered that spiritual effort is exciting, rewarding, and results in gratification and benefits that eventually reach the level which can only be described as 'miraculous' because they emerge spontaneously out of the power of nonlinear context rather than being 'caused' by linear content.

Meaning, significance, and value are experientially revelatory in their emergence rather than seeming to occur as a consequence of presumptive, logical 'cause and effect'. The laws of context are those of dominance, influence, and increased likelihood that are therefore dissimilar from the content of ordinary mentation.

With advancement of consciousness, the truths of spiritual realities become spontaneously obvious, even though they may not be logically comprehensible to the thinking mind. The witnessing of events results in a greater contextualized comprehension that is beyond the ordinary. This transition becomes quite marked at consciousness levels 540 and above, by which all experience is transformed. By consciousness levels 570 to 590, there is a continuous unfolding of ever-increasing beauty and perfection, and the witnessing of the seemingly miraculous can become almost constant.

Development of Faith

The individual's psychological capacity for the development of faith begins with childhood dependency on reliable parenting where nurturance is provided in accord with the infant's tolerance levels. With adequate training, the tolerance of delay increases as faith is linked with expectancy. This phase also influences later propensity for optimism versus pessimism, as well as confidence in authority figures.

Parental guidance rewards positive behaviors, and the withholding of it for negative behaviors can even be accompanied by punishment for noncompliance. The ego/self then integrates the parental pattern of 'good me' versus 'bad me' as well as 'good-versus-bad' concepts of authority. Out of this dichotomy arise guilt and self-hatred versus approval. The pain of guilt is assuaged by the discovery of blame, excuses, and rationalizations. The propensity for trust becomes incorporated in later development as spiritual expectations and beliefs in God and spiritual truths.

Everyone already has a calibratable level of consciousness from the very moment of birth, which is independent of worldly factors or circumstances. This is in accord with the classic principle of karma that, although not a Western term, finds its corollary expressions in Western religions (fate, destiny). (The calibratable level of truth of the principle of karma calibrates at 1,000.)

The calibratable level of an infant's consciousness at birth roughly indicates the degree of spiritual evolution that has already occurred and also implies the amount of work yet to be done. There is widespread recognition of this basic principle in all the major religions of the world, as well as agreement that the characteristic of the afterlife of the spirit is the consequence of spiritual choices made during earthly life.

To facilitate the acceptance of man's fate are the great teachings that emphasize the availability of Salvation and/or Enlightenment, accompanied by the benefits of Grace which ensue from faith. Therefore, the teaching "But believe in my name" emanates from the teachings of Krishna, Buddha, Jesus Christ, Muhammad, and the great, ancient Aryan sages. That "The kingdom of God is within you" is confirmable by consciousness calibration as well as by the subjective human experience of the shift of identity from the self to the Self (Hawkins, 2007).

That faith may be naïvely and mistakenly placed in inadequate or nonintegrous teachers or erroneous pathways was described in detail in *Truth vs. Falsehood*. Misplaced faith is the basis for great disasters, both personal and collectively, whereby the innocence of naïve devotees is exploited by leaders and teachings that calibrate at only 90 or below. Therefore, faith in verifiable truth is the royal pathway to Salvation and Enlightenment. In contrast, faith in that which is erroneous is a trap for the unwary. Thus, Jesus Christ, the Buddha, and all the other great teachers taught that man's basic error is due to ignorance, and his long-term destiny is dependent on overcoming that ignorance. Therefore, identification and verification of truth are critical to human destiny, both collectively and individually. As we can see by historical analysis, the consciousness level of mankind has progressively risen over the centuries.

Theism and Deism in the United States

Although secularism is promulgated via well-funded legal/political activist groups, the majority of Americans (ninety-two percent) believe in God, and ninety percent have a religious or faith-based affiliation (*Baylor Survey of Religion*, 2006). Only five percent are atheists (which is the same as the worldwide rate). The survey reported that God may be conceived of as authoritarian (thirty-one percent), benevolent (twenty-three percent), critical/judgmental (sixteen percent), or distant (twenty-four percent). Of nonaffiliated people, sixty percent believe in God. Thus, the great majority of Americans have faith in a Higher Power.

Commonly, degrees of faith, affiliations, and concepts of God fluctuate during people's lifetimes, resulting in periods of great faith as well as periods of neglect. Then later, there is a resurgence, especially in response to stress and calamity. Thus, faith may be active or merely dormant.

The Necessity for Reason

As is readily apparent, innocent trust and faith can lead to serious error without the counterbalance of reason, logic, and education. Thus, credibility of sources of information indicates the importance of the capacity to discern verifiable truth from falsehood. Rationality requires accurate information plus the capacity to process data through experience and mature as the progressive wisdom and authenticity that is the final product of experiencing. Thus, by processing, the linear becomes integrated and synthesized within the context of the nonlinear overall field of comprehension and understanding.

Without the leavening and contextualization of reason, religious faith can lead to irrational extremism and destructive excess of religiosity as fanaticism. Thus, genocide and barbaric mayhem have occurred throughout history and are now expressed as Islamic terrorism and fascism.

As demonstrated worldwide, Islam is currently at war in many countries, with no counterbalance of reason or rationality. The current international criticism of Islam is that it is immune to reason and unable to even comprehend its value (Warraq, 2002). The difficulty is due to Islam's denunciation of reason as a threat to faith (as per the Koran).

Influence of Religion in United States Society

The overall cultural impact of the various religions or belief systems currently calibrate as follows:

Atheism	165	Libertarianism	185
Academia	190	Hedonism	180

Relativism, Moral	180-185	Judaism	450
Sophistry (Political)	185	Catholicism	450
Islam	190	Protestantism	450
Secularism	190	Traditionalism	450
Academia	190	Buddhism	455
Hollywood	190	Chivalry	455
Evolutionary Psychology	210	12-Step Programs	525
Christianity	450		

As shown above, the source of socio-political-philosophical conflict and debate is between the segments of society that calibrate below 200 and those that calibrate in the 400s. This demonstrates the old American Indian legend that inside everyone there are two wolves. One is evil and angry, jealous, greedy, arrogant, and given to false pride and prideful ego. The other is good and is joy, peace, love, hope, serenity, humility, kindness, generosity, and truth. Therefore, be careful which wolf you feed (Wheat, 2007). One wolf leads to enslavement, the other to freedom and liberty (Williams, 2007, quoting Alan Keyes).

Faith as a Cornerstone of America

Deistic/theistic faith has been the primary foundation of America since its founding and continues to be the very basis for its continuance of freedom, opportunity, and strength as guaranteed by the United States Constitution itself. The details were well explained in *God and Religion in America* (Gingrich, 2006) and *The Preacher and the Presidents* (Gibbs and Duffy, 2007). It is clear from all the above that faith itself is of such power that it sustains moral integrity in the face of worldwide challenge and threat of destruction. The presidents thus bulwarked reason with extensive ethical investigation and pastoral discourse.

The Reverend Billy Graham served eleven American presidents and the country for fifty years. Thus, faith is not only inspiring but ultra-practical in its capacity to contextualize logic and reason. The grim decisions of war were the consequence of the overall historical context of the threat of survival. In sequence came the great challenges of totalitarian aggression (e.g., Imperialist Japan and the Nazi regime), then communist militancy, and currently, Islamic totalitarianism and attack on the United States itself.

Another stress of the presidency is the constant risk of assassination by which many former presidents were either injured or killed. Another formidable stress is the constant stream of hatred directed at every president by every form of vilification and threat. Without faith, function would be impossible.

CHAPTER 10

Experiential vs. Conceptual

The word 'know' can imply multiple levels, such as 'heard about', 'learned about', 'presumed', or 'be familiar with'. It can also mean 'formally studied', or even 'expertise in a given subject'.There are levels of knowing that most accurately can be described as provisional, presumptive, hypothetical, or conjectural likelihoods. There are also degrees of conviction, certainty, and convincingness. Thus, each level implies degrees of certitude or reliability based on experiential information in contrast to intellectual constructs of mentation.

To 'know about' means that although the information itself is familiar, its reality and truth remain to be confirmed experientially. In the final stage of achieving certainty, to really know means to 'be', and thus both subject and knower are unified.To know 'about' is mental; to know experientially is accepted as confirmatory. ("The proof of the pudding is in the eating.")

In the familiar linear and conceptual levels of life, confirmation is relatively easy and practical. In contrast, in spiritual matters, the entire process is of a different, subtler nature that involves modalities other than just thought, emotions, or mentalized constructions. The confirmation of spiritual realities requires the development of other qualities and capacities of consciousness by which the nonlinear realities can truly be known (e.g., via identity).

Who Is the Knower?

The mind naïvely assumes that it is the real 'me' who is searching for truth because it assumes that its ego/self is primary and is the sole author of intention as well as action, and therefore the arbiter of reality. This implies motivation as well as a presumptive goal. The motivation for knowingness can be simply mere curiosity or the desire for gain, but with spiritual motivation, there also arises the inner necessity to ascertain certainty of the innate truths of various teachings, pathways, and religions. The desire for meaning, truth, and spirituality has biological roots that correlate with brain physiology (Newberg, 2006).

Traditionally, the readiness for spiritual learning has been termed 'ripeness', indicating a fortuitous combination of sincere intention plus maturity, progressive evolution of consciousness, and activation of the desire for experiential learning. Although it may start with only mild curiosity, interest then gains momentum with intensified progressive awareness of the importance of spiritual learning and the implication of its long-term personal consequences. There develops an enthusiasm and eventually a dedication, and spiritual goals and values progressively replace the lesser ones of the worldly ego. Utilization of spiritual information results in progressive inner experience and wisdom that further increase incentives. Spiritual premises experientially become progressively real and lead to conviction as the 'knowing about' converts to actually knowing by virtue of experiential becoming.

Progress is best described as the unfolding of realizations and spontaneous revelation that are often ascribed to intuition and inner guidance. Many people speak of spiritual guides as experiential realities. As spiritual work advances, the self progressively dissolves and merges into the Self, which has its own learning capacities that differ from those of the ego/mind.

Sovereignty

Whereas the narcissistic core of the ego presumes that it is the source of experiential reality and seeks credit, spiritual processing brings about an ever-deepening humility and eventual inner gratitude. Spiritual intention activates the Self to become progressively dominant, and surrender of positionalities becomes easier and more natural. There is a subtle shift of allegiance from the presumptively known to the still unknown. Then arises the inner discipline for perseverance and the resolve to transcend resistances. Success brings ever-greater strength, faith, and conviction in the spiritual process itself. The weakened ego gradually recedes and surrenders its illusions of sovereignty, allowing the seeker to be led by the influence of the Presence of the true Higher Power.

Spiritual Intention

Most commonly, the original source of spiritual information is via a form of religion or spiritual organization that is endemic to the culture of one's family and birth. With acceptance and maturation, nothing more is actually required since spiritual progress is the result of dedication. Alignment with traditional religions and their teachings provides a core of spiritual truth that subtly becomes intuited in its differentiation from ecclesiastical elaborations that seem more appropriate to other cultures and times.

Whatever their presumptive limitations, traditional religions suffice for the majority of people, but for some individuals, there is doubt. Classical teachings seem insufficient and problematic. This is especially so for the educated person of today for whom reason, science, and the intellect can bring disquieting doubts (e.g., the Scopes trial dilemma). Thus, modern man rejects and yet accepts both sides of the Scopes trial. The requirement is one of integrating faith, traditional religion, and scientific realities as well as logic and the reason of the intellect.

A common life experience is for formal religion to be an accepted part of childhood and early life. This then becomes neglected or abandoned by the pressing requirements and time demands of adulthood and family life in the modern world. Although a return to simple acceptance is desired, questions and doubts have arisen that have to be answered. With maturation and advancing age, denial of mortality diminishes, and the necessity arises once more to look into religious/spiritual teachings. To discern their inherent reality becomes progressively more important. This importance can be precipitated by serious life events, either personal or social, that are confrontive, such as severe illness, death, or calamities.

Interestingly, almost all survivors of major disasters spontaneously recount that they prayed in earnest (actually ninety-nine percent), and some even went into a state of profound peace subsequent to prayer and surrendering to God. This, surprisingly, is very characteristic of people who have been lifted high up in the air into the eye of a tornado. They reported being in a state of profound stillness and peace that was outside of time, and they were almost sad when the tornado came to an end and they returned to a normal mental state. These personal experiences reflect the dictum, "Man's catastrophe is God's opportunity." Night after night on television's Weather Channel, one can hear the spontaneous testimonies of the survivors of disastrous events.

The discoveries of the Reality of Divinity consequent to personal or group disasters have traditionally been ridiculed by the skeptic as 'foxhole religion' due to the presumption that the motivation is merely situational fear. In reality, this discovery is made only after the fear is surrendered. Fear itself actually precludes the awareness of the Presence of God. Only when it is abandoned does profound surrender of the resistant ego reveal a Peace beyond understanding. Its profundity has to be experienced to be understood as it cannot really be described in words. Its net effect, however, is transformative and life changing, and those who have been transformed by the great depth and profundity of the experience acquire a radiance that shows through many years later.

The discovery of the Presence of God is not due to fear but to the surrender that was precipitated by the fear. The profound states of Infinite Peace in the very eye of disaster calibrate at 600, are life transforming, and result in a permanent loss of fear of death.

Verification of Spiritual Realities

Whereas most people have the capacity to accept the truths taught by the great religions and spiritual teachers of history, the modern mind now often poses different requirements due to the impact of the media, modern skepticism, secularism, and the undermining of traditional values. In addition, the modern college education involves subtle as well as overt programming that discredits and undermines those values. There is a pervasive, strong, open academic hostility towards spirituality, religion, and even traditional moral and ethical values (Kupelian, 2005). This indoctrination is fortressed by inculcation of postmodern, relativistic philosophical belief systems, the inner fallacies of which are revealed by calibrating the levels of truth of the teachings (160 to 180), which are shown thereby to be inherently false.

The intellectual trends of today's academia calibrate at 180-190. This is further buttressed by political ideologies that calibrate from 160 to 190 or even lower and result in sympathy and apologists for the falsehood of sophistry. Thus, today's college graduate actually has an inculcated limitation of intelligence and impaired reality testing, especially of intellectual integrity and the capacity to discern the fallacies of rhetoric.

While the 'ignorance' of previous generations was primarily due to that which is inherent within the ego/mind structure, the problem is now compounded by additional layers of actual subtle intellectual indoctrination and programming. While such indoctrination is cleverly hidden under the cloak of supposed idealism, its real appeal is to that of the intellectual pride of being superior and other attitudes of self-aggrandizement.

All the predominant, currently fashionable relativistic sociopolitical philosophies and systems calibrate below 200, and their attraction is universally their appeal to narcissism and especially attractive to the 'YouTube/me' generation, as per the famous *Time* magazine cover of December 25, 2006. The benefit of the now-surfaced recognition and acknowledgement of social 'ego worship' is that it is necessary before it can be transcended.

Consequent to all the above, it is now more necessary than ever before to be able to formally validate the level of truth of any teacher, teaching, spiritual religious group, university faculty, organization, etc. Thus, the first requirement for successful spiritual endeavor is intellectual humility from which investigation can profitably proceed.

Whereas the calibration level of America overall is currently at 421, the culture of academia now calibrates at a shocking 190. The narcissistic ego appeal of postmodernism or anarchism results in the deification of hedonism, nihilism (Marcuse, Chomsky, et al.), and the discarding of the philosophical wisdom of *The Great Books* (cal. 460). The intellectual integrity of those great classic books was formerly the backbone of a college education. Now, however, as mentioned previously, Ivy League, 'Big Ten', or even Jesuit universities, such as Notre Dame, want to be 'modern' and incorporate speakers and politicized teachings (Goshgarian, 2005) that calibrate far below 200. Thus, the decline of Western civilization is a consequence of both relativism itself and its consequent subservience to Islamic triumphalism as was described by Pope Benedict (2006) and multiple news analysts (e.g., Beck, 2006). This decline is an example of the effect of 'iteration', a term from nonlinear dynamics, which states that even a small stimulus, if frequently repeated, can result in a major change (see *Power vs. Force*.)

For all the reasons mentioned above and others we have not yet discussed, it is now more important than ever before to be able to formally validate the truth of the teachings of any philosophical, political, spiritual, or religious group or organization. Thus, the first requirement for successful spiritual endeavor is intellectual humility from which investigation can beneficially proceed.

For convenience, the characteristics of integrous, legitimate spiritual teachers, teachings, and spiritual organizations are identified by the following list (reprinted here from *Truth vs. Falsehood*):

Identification and Characteristics of Spiritual Truth, Integrous Teachers, and Teachings

1. **Universality**: Truth is true at all times and places, independent of culture, personalities, or circumstances.
2. **Nonexclusionary**: Truth is all-inclusive, nonsecretive, and nonsectarian.
3. **Availability**: It is open to all, non-exclusive. There are no secrets to be revealed, hidden, or sold, and no magical formulas or 'mysteries'.

4. **Integrity of purpose**: There is nothing to gain or lose.
5. **Nonsectarian**: Truth is not the exposition of limitation.
6. **Independent of opinion**: Truth is nonlinear and not subject to the limitations of intellect or form.
7. **Devoid of Positionality**: Truth is not 'anti' anything. Falsehood and ignorance are not its enemies but merely represent its absence.
8. **No requirements or demands**: There are no required memberships, dues, regulations, oaths, rules, or conditions.
9. **Noncontrolling**: Spiritual purity has no interest in the personal lives of aspirants, or in clothing, dress, style, sex lives, economics, family patterns, lifestyles, or dietary habits.
10. **Free of force or intimidation**: There is no brainwashing, adulation of leaders, training rituals, indoctrinations, or intrusions into private life.
11. **Nonbinding**: There are no regulations, laws, edicts, contracts, or pledges.
12. **Freedom**: Participants are free to come and go without persuasion, coercion, intimidation, or consequences. There is no hierarchy; instead, there is voluntary fulfillment of practical necessities and duties.
13. **Commonality**: Recognition is a consequence of what one has become rather than as a result of ascribed titles, adjectives, or trappings.
14. **Inspirational**: Truth eschews and avoids glamorization, seduction, and theatrics.
15. **Nonmaterialistic**: Truth is devoid of neediness of

worldly wealth, prestige, pomp, or edifices.

16. **Self-fulfilling**: Truth is already total and complete and has no need to proselytize or gain adherents, followers, or 'sign up members'.
17. **Detached**: There is noninvolvement in world affairs.
18. **Benign**: Truth is identifiable along a progressive gradient. It has no 'opposite' and therefore no 'enemies' to castigate or oppose.
19. **Nonintentional**: Truth does not intervene or have an agenda to propose, inflict, or promulgate.
20. **Nondualistic**: All transpires by virtue of intrinsic (karmic) propensity within the field by which potentiality manifests as actuality rather than by 'cause' and effect.
21. **Tranquility and Peace**: There are no 'issues' or partialities. There is no desire to change others or impose on society. The effect of higher energies is innate and not dependent on propagation or effort. God does not need help anymore than gravity needs the 'help' of an apple's falling off the tree.
22. **Equality**: This is expressed in reverence for all of life in all its expression and merely avoids that which is deleterious rather than opposing it.
23. **Nontemporality**: Life is realized to be eternal and physicality to be a temporality. Life is not subject to death.
24. **Beyond proof**: That which is 'provable' is linear, limited, and a product of intellectualization and mentation. Reality needs no agreement. Reality is not an acquisition but instead is a purely spontaneous, subjective realization when the positionali-

ties of the dualistic ego are surrendered.

25. **Mystical**: The origination of truth is a spontaneous effulgence, radiance, and illumination, which are the Revelation that replaces the illusion of a separate individual self, the ego, and its mentation.
26. **Ineffable**: Not capable of definition. Radical subjectivity is experiential. It is a condition that replaces the former. With this event, context replaces content, devoid of temporality and beyond time. Reality does not exist in time, or of it, or beyond it, or outside of it, and it has no relationship to that which is an artifice of mentation. It is therefore beyond all nouns, adjectives, or verbs, transitive or intransitive.
27. **Simplistic**: One sees the intrinsic beauty and perfection of all that exists beyond appearance and form.
28. **Affirmative**: Truth is beyond opinion or provability. Confirmation is purely by its subjective awareness; however, it is identifiable by consciousness calibration techniques.
29. **Nonoperative**: Truth does not 'do' anything or 'cause' anything; it is everything.
30. **Invitational**: As contrasted with promotional or persuasive.
31. **Nonpredictive**: Because Reality is nonlinear, it cannot be localized or encoded in restriction of form, such as secret messages, codes, numbers, and inscriptions, or hidden in runes, stones, the dimensions of the pyramid, the DNA, or the nostril hairs of the camel. Truth has no secrets. The Reality of God is omnipresent and beyond codification or exclusivity. Codes are indicative of man's imagination and not

the capriciousness of Divinity.

32. **Nonsentimental**: Emotionality is based on perception. Compassion results from the discernment of truth.
33. **Nonauthoritarian**: There are no rules or dictates to be followed.
34. **Non-egoistic**: Teachers are respected but reject personal adulation or specialness.
35. **Educational**: Provides information in a variety of formats and ensures availability.
36. **Self-supporting**: Neither mercenary nor materialistic.
37. **Freestanding**: Complete without dependence on external or historical authorities.
38. **Natural**: Devoid of induced, altered states of consciousness or manipulations of energies by artificial exercises, postures, breathing, or dietary rituals, (i.e., nonreliance on form or physicality; no invoking of entities or 'others').
39. **Complete**: Devoid of exploitation or gain.
40. **Nonviolent**: Not coercive; benign; nonthreatening.

In addition to the above requirements, for convenience, the following list of the calibration levels of major established world teachings is also provided (from *Truth vs. Falsehood*):

Spiritual Teachings

Abhinavagupta (Kashmir Shaivinism)	655	Aggadah	645
		Apocrypha	400
A Course in Miracles (workbook)	600	Bodhidharma Zen Teachings	795
A Course in Miracles (text)	550	Bhagavad-Gita	910

Book of Kells	570
Book of Mormon	405
Cloud of Unknowing	705
Dead Sea Scrolls	260
Dhammapada	840
Diamond Sutra	700
Doctrine and Covenants:	
Pearl of Great Price	455
Genesis (Lamsa Bible)	660
Gnostic Gospels	400
Gospel of St. Luke	699
Gospel of St. Thomas	660
Granth Sahib-Adi (Sikhs)	505
Heart Sutra	780
Huang-Po Teachings	850
Kabbalah	605
King James Bible (from the Greek)	475
Koran	90-700
Lamsa Bible (from the Aramaic)	495
Lamsa Bible (minus the Old Testament and Book of Revelation, but including Genesis, Psalms, and Proverbs)	880
Lao Tsu: Teachings	610
Lotus Sutra	780
Midrash	665
Mishneh	665
New Testament (King James Version after deletion of the Book of Revelation)	790
New Testament (King James Version from the Greek)	640
Nicene Creed	895
Psalms (Lamsa Bible)	650
Proverbs (Lamsa Bible)	350
Ramayana	810
Rubaiyat of Omar Khayyam	590
Rig Veda	705
Talmud	595
Tibetan Book of the Dead	575
Torah	550
Trinity (concept)	945
Upanishads	970
Vedanta	595
Vedas	970
Vijnane Bhairava	635
Yoga Sutras, Patanjali	740
Zohar	905

Spiritual endeavor starts with taking responsibility rather than depending on naïve impulsivity or proselytization. It is important to realize it is not just a literal wording of teachings but also the entire energy field of a teacher or organization that has a subtle, unseen field effect upon students. There is wisdom in the old dictum to "stay with holy company" and avoid that which is nonintegrous. Just on the face of it, it would appear to be foolish to disregard the teachings of Jesus Christ, the Buddha, or Krishna, all of which calibrate at 1,000, and substitute for them the pseudodeification of the teachings of atheistic anarchists whose false teachings have brought on the death of literally hundreds of millions of people just in this lifetime.

Experiential Validation

Spiritual alignment and intention plus dedication are inherently transformative and bring about a progressive change in the quality of life experience. This occurs automatically as a result of the field effect and is therefore not 'caused' by the personal will. The incorporation of spiritual values should be for its own sake rather than for some imaginary gain or control that paradoxically counters and obstructs the primary intention.

A subtle inner pleasure accompanies true spiritual endeavor. An inner quality of peace and fulfillment accompanies the subtle inner knowingness that one is finally 'homeward bound' in the transition from the world of the self to the expanded awareness of the Self. There is also relief from inner spiritual guilt that accompanies spiritual negligence and willful indulgence of the ego's demands and desires for gain.

Resistance

The source of resistance to spiritual endeavor is the narcissistic core of the ego itself, which secretly claims sovereignty and authorship of one's existence, decisions, and actions. Thus, despite one's best efforts, willfulness and desire for gain or control continue to erupt repetitiously. This pattern can be diminished simply by accepting that it is natural for the ego to be vain, greedy, hateful, prideful, resentful, envious, and more.

These were learned accretions to the ego during its evolutionary development over eons of time. Therefore, it is not necessary to feel guilty because these primitive emotions merely need to be outgrown and discarded in the transition from self-interest to Self-interest.

Spiritual Progress

The true validation of spiritual truth is subjective, experiential, progressive. It often takes the form of spontaneous discovery, subtle revelation, and emergence of a new, more expanded awareness. This is consequent to the transition from identification with content to that of context. A subtle satisfaction accompanies inner growth that is affirmative as a knowingness consequent to surrender, which invites Divine Grace. These are recognized to be gifts rather than acquisitions or consequences of one's personal efforts. One experiences that gains have not been acquired but have been granted; thus, gratitude replaces spiritual pride or the vanity of the spiritual ego that seeks to claim credit.

Spiritual progress is unpredictable and influenced by unknown factors, including karmic propensities. The 'spiritual ego' is tempted to arise when the seeker begins to experience the phenomena of the so-called *siddhis* that characteristically appear in the energy field of 540 and especially on up to around level 570. (These levels have been previously described in detail.) They should not be pursued for their own sake, nor should a person take credit for them as the phenomena are autonomously consequent to the rise of the spiritual/

kundalini energy itself. They are gifts of the spirit to be accepted with gratitude. The phenomena cannot be controlled but merely witnessed.

The miraculous nature of the siddhis is indeed quite astonishing and impressive when they begin to occur and can eventually become almost continuous. Humility allows for the witnessing to happen without claim to authorship, which is a pitfall and error for students who have not been forewarned.

Imitations of the genuine siddhis are peddled for profit by nonintegrous, self-seeking organizations. The creation of imitations of genuine siddhis is endemic in many cultures, such as with the so-called 'holy men' of India. Claims of 'performing miracles' are also common in cult leaders, which lead to aggrandizement. There are, however, spontaneous cures that are the result of hypnotic suggestion induced by theatrical healers via suggestion plus dramatic displays.

As described previously, the miraculous phenomena of the siddhis may last for some years, and they come and go. They can indeed, as said above, be very astonishing and impressive because they occur without any personal volition. They are very real, confirmable, and can be incredibly accurate. They account for 'spontaneous remissions', which are known to occur in patients with almost any or all diseases and are well documented.

The miraculous phenomena are due to the activation of the principle of potentiality becoming actuality when conditions are appropriate, such as the presence of the power of advanced spiritual energy fields. These influential energies have traditionally been called 'kundalini', which is merely a name for the spiritual energy that runs through the inner energy system and eventually energizes and lights up the higher etheric, spiritual energy bodies.

This spiritual energy emerges and begins to rise at consciousness level 200. Its initial benefit is that it changes brain dominance and neurotransmitters. It also triggers the release of endorphins so that brain processing of information is not only altered but also brings about changes of perception that are transformative (Newberg, 2006). Thus, at the higher spiritual levels of consciousness, miraculous healings occur, which is why a well-known spiritual pathway is called "A Course in Miracles." Clinical experience confirms that potentiality is activated as actuality by the power of the field of consciousness.

Spiritual endeavor has many benefits, both seen and unseen, and studies abound which reveal increased social capacity as well as greater health and behavioral benefits that accrue to the family as well. In addition, the overall level of happiness is directly related statistically to the prevailing level of consciousness, shown here for convenience from *Transcending the Levels of Consciousness*.

Correlation of Levels of Consciousness and the Rate of Happiness

LEVEL	LOG	PERCENT
Enlightenment	700-1,000	100
Peace	600	100
Joy	570	99
Unconditional Love	540	96
Love	500	89

Correlation of Levels of Consciousness and the Rate of Happiness

LEVEL	LOG	PERCENT
Reason	400	79
Acceptance	350	71
Willingness	310	68
Neutrality	250	60
Courage	200	55
Pride	175	22
Anger	150	12
Desire	125	10
Fear	100	10
Grief	75	9
Apathy, hatred	50	5
Guilt	30	4
Shame	20	1

Just as the lower energy fields attract that which is associated with negativity, including squalor and crime, the higher energy fields attract that which is positive and supportive of life. While the positive benefits of spiritual endeavor are substantial and may even be profound or miraculous, they, like the siddhis, should not be sought for gain but instead humbly accepted with gratitude. Humility arises from intention and desire to serve God or to reach Enlightenment, both of which are very powerful catalysts.

In summary, we can see that the subjective experiential world is a consequence of the calibrated level of consciousness arising from within, independent of external events. Thus, it is impossible to accurately ascertain the true reality of the world as it is because one only experiences the world as it is perceived.

When seen from the highest level, the world is perfect as it is because it offers the maximum opportunity for spiritual evolution.

CHAPTER 11

Belief, Trust, and Credibility

Social Matrix: Information/Disinformation

Faith, belief, and trust are problematic in today's world where the media and the Internet are a dominant theater of contentious bias and severe distortion (Kupelian, 2005). World leaders make overt, grossly fallacious statements, such as "The holocaust never happened," or "The U. S. engineered the 9/11 catastrophe," and public figures knowingly make grossly false statements. Research shows that many politicians distort the truth routinely as do the majority of foreign politicians and members of the United Nations.

In the limelight also are judges who consistently rule in favor of recidivist felons and child abusers; the ACLU sides with child rape pederasts and child pornography; the *New York Times* is transparently, overtly, and even admittedly biased (its editorials calibrate below 200); Hollywood backs seditious absurdity; and media financiers back anti-American hate propaganda (cal. 70) against their own country that made them rich. (Note that all proponents of hate calibrate below 200, as they themselves are the victims of their own hatred.) Supposedly antiwar moguls buy hundreds of millions of dollars of stock in companies that make many billions of dollars on war.

Child pornography is 'proudly' made freely available in a local public library, and 'free speech' is the Trojan horse and standard fatuous excuse for even psychotic degrees of falsehood. The list of propagandized and financially well-supported avenues of falsehood grows longer daily and is passively assented to by the benumbed populace that retreats into confused resignation.

The technique of purposely presenting propagandized falsehood has been progressively and professionally refined. One strategy calls for first intentionally creating shock by a purposefully extreme statement, subsequent to which the public will be less likely to protest the false program, which is the propagandized rhetoric that has been carefully prepared and then sold via the media to the public by perpetrators who seek control. Another favorite ruse is 'salting the mine' with fallacious statements to be later quoted. The 'straw man' attack is also common.

The current media barrage, as would be expected, calibrates at only 160, which represents fallacy as a consequence of prevalent philosophical systems that declare all truth to be merely arbitrary, subjective bias. Inasmuch as there is supposedly no such thing as objective truth, distorted and biased subjective value judgments are purported to be of equal merit. These then often become memes (slogans) that convince listeners of their purported truth by sheer repetition. For example, the seductive phrase "One man's traitor is another man's freedom fighter" calibrates at 180 and represents the clever, misleading downside of relativism. (Famous recent spies calibrate at 80; a currently arrested traitor is also at 80; 'freedom fighter' calibrates at 200, and 'terrorist' calibrates at 30.) The net result of the above programming is an actual diminution in the human capacity and capability for reality testing. Thus, there is the actual destruction of the very ability to discern truth from falsehood at even the most basic levels.This has also been noted and documented by social critics and commentators (Bruce, 2003; Klein, 2007; Marzeles, 2007; Krauthammer, 2007, and many others).

The rationalization for moral anarchy is termed 'ethical relativism' (cal. 155) by which good and evil become equated. By epistemological sleight of hand, however, this reversal of good and evil itself is viewed as a 'good', and traditional ethics then become a 'bad'. Fallacy is fashionable but its calibration at 155 indicates a more serious violation of truth than does philosophical relativism (cal. 190), which is operationally primarily intellectual error.

Survival of Belief and Trust

The public's propensity to believe and trust information which is fallacious paradoxically is evidence that naïve innocence, belief, faith, and trust are intrinsically still very much alive, operative, and actually as strong as ever. In fact, that very bedrock of naïve human nature enables falsity to gain so much momentum and support.

Like lambs led to the slaughter, the naïve innocence of millions of people is savaged, and there is no dearth of eager young recruits for the most ghastly extremes of depraved behavior via which, for example, the purposely slow beheading of innocent women is applauded and paraded on world television (cal. level 10). The self-aggrandized perpetrators, however, hide behind facemasks, and meanwhile, apologists propagandize that the mayhem is in the name of 'freedom fighters' or a 'religion of peace' (Spencer, 2005), which, by mass hypnosis, demonstrates and screams, "Death to America," "Death to Israel," "Death to Christians," "Death to Jews" (and paradoxically threatens to kill anyone who states that it is not a 'religion of Peace' (Goldberg, 2007). Meanwhile, the citizenry is admonished to 'accommodate' the harbingers of social/cultural destruction and fomentation.

Loss of Reality Testing

To protect itself from conflict and stress, the mind seeks refuge through denial or withdrawal, or, paradoxically, by throwing all caution to the wind and wildly jumping into one extreme or another over the conflict. Thus, there is even the parading of denial to an exaggerated and absurd degree, such as Hollywood celebrities rushing to embrace terrorist leaders (cal. 90) who torture women and murder their own countrymen by the hundreds of thousands.

The style and technique of public information presentations often unwittingly or purposely follow the very same systems as employed with brainwashing techniques, which are also designed to destroy self-trust and confidence in one's own mind and its capacity to comprehend reality. The mind then surrenders to the proximate authoritarian figures such as seen in the purposeful indoctrination of young, impressionable college students in the United States, Islamic terrorist recruits worldwide, or brainwashed prisoners (Zimbardo, 2004, 2007; Milgram, 2004).

The syndrome of induced impaired-reality testing has already happened to a large percentage of the world population that has capitulated autonomy and taken the easier road of simply surrendering and parroting slogans and the memes of 'pop' attitudes. This damage has already seriously occurred in forty-five percent of the population in the United States. Also of serious note is the decline in 2006 of the overall consciousness level of America from 426 to its present level of 421 in 2007.

In the United States, falsity is often rewarded by media focus, publicity, and its monetary benefits. The vanity of the narcissistic ego is paraded and presented as being 'important'. Extremism and the grotesque and bizarre have become a quick and easy road to fame and fortune, even if it means selling out integrity, ethics, and morality for profit. Exploitation of innocent human ignorance and naïveté is now a routine occurrence. Being 'bad' is celebrated, and 'girls being bad' is a popular program. Even gross evil is promoted and slyly promoted.

Falsity is not the opposite of truth but merely its absence, for in reality, truth has no opposite, just as cold is not the opposite of heat, nor is light the opposite of darkness. (Darkness represents the absence of light, just as cold indicates the absence of heat.)

Psychosis

One of the most critical blind spots of the public, both in the United States and worldwide, is the inability to recognize blatant, overt psychoses or severe mental disorders, even when accompanied by gross delusions. They are even more difficult to identify if the delusions are cleverly rationalized and defended by politicized rhetorical argument and pseudoevidence. Delusional beliefs spread via memes that become believed as truth solely by virtue of their sheer repetition. False rumors also propagate due to disguised malice reinforced by rationalized distortion and inference. As a consequence, psychotic, grossly delusional professors are invited to speak at prestigious universities that themselves are subject to academically popular delusions (e.g., relativism).

While the above absurdity can be excused by using the pretexts of 'free speech' and 'academic freedom', it is quite strongly remarkable that delusional paranoids are not tolerated in the business world where rationality remains grossly intact. Nobody who believes "the United States caused 9/11" gets hired by business to handle financial decisions. Thus, the job market retains its sanity rather than ignoring the 'elephant in the living room'. While it may be 'fashionable' to agree with anarchy via gross loss of reality testing, psychotic delusions do not escape the sanity of the marketplace. Thus, the recognition of psychotic delusional disorders is quite possible (e.g., common sense) without psychiatric training. (All delusional disorders calibrate below 200.)

Messianic delusional disorders (malignant messianic narcissism) are almost universal in dictators (who commonly calibrate at level 90) in recent history as well as currently. Failure to recognize this disorder has cost the lives of multimillions of people worldwide in the last century. The current world leaders with this disorder threaten nuclear war. (The calibration level of the 90s is also characteristic of child predators and recidivist criminals.)

Extremism

Extremism, especially excessively savage brutality and overt demonstrations of group bloodlust, expresses the most atavistic instincts that are normally rejected and repressed into that area of the unconscious that Sigmund Freud termed the "Id," and Carl Jung termed "the shadow." The bloodlust is exhibited by animal-pack killing; dog-fighting 'sport' by famous athletes; student-homicide spree killing; frenzies; and rabid, frantic group savagery, such as lynch mobs; the Japanese slaughter in Manchuria; mob violence; Ku Klux Klan hangings and torture; the blowing up of innocents by insurgents; the berserk, savage riots in Haiti; and the civil wars in African nations with their machete-wielding participants. In addition, there are the Taliban beheadings and Gestapo slaughters, as well as concentration-camp and gulag mayhem by both Nazis and Stalinists.

The French Revolution was celebrated by the slaughter of fourteen thousand people by the guillotine. Religious cults slaughter themselves and each other, as well as the children. The atavistic trend is glorified currently by Islamic terrorism and mass violence in the name of Apocalyptic Triumphalism by which, via nuclear means, two-thirds of mankind will be annihilated in order to precipitate the appearance of the 'mahdi' (12th Imam) who will convert the world to a paradise similar to the Apocalypse of the Book of Revelation. (This is the stated position and belief system of Iranian president Mahmoud Ahmadinejad [Netanyahu, 2006] who was invited to speak at Columbia University in 2007.) Note that all apocalyptic theories calibrate at an extremely low level of 70, which denotes very serious and fatal falsity.

All the above behaviors have classically been termed 'satanic' and indicate a dark reservoir within human consciousness that can be unleashed under certain circumstances, even by seemingly innocent children (e.g., *Lord of the Flies*). Note that current popular video games often calibrate as low as 90, celebrating murder and rape. This 'dark side' tendency (e.g., the movie *Black Christmas*) was studied and documented by psychological experiments where even ordinary, 'normal' people exhibited cruelty at the behest of authority figures. Even under scientifically controlled prisoner/guard experiments with volunteers, cruelty surfaced among the paid volunteers (Zimbardo, 2004, 2007; Milgram, 2004).

Rampant genocide has been endemic and characteristic of conquering barbarian forces for millennia (e.g., Genghis Khan; the Vikings, Huns, and Goths). Only centuries later was this savage trend incorporated into religious apocalyptic scriptures of Islam and Christianity.

Reversal of Truth

Under the influence of authority, propaganda, and brainwashing techniques, plus group agreement, the human psyche's capacity for reality testing crumbles, and falsity reigns as truth, even to the point of religious worship (the Inquisition). It was an excuse for such events as the Salem witch trials. This phenomenon as an occurrence in religion is also exhibited by the decline of the teachings of Muhammad as a consequence of the cultist teachings of Muhammad Ibn Abd al-Wahhab (cal. 20), and Sayyid Qutb (cal. 75), out of which emerged Hamas (cal. 40), al-Qaeda (cal. 30), and bin Laden's Jihad (20).

It is significant that whole countries, cultures, and religions can, even for decades or centuries, represent the very opposite of their own teachings under certain conditions. The most important mechanism is the claiming of the authority of God in the name of which the most savage and ungodly of nascent human-animal instincts are rationalized, encouraged to be acted out, and even applauded; thus, the killing of innocents by simultaneous suicide (in the name of 'Allah, the All Merciful').

This phenomenon is also exhibited by cults that end up as group suicides (e.g., Jonestown, Heaven's Gate, and Hale-Bopp). All these catastrophes indicate that an aspect of the human consciousness is its tendency to follow politicized authority figures. As history demonstrates, all these charismatic leaders are characterized by the syndrome of 'malignant messianic narcissism', which is defined in detail elsewhere (*Truth vs. Falsehood*, Chapter 14). History repeats itself century after century, up to the present-day world where messianic leaders continue to claim God's authority by which they can rationalize the slaughter of millions of even their own countrymen and families.

The deification of hate and evil (e.g., bin Laden's "We worship death, not life") calibrates at level 10 (primitivism). In today's world, it represents that which over the centuries has been theologically defined as 'satanic reversal'. Its impact on Islam is described in scholarly detail in Ibn Warraq's authoritative study, *Why I Am Not A Muslim* (1995), which calibrates at 410. Other authoritative depictions of this phenomenon are provided by well-known writers, such as the famous long tribulation of Salmon Rushdie subsequent to the Ayatollah's 'fatwah', which is well known worldwide.

'Lucerific reversal' of truth occurs in the switching of conceptual premises whereby truth and falsehood are reversed via the prideful greed of the narcissistic ego which unconsciously sees God as its enemy. This grandiosity represents succumbing to the temptation of what might be called 'godification', into which many world-famous leaders have fallen via greedy financial and sexual exploitation, control, and manipulation of followers for personal gain (representing the dictum, "Power tends to corrupt; absolute power corrupts absolutely." [Lord Acton]).

From all the above, it is apparent that the human ego/mind/self is prone to deception and error due to ignorance of its own limitations, weaknesses, and vulnerability. These limitations are due not just to the well-known psychological mechanism of denial but are evidence of the limitation of the evolution of consciousness itself in its biological as well as karmic attributes. (Eighty-five percent of the world's population calibrates below level 200.)

Acceptance of the ego/mind's intrinsic and innate limitations results from humility, out of which emerges a wisdom that respects and therefore compensates for inherent restrictions. The unwary set sail without a compass or instructions from capable, experienced guides who have successfully traversed the route and left a map for others to follow.

In spiritual work also, there are risk and opportunity for error, just as there is in mountain climbing. (Mt. Everest has already claimed more than one hundred sixty people, with no end in sight.) Therefore, out of integrity and respect rather than fear, the verifiable truth of any pathway, teacher, or spiritual/religious organization should first be verified. There are no secrets of spiritual truth, so the wise avoid the seductive temptation of the narcissistic ego's attraction to the specialness of becoming privy to 'ancient mysteries' and 'secret teachings' (available for a price, financial or otherwise). That which is integrous has no need to persuade, proselytize, glamorize, or control.

Credibility, truth, and integrity are instantly revealed and recognized by simple consciousness calibration techniques by which essence becomes obvious and transparent. To save spiritual aspirants time and trouble, extensive lists of qualified, verified, integrous teachers, teachings, and organizations have already been provided herein, along with charts and lists in *Truth vs. Falsehood*.

It would seem that truth and its pursuit are attractive to attack by supporters of falsehood for they threaten the gains of egotism as well as its narcissistic pride. The payoff of falsity is so valued that it actually takes the most extreme forms, such as denying God, opposing any reference to Divinity, or, alternately and paradoxically, claiming the authorship of God for extremist actions. The gravity of spiritual error due to the narcissistic core of the ego is demonstrated by the famous character of Dr. Faustus who progressively sells his soul for worldly gain. Audiences of the drama, especially in its operatic form, actually shudder as the final catastrophe and fate of the soul of Faustus are revealed.

Because of the gravity of extreme spiritual error, the Vatican historically tried to provide spiritual safety for Catholics by its approval or disapproval of written works. Thus, the formal 'imprimatur' meant that the work was safe and not a threat to the soul, but on the other hand, if it was placed in the index of forbidden works, that indicated the book was likely a seduction to evil. While current-day libertarians would consider such action as repressive, the intention was integrous, as indicated by its calibration of 370. The Catholic Church merely sought to establish safe parameters and provide guidelines in order to protect the innocent and uneducated whose gullibility and ignorance, as well as intrinsic innocence, made them vulnerable to seduction by the pandering of lust as well as blasphemous belief systems.

Authority

The foundation of true authority is integrous credibility plus responsible leadership and stewardship of authenticated information. True authority, by virtue of its level of truth, is thus due respect as it has been considered throughout history to be a major social asset and intellectual and moral guide. True authority is an abstract principle that transcends literal examples of its application to specifics. The failure by individuals to exemplify the ideal does not disprove the authenticity of the principle but merely the failure of its true application in a specific instance. For example, that civil authority is sometimes abused or makes mistakes does not mean there is no such thing as true integrous authority.

The implied authority of titles does not automatically confer true authority, which is vulnerable to conditions of sociopolitical positionalities. That authorities fail in the personal execution of their responsibility is, of course, a widespread phenomenon. In this generation, it is perhaps demonstrated by the failure of even the federal government to respect and enforce its very own laws for decades, which has subsequently created very major conflicts and dilemmas as well as loss of sovereignty.

Aside from its political definitions, what actually is the essential nature of true authority? It speaks for itself by its innate authenticity, such as knowledge, expertise, experience, and capability (e.g., an airline pilot). Thus, perception has to be backed up by essence. Whether this is actually so in a given instance is often obscure and only resolvable by the application of consciousness research techniques.

Historically, true authority has been represented most often by the founders, originators, and authors of disciplines or bodies of knowledge, such as represented by the great scientists of history as well as the founders of integrous philosophical systems. Other true authorities are represented by the greats of music, art, religion, and spiritual discovery. Confirmation of authority is by demonstration as well as experiential validation and corroboration via some objective means, such as that represented by consciousness calibration, which has no vested interest in the levels of truth that are revealed.

Thus, true authority is characterized by excellence through which it is authenticated. Respect is due to true authority as humanity relies on it for survival as well as guidance. Misplaced reliance on false authority has grave social consequences that often result in widespread death, devastation, and the suffering of millions of people (e.g., Chairman Mao, cal. 185; Karl Marx, cal. 130; and Stalinist and Nazi theories). Both Hitler and Stalin usurped unauthentic military roles as well as political powers that had disastrous results. The terrorist doctrines of Lenin (cal. 80) persist to this day.

In today's world, we see the fatal consequences (e.g., the 9/11 bombings) of the doctrine of Wahhabism (cal. 30). There is probably no greater error that mankind can make than the deification of falsehood and the worship of corrupt leaders. The naïve populace confuses egoistic vanity with greatness. Note that malignant messianic narcissism is accompanied by and gains momentum via hatred (class, nationality, religion, race, or revenge). The chant, "Death to America," or depiction of the United States as the 'Great Satan', calibrates at level 20 (satanic/demonic). Of importance for students of truth is that apologists for malignant falsehood thereby take on concomitant karmic responsibility and accountability.

Loss of the Asset of True Authority

It is difficult for the current culture to understand the value of true authority, to be able to identify it, and to disentangle it from politicized public image. Great social forces are comparable to tectonic plates whose movements eventually cause earthquakes and disruption. Authority figures are commonly blamed for these catastrophes that, in their extreme social expression, erupt as war (which has prevailed ninety-three percent of the time in recorded human history). Thus, it could be said that failure occurs not because of true authority but in spite of it.

In the current world, truthful authority itself is the target of philosophical relativism, which rhetorically denies that true authority (truth) even exists or has any possible validity; thus, politically and philosophically, it condemns absolutism. The paradox is that relativism does not destroy authority but merely claims it as its own via narcissistic, postmodernistic doctrines and theories. Thus, in essence, relativistic argument, theory, philosophy, and dogma claim the moral authority that it ostensibly disputes. Relativistic postmodern doctrines conceal the paradox that if truth is merely arbitrary, then their own dogma is fallacious (e.g., it claims that morality is 'wrong' and therefore immoral). Thus appears the unctuous bumper sticker, "Question Authority" (cal. 180).

True, valid authority originates from essence (Reality) and not from appearance, titles, attributes, or perceptions, nor does true authority stem from media approval. That which is nonintegrous, unauthentic, and calibrates below 200 (adolescent rebellion) supports disrespect for true authority because authoritative truth based on essence (absolutism) does not support false perception, which stems from the narcissistic ego.

In current society there is the popularity of having

an overt, strident anti-American antiestablishment attitude ('Hollywoodism', cal. 170 to 190) that profits as media attention and appeals to the narcissism of the 1960s' generation which now constitutes the current age group of college professors. Philosophical posturing is appealing to the naïve ego's vulnerability to rhetoric as it is self-inflationary and blind to its own innate limitation. If, as relativism states, "Absolutism is false," then that very statement is also fallacious by its own definition of falsehood.

Limitations

Authority is not omniscience and therefore not immune to error due to the fluctuating nature of the human condition and its state of evolution. Thus, errors occur that are recognized as being consequent to mortal limitation. These are due to misinformation, miscalculation, erroneous data, shifts of prevailing conditions, and unknown or hidden factors and influences. Deception and misinformation tend to prevail in international relations and are very overtly displayed in the ceaseless turmoil of the United Nations (cal. 190). Domestic issues are transitional in all countries because of the constant shifts in economic and population factors as well as natural disasters and the low prevailing level of consciousness of many countries, their political leaders, and subpopulations.

Despite error or defects, true 'greatness' is recognized worldwide as a composite of strengths, character traits, and virtues as exemplified by Theodore and Franklin D. Roosevelt, Benjamin Franklin, Winston Churchill, Ronald Reagan, Gerald Ford, Mahatma

Gandhi, Parks Reese, the astronauts, Susan B. Anthony, Martin Luther King, Jr., and others (see *Greatness* by Hayward, 2005). These all exemplify stature and alliance with integrity and valor (cal. 460 to 700).

Historically, all presidents, especially during times of war (e.g., Abraham Lincoln), have been subjected to critical attack, extremes of vilification, or even assassination and have had to go through agonizing moral crucibles, such as Truman's painful decision of whether to resort to the atomic bomb to end World War II. This event turned out to be extremely fortuitous, for decades later, records revealed that Japan was planning and preparing to drop a nuclear bomb on the United States (Kuroda, 2007). Thus, the 'morality' of every war is situational and a matter of debate and discussion for many decades and even centuries, during which context becomes progressively comprehended and appreciated.

Autonomy

In childhood, age two is characterized by rebellion and the negativity of the developmental phase of the 'no's,' as every parent discovers. The issue is one of control, and a power struggle ensues in family interaction. The qualities of age two become the character traits of rebellious defiance (Freud's toilet-training phase of 'anal defiance' aggression). This conflict is an expression of the narcissistic ego that is characterized by willfulness, selfishness, lack of respect for others, and the perversity of pleasure in being 'God'. With artful parenting, this is surrendered out of fear of the loss of parental protection as well as the emergence of love for the parents. The conflict over autonomy and control resurges in adolescence (e.g., drugs, rap music, punk rock, lowered pants, and references to women as whores) when defiance of authority and its societal representations are again seen as restrictive to instinctual gratifications.

The cost of unresolved defiance of true authority is revealed by high-school dropout rates of thirty to even fifty percent, with consequent social and economic results. Rebellion includes disparagement of all forms of authority, including morals, ethics, and legal standards of conduct. This results in subcultures of hedonistic self-indulgence, with associated major sociological problems that frequently eventuate as the cultures of prison populations. Failure to resolve the issues also results in the disorder termed 'Oppositional Personality Disorder,' whose victims constitute a large percentage of 'protest' movements, 'nutty professors', conspiracy theorists, and mob violence. Whereas contrariness is infantile in its origins, it has become a stylish play for media attention.

Many of the leaders of the counterculture of the Vietnam era later regretted their actions and actually published articles about them because, with maturity, they realized they had merely prolonged the war, increased suffering and the casualty rate, and had given aid and comfort to the enemy. The narcissistic ego likes to see its adolescent rebellion labeled as 'noble' and 'idealistic', or 'elite'. The terms themselves glaringly reveal the appeal of such attitudes to narcissism, egotism, and vanity cal. 170).

Rebellion often results from confusing repressive

authoritativeness with authentic expertise of true authority. Paradoxically, the antiestablishment, anti-authority attitude itself then becomes abusive, authoritative, coercive, and stridently demands compliance. Much that parades as free-speech superiority is actually only the exhibitionism of the neurotic personality disorder termed 'contrariness' (cal. 190).

History is replete with the settings and social circumstances that led to the great revolutions which shaped both ancient as well as modern civilizations. Some brought about great benefits, and others precipitated great disasters and widespread death and starvation. Each rebellion had its ostensible heroes as well as villains, along with its benefits and tragic costs. Such conflicts have been the subject for study and argument for centuries. The question is always whether the benefit was worth the cost of the loss of life and suffering. The same discourse prevails in the current world dialogue so well addressed by Shakespeare as suffering the slings and arrows of outrageous fortune or taking up axes against it. Each generation makes its own decision.

What are the options? The rebellious are too often merely juvenile malcontents or hostile narcissistic denouncers who fail to see that there is a mature option of dissent and disagreement rather than the hate-monger type of vilification. America is currently again viewed as using coercion to force its ideals on a foreign culture as its critics proclaim. 'Choose democracy' is up against 'choose Islam' as the core of world conflict.

In the past, it was conflict between the 'Divine

Right' or hereditary monarchies versus 'equality, liberty, and fraternity'. Communism (cal. 160) appealed to 'throw off the chains' of servitude for collectivism and radical socialism. And so the great social tectonic plates underlying civilization continue to grind and perpetrate war and conflict. As is readily apparent, the basic conflict is repetitively between different depictions of levels of truth and their implied moral authority. Thus, levels of consciousness are determinative of conflict as well as its resolution. Reading Winston Churchill's *The New World: A History of the English Speaking Peoples* results in a modesty about having pat answers to the human condition itself.

Refutation of Religion

Because of its absolutist doctrines as well as moral authority, religion has periodically been the target of hostile extremism throughout history. Thus, the truth of religion becomes vulnerable to attack because of its misuses and abuses by man's ego. Militant religionism prevails in today's world as the prime source of war and potential for mass destruction as used 'in the name of God'. It is the ego that thus usurps the authority of Divinity to justify actions that calibrate at the levels of 10 to 90 (those of criminality).

Current popular culture is characterized by the aggrandizement of adolescent rebellion. Its appeal to being fashionable is thus based on the desire for approval. Even great universities succumb to the desire for approval by inviting so-called "nutty professors" to teach.

The differentiation of oppressive authoritarianism

from true reality-based authority is a matter of discernment and therefore also depends on context. Thus, civil rights and liberties depend on circumstances as well as intention. Some situations can be clarified only by calibrating the levels of consciousness, which reveals the actual essence of a positionality. The most obvious examples are those of restrictions consequent to a state of war, an infectious disease epidemic, or an emergency that threatens survival.

Similar discernment is necessary to understand rational liberty from anarchy or extremes of libertarianism. Liberty means freedom from undue restraint but within rational parameters (e.g., shouting "fire" in a theater). Free speech also has consequences even though it may be legal. Libertarianism pushes the envelope and consequently precipitates restrictive social reaction (e.g., Ku Klux Klan incendiary rhetoric). Thus it is said that those who do not respect and value their freedoms soon lose them, which means that freedom is dependent on responsibility and discernment of social realities (time, place, circumstances, etc.).

Historically, purported liberators and revolutionaries eventuate into repressive dictators and become the new oppressors (e.g., Che Guevara, Fidel Castro, and Hugo Chavez) ideologically as well as politically. Thus, the principle of balance becomes operative, which then becomes a new arena for discussion and contention. The successful resolution is concordant with and subsequent to the calibrated levels of consciousness of the contenders.

The necessity of defining parameters and balance is also seen in the current social dialogue on the concept of 'tolerance', which can represent a valid democratic ideal or become a fallacy when pushed to the extreme to excuse and even justify horrendous excesses, including mass murder, criminality, and sexual savaging of innocent children (Dierker, 2006). In psychoanalysis, this proclivity is termed 'identification with the aggressor', which is then supported by pseudophilosophical rationalizations and seemingly idealistic platitudes. Alternatively, there is the option of being compassionate towards savage aggressors without going into agreement, support, and maudlin sympathizing. Discernment is not prejudice. It is not necessary to plant crabgrass in one's lawn in order to institute 'moral equivalence'.

From the above discussion, it becomes apparent that all acts carry degrees of responsibility as well as culpability and accountability. There is the dictum of 'impaired capacity'. Humanitarianism takes into account human limitation and is therefore flexible but not foolish or maudlin. An act may be committed in error yet simultaneously have consequences, such as severe social approbation or even death or war.

After World War II, survivors on both sides forgave the other because of the severity of the circumstances. This principle is currently operative as a consequence of realizing the severe indoctrination inculcated by the programming of Islamic terrorist ideologies that result in militant suicide bombers who operate from induced authoritative belief systems.

Compassion includes recognition of social realities rather than denial of them. We can love and appreciate all the natural beauty of the wild tiger, but it is only the foolish who think they can safely just play with it. As said previously, reality is a consequence of essence and not appearance.

It is important to realize that an apologist for evil shares the consequences with varying degrees of karmic responsibility. This is subserved within the common lament, "What did I ever do to deserve this?" This also explains group cultural and national calamities whereby Divine Justice operates via principles of the laws of karma (i.e., "Every hair on your head is counted" [calibration level 1,000]).

Resolution

It is often said that successful recognition and acceptance of true authority are dependent on having had positive and rewarding experiences with one's parents during childhood and adolescence during which support and love more than compensated for relinquishment of willfulness and self-centered control issues. The adequate parent is seen as supportive, protective, and a source of pride with which one identifies. The lack of a successful resolution results in lingering resentment or even hatred of all authority figures or their symbols, including God.

Sometimes it is only by catastrophe that the self capitulates to the Self. The true Self is solely aligned with the victory of the soul and the breakthrough of spiritual reality. In the course of human events, there is the fulfillment of the dictum that "Man's extremity is God's opportunity." Thus, calamitous disasters and worldly catastrophes are paradoxically often the only means remaining for salvation. God is not discovered as a consequence of fear but only when that fear is surrendered.

Honor

We honor that which we esteem in others as well as ourselves. Out of this, one honors one's own humanity and that of others and ends up honoring all of life in all its expressions by resignation to Divine Will. With surrender of the ego, the spirit becomes aware of the sanctity of existence.

Out of self-honor arise chivalry (cal. 465) and respect for countrymen as well as heritage and appreciation for the valor of true responsibility. From self-respect arises respect for the rights of others as well as responsibility for personal accountability. Honor is far beyond pride and is, at its very core, humble, thankful, and grateful, out of which one senses the divinity of Creation and the Knowingness, which is expressed by the exclamation, "Gloria in Excelsis Deo!"

CHAPTER 12

God as Hypothesis

Introduction

Discussions and speculations about the nature of Divinity have historically been the province of theology and religion. Despite the erudition of such writings, the average person is often actually puzzled as to the true nature of the ultimate Reality, and in today's world, there is little personal time to study or contemplate the subject in depth.

In general, God is pictured as being 'up there' and, although accessible by prayer, does not really exist at the same level as perceived worldly phenomena. In everyday life, the sense of 'reality' is primarily based on sensual validation plus conceptual and emotional elaborations. For many people, God is primarily a belief system and as such is subject to the vicissitudes of the individual psyche over one's lifetime. Thus, the subject may be neglected for decades or may be compartmentalized to Sunday morning only. Many people merely decide that they will seriously get around to dealing with the subject later on in life.

Historic Depictions

Almost universally, as was mentioned, God is imagined and pictured to be elsewhere, such as being located within the heavens and therefore at some actual physical distance. God is depicted in art as being large in size, situated against stars and clouds, with perhaps some angels and cherubs floating nearby. Classically, the depiction is a similar to that of the ceiling of the Sistine Chapel, with God having long hair, being large and somewhat elderly, and suspended in space, perhaps reaching down towards man in ancient times.

God as a Concept

The concept and definition of God as 'Creator' rather than timeless Presence and ever-present, constant, ongoing Source results in conceptual limitations whereby God is defined in terms of time and causality and thus conceptually linked with the linear, observable daily world. Time itself is a cognitive and perceptual illusion and merely a projection of consciousness, as previously stated (Hawkins, 2001). This realization has been confirmed by expansions of advanced quantum physics theories (Lynds, 2006), which conclude that without consciousness, no independent universe even exists (Stapp, 2007; Rosenblum and Kuttner, 2007).

God is considered to be not only a 'what' but also a 'who,' as well as a 'when', with personality characteristics that are primarily anthropomorphic (human-like), and particularly so as depicted by the Old Testament. God is therefore seen as having all the failings of the human ego—anger, vengeance, primitive, retaliatory, jealous, and judgment, along with benevolence, if pleased. Such a God is also seen as somewhat capricious in that people are seemingly created as grossly unequal and yet responsible for their defects, even though they are created as deficient (ignorant). Thus, mankind requires both God's Mercy and Salvation.

Out of these anthropomorphic projections arises an image of God about which the human is understandably somewhat ambivalent in that God is perceived as benevolent but, paradoxically, also capable of even throwing one's soul into Hell. Thus, God is perceived as being loving but also limited and likened unto one's human parent. This, of course, was looked into by Sigmund Freud who discarded the idea of God as being merely an anthropomorphic projection from the infantile unconscious. While he threw out false depictions of God, he then made the mistake of concluding that a real God did not exist, which was an error, that is, the fact that anthropomorphic depictions of God were false did not disprove the Reality of Divinity. The seeming unfairness of human destiny is countered by more sophisticated religions such as Buddhism and Hindu, which teach the laws of karma.

Fear of God

While the anthropomorphic depictions result in fear of God's judgmental anger, another source arises out of conceptualizing God as the Source and cause of all earthly as well as human calamities. Thus, God is seen as the author of storms, droughts, floods, earthquakes, volcanic eruptions, etc. In primitive societies, this led to attempts to assuage God by human or animal sacrifices, and in Incan, Mayan, and most other primitive religious rituals, sacrifices were made, often to bizarre extremes. Animal sacrifice was also widespread and innate to ancient Hebrew and other cultures. In today's world, the same primitivism is seen in Islamic worship of suicide and killing of innocents or 'infidels' to please God and thus win Divine favor as well as heavenly gifts and indulgences. The same type of thinking is involved in the giving of alms or sacrifices to please God. The concept that God can be pleased, angered, placated, 'bought off', or flattered by worship is an elaboration of anthropomorphism. As with other religious practices, the important quality is the intention and faith that are involved.

God As Creator

The defining attributes of God have been classically described as omnipotence, omnipresence, and omniscience. God is the primary origin, source, and therefore, the Creator. The human mind thinks in terms of causal sequence over periods of time. It presumes that time, sequence, and causation are 'out there' in the perceived linear world and therefore represent reality (the confusion of Descartes' *res interna [cogitans]* vs. *res externa [extensa]*). This conceptualization is further confirmed by the sequential nature of mental-image processing. Thus, the mind constructs a 'timeline' with a beginning and an ending, which requires a 'primary cause' of origination and authorship.

God is considered to be a primary 'first cause'. Creation is pictured to be a sequential linear process, as described in Genesis, by which the universe is the caused product, and time is set. The conceptual limitations inherent in this logical progression were pointed out by Immanuel Kant in 1781 in *Critique of Pure Reason*, and later elaborated consequent to the emergence in quantum mechanics by Stephen Hawking who, in 1993, included the pragmatic value and usefulness of 'imaginary time' in theories of quantum gravity.

The Old Testament cognitively separates Creation from the Creator by virtue of dualistic languaging of subject, object, and transitive verb. Thus emerges the common 'roll of the dice' concept that is concordant with the ego/mind's style of processing.

Beyond limitations of conceptualization, it is seen that creation is actually outside of time. Thus, 'then' and 'now' are bypassed by the realization of eternity as alwaysness, with no beginning and no end; no past, future, or now; and no progression of time because what actually progresses is merely human witnessing. The witnessing is sequential and experienced as being placed in the unfolding of time and potentiality. 'Existence' itself is a selective interpretation because, in reality, the universe and Divinity are unitary.

God is the Source and ever-present substrate rather than the 'cause' of the universe; therefore, evolutionary creation represents the consequences of the unfoldment of the infinite potentiality of omnipotence into the actuality of existence. The enfolded universe of the Godhead emerges into beingness and the unfolded universe of life and existence. In this transformation, existence does not require the confirmation of witnessing. The universe is the content of which Divinity is the context and Source. Thereby, it can be seen that essence is not 'cause' but permanent, ongoing, ever-present primordial Self-existent Reality.

It can be intuited and said as well as comprehended at a high abstract level that *All Is* and has its existence by virtue of Divine Ordinance. It is a reflection of God's grace whereby the enfolded potentiality manifests as the unfolded linear observable universe (Bohm, 1980.) Thus does the Godhead of infinite potential actualize as existence so that the linear emerges out of the nonlinear. Classically, elaborations of the above are the subject of ontology, the branch of philosophy concerned with the science of being. The biblical interpretation is expressed in the Gospel of John, Chapter 1, which states that in the beginning was God as the Word (Godhead), out of which emerged all of existence, including the Light of Life and human consciousness (calibrates at level 1,000). Thus, God is both Source and Creator.

God and Creation in Terms of Modern Science

In quantum mechanics, the active physical world is revealed to be the consequence of the 'collapse of the wave function' from potentiality (wave principle) to physical manifestation as 'particles' via the Heisenberg Uncertainty Principle, whereby consciousness and intention are the catalysts. This propensity is increased by the calibratable power of the consciousness level of the intention. Inasmuch as the consciousness level of God is infinite and beyond time or limitation, Creation and its evolutionary appearance (emergence) are absolutes. Thus, out of the 'Godhead' of infinite potential by virtue of 'God's will' (omnipotence) arises the manifestation (omnipresence) and the omniscience of Infinite Consciousness whereby all is known forever.

God As Experiential Reality

The intellectual depictions of Divinity arise from mental images and the constructs of mental processing of linear logic and meaning. Thoughts and ideas about God are intellectualizations that are consequent to the consciousness calibration range of the 400s.

Completely independent of such intellectualizations, human experience throughout time has included awareness of the presence of God as contextual power, the Divine nature of which is an overwhelming revelation from beyond mind itself and transformative in its profound impact. As spiritual evolution progresses in the individual, spiritually transformative events may occur, and by consciousness level 540 to 570, they often become frequent and form a recontextualization of one's subjective experiential sense of the reality of life.

By consciousness levels 540 to 570, spiritual concepts are no longer merely intangible but begin to emerge as the very experiential fabric of life itself. Sharing of such experiences with others of a similar level of consciousness brings about corroboration, and one finds a common ground that is experientially substantiated. In such spiritual communities, God's 'Will' is accepted as influential, present, innate, operative, and omnipresent (e.g., context). It is thus part and parcel of the subjective phenomenal world. The presence of Divinity is comprehended to be all encompassing and thereby becomes termed 'the Higher Power' of faith-based groups that seek to increase conscious contact with God through prayer, meditation, and selfless service. From humility, it also becomes apparent that because of one's own personal limitations, one is responsible for the effort but not the result, which is up to God's Will.

As the payoffs of the ego are refused and surrendered, its grip on the psyche lessens, and spiritual experience progresses as the residuals of doubt are progressively relinquished. As a consequence, belief is replaced by experiential knowledge, and the depth and intensity of devotion increases and may eventually supersede and eclipse all other worldly activities and interests.

Experiential Validation of God As Primary Reality

Spiritual evolution gains momentum as it becomes the primary focus, and its progressive stages have been described rather specifically in the series of books by this author, including *The Eye of the I*, *I: Reality and Subjectivity*, and *Transcending the Levels of Consciousness*. Descriptions and testimony as to subjective states of realization of the presence of God have been recorded throughout history and restated in the author's *Discovery of the Presence of God: Devotional Nonduality*, as well as in Chapter 17 of *Truth vs. Falsehood*. In all the books cited, evidence as well as experience of Divine Reality have been corroborated by consciousness calibration, first described in *Power vs. Force* (Hawkins, 1995).

In addition to the cited accumulation of confirmatory evidence, students and study groups worldwide over recent decades have added further information and contributed a mass of concordant, supportive group and individual experience reflective of advanced awareness (Grace, 2007). Notable among all the spontaneous contributors has been the lack of personal ego investment, and many such reports are actually anonymous in the typical form of "George P. from New Zealand," or "Mary S. from Germany."

The subjective experience of spiritual realities has been universally reported by mankind throughout all time and subsequently documented and confirmed by consciousness calibration, which is currently ongoing and conducted by widely separated individuals and groups.

Impediments

The reality of Divinity can be rejected at any and all levels by individuals, groups, or even whole cultures by virtue of free will. The underlying motivations are personal as well as social/psychological and actually represent the evolutionary nature of consciousness, both individual as well as collective. These are influenced in turn by both individual and collective karmic propensities. In the individual, spiritual awareness is influenced by tradition, intelligence, education, and personal experience, including emotional and family relationships. Also influential is the availability of integrous spiritual literature as well as adequate teachers. Degrees of personal motivation also reflect the influence of other factors, such as age, personality, psychological typology, aptitudes, talents, and Jung's balance of introversion versus extroversion.

Certain attitudes may obstruct the emergence of spiritual awareness, such as the predominance of narcissism, skepticism, doubt, mistrust, negativity, as well as opposition, defiance, and even paranoid orientation as discussed in Chapter 13. In addition, there is immaturity or delay of spiritual evolution. Religious or spiritual disappointments also may occur due to unfortunate experiences with religious figures or even dismay in public examples of failures of religious integrity, such as church scandals.

In addition to personal factors, there is the overall cultural impact of the media, including their well-financed, organized attacks on religion and spirituality to the point of trying to eliminate even mention of the word 'God'. These antireligious or antispiritual movements are based on the narcissistic appeal of trendy political positions of secularism that paradoxically become a new, oppressive 'religious fervor'. The secularist movement is further supported and energized by philosophical systems of postmodernism and relativism, all of which calibrate below 200 (see *Truth vs. Falsehood*).

During maturation, people may have alternating periods of either attraction or aversion to religion and religiosity at various stages of their lives. There is the defiance of childhood, the rebelliousness of adolescence, and then preoccupation with the responsibilities of marriage and raising children. These are subsequently replaced by the concerns of older age and the confrontation with the limitation of the temporality of human life because in later life, it becomes a priority. Under the pressure of the anticipation of the inevitable, there is a resurgence of faith and hope, not only just out of fear of death but also out of acceptance. The Reality of God then becomes an expectancy, and fear and doubt are replaced by the peace of surrender to God's will and human destiny.

Other Depictions of the Ultimate Reality

Monotheism (Hebrew, Christian, and Islamic) tends to result in a depiction of the Ultimate Reality as a definable entity as though it were a unitary super-personality with specific characteristics that are suprahuman. As a specific entity, God is then pictured to be located in space, time, and even location. In addition, as mentioned previously, God is then further defined with anthropomorphic (human-like) attributes, such as motive, will, intention, preferences, and predilections. Thus, any of these may also be refuted, and the 'nature' of God is thus subject to theological debate and intellectual hypothecation.

Unfamiliar to monotheistic cultures and religions are the older depictions of the Ultimate Reality as understood by the cultures of ancient India or the Far East. These arise not from historical mortal depictions but from revelations from the essence of consciousness itself. Thus arose the revelation of Krishna, the Buddha, and the rishis and sages of the ancient *Vedas*. These are references to the ultimate Revelation as a consequence of Enlightenment.

The knowingness that arises from within is innate, accessible, experiential, and beyond definition or description as the primary, confirmable, universal substrate power and energy out of which arises the possibility as well as actualization of existence. This ultimate Reality is revealed via the search into the substrate and source of consciousness itself, which is the ultimate nonlinear context beyond all definition. Thus, via the pathway of Enlightenment, there is no separate relationship of 'you-God' vis-à-vis 'me-human'. This is the meaning of the Advaita (nonduality) terminology of Self as compared to self. This is the illuminated core of the mystic by which the ultimate nonlinear Reality is self-revealing when the obstacles of the linear ego have been relinquished.

Mystic revelation is the inner pathway of the contemplatives of Hebrew and Christian ("Unio Mystica") tradition and the Sufis of Islam. It is the 'pathless' way of Zen and the core of Buddhism as well as the Hindu tradition of the classical yogas. The Presence that is revealed and realized is beyond description, depiction, or nominalization and is therefore beyond dispute, agreement, or theological discourse. Devoid of definable qualities, the ultimate Reality is also beyond nominalization or characterization and outside the constrictions of linear concepts such as causality, space, time, or location (Grace,2007).

The pathway of radical subjectivity reveals the intrinsic core of consciousness itself, which is beyond hypothesis as it is the primary substrate and source of the capacity for experiential awareness. Thus, the hypothetical is ultimately answered by its transcendence.

The nondefinable nature of the core of Reality results in the previously mentioned impossibility of definition or nominalization.Thus arise such references as the 'Buddha nature', which is seemingly paradoxically impersonal yet the very substrate of the experiential. This nondefinable quality is an ever-present, necessary, all-prevailing, a priori condition whose closest corollary in Christianity is indicated by the term 'Godhead', out of which arises the term 'Creator' when applied to the existence of the universe.

The realm of the describable linear arises out of the indescribably nonlinear Source. The Realization of the ultimate substrate core of all Reality is consequent to the condition termed 'Enlightenment', which is thus the province of the mystic whose inner state is characterized by the term 'ineffable'. It can be confirmed experientially and corroborated by consciousness calibration research and is beyond intellectual comprehension or definition. It is therefore beyond the intellection of hypothetical propositions or argument. (The above calibrates at 1,000.)

The resolution of all intellectual doubt is experiential, and the means is described in *Discovery of the Presence of God*.

Resolution

Hypotheses about the existence and nature of God have been the subject of discourse and debate by the greatest minds of Western culture over the centuries. The discourses collectively display a massive erudition as well as brilliant intellectual acumen, together with the collective wisdom obtained by intensive effort and dedication. The integrity of the greatest thinkers of all time is obvious and inspiring.

To this impressive human effort of Western civilization, modern man also has access to the accumulated wisdom of the Middle and Far East. Even in modern China, Confucianism forms a supporting matrix to a giant and rapidly evolving society. India, the other giant emerging culture, has an ingrained Hindu cultural/religious fabric that reflects the distillation of many centuries of collective wisdom. In America, the Native culture of its earliest inhabitants had universally discovered the Great Spirit, and widely separated aborigine cultures of Africa and South America also worshipped deities.

Ancient Germanic tribes as well as the societies of pre-Christian Greece and Rome all had gods. Thus, it could be said that, although differing in depiction, mankind has collectively understood that Divinity is the Source of life and existence.

Thus, the atheist is faced with the dubious intellectual task of purportedly refuting all mankind over all of human history. Despite pretenders to the task, none has ever succeeded in doing so despite intellectual pretenses. This failure is due to the inescapable fact that that which is not provable therefore cannot be disproved.

The prudent mind would conclude that the reality of Divinity is a tentative probability whose resolution invites further clarification by the evolution of consciousness itself. The ultimate resolution occurs on a higher plane and in greater dimension than the limited realm of the intellectual, which is confined to the consciousness levels of the 400s. By self-honesty, it is discovered that intrinsic to the mentalizations of the 400s is an innate unconscious, blind pridefulness. Every 'thinker' secretly believes that their mind is really superior to that of everyone else. That is the psychological basis of the 'feel good about yourself', wonderful 'You' generation a la *Time* magazine's cover (25 December 2006).

The mind's illusion that it is capable of actually knowing reality is not the result of just ordinary pridefulness but is instead an intrinsic defect of the construction of the mind itself as a consequence of its evolutionary development. Biological life had to have certainty, and the organism sampled the environment (e.g., via the function of the 'experiencer' aspect of the ego). Thus, to survive, faith evolved in the accuracy of sampling the *linear* domain. However, the linear processing function of the ego apparatus did not acquire the capacity for discovering the reality of the nonlinear dimensions of existence or reality. Thus, only after eons of evolutionary time did the human consciousness evolve to discern context from content. That capacity is still absent in eighty-five percent of the human population in the world today.

The resultant limitation means that the majority of mankind requires reliance on its most advanced members to explain the nonlinear Reality that is the context and source of existence. Thus, the value of consciousness calibration is that it opens the avenue to higher knowledge (discernment of essence) that would not otherwise be available. Just as the telescope expands the range of human vision to the otherwise unseen and undetected, consciousness research reveals truth beyond ordinary perception and holds untold and as yet undiscovered benefits.

Recovery from Innate Limitation

The basic purpose of spiritual work and dedication is to transcend the innate evolutionary limitations of the ego and thereby access and develop the nascent capacity of consciousness itself, which bypasses all the limitations of the ego/self. Truth then presents itself by virtue of Divine Grace. Divinity reveals Itself to those who call upon It (calibrates as true) in God's time. The pace of spiritual evolution can seem slow, but spiritual endeavor is never futile. Progress can become very sudden and very major in dimension and impact.

Problematic Religious Doctrines

Due to the proclivity for error and suggestibility of the human mind, segments of major religions have been pirated by splinter groups that use the name of a bona fide religion to give credibility to separatist offshoots, which often represent the exact opposite of the claimed religion. This is most obviously represented by the endless religious wars as well as the historic Inquisition.

Religion is relatively easy to politicize, and thus, "In the name of God" all manner of horrific militant ravages have massacred millions of people for many centuries. These are commonly in the form of 'holy' wars, from the historic Crusades to the centuries-long militancy of the Ottoman Empire to modern-day Jihadists (cal. 30), Islamic terrorist triumphalism (cal. 90) based on Wahhabism (cal. 30) and apocalyptic Islamic legends (cal.70), such as the return of the 12th Imam, the Madhi (savior). Importantly, Islam's texts (e.g., the Koran) make no distinction between religion and the State. The religion *is* the State (the 'House of Islam').

Interestingly, all apocalyptic visions calibrate between 60 and 70 and arise from Carl Jung's archetype in the unconscious of the 'Shadow', or Freud's 'Id.' There are the periodic personal reports of 'lower astral' visions that are repeatedly visited by the minds of human beings in altered states of consciousness (e.g., trance, demonic possession, psychedelic drugs, temporal lobe brain dysfunction, and psychotic, post-convulsive, and hallucinatory states). These repetitiously reappear over the centuries and often result in survivalist communities and formation of extremist cults with messianic charismatic leaders.

Religious Deviations

As previously noted in *Truth vs. Falsehood*, there are sections of possible error in traditional scripture in world religions. These were not diagnosable before the discovery of consciousness calibration; thus, potential error went undetected. The New Testament calibrates in the 800s, but the Book of Revelation is at the extremely low level of only 70 (as is the calibration of its author, John).

The Koran overall calibrates quite high as it is monotheistic and devout, but thirty percent of its verses calibrate below the level of truth (200), and fourteen percent are severely below level 100. There are also negative depictions of God in the Hebrew Old Testament, and savage depictions of Divinity occur routinely in primitive religions (e.g., Incan, Mayan, and Easter Island).

The above paradoxes are classically explained as the consequence of the attack of evil energies/entities in their struggle for survival (Luciferic, Satanic, plus their leading edge of the energy of confusion). The Buddha noted that he was beset by demons as he neared enlightenment, and Jesus Christ sweat blood while under similar duress. Also notable is that many spiritual teachers and gurus calibrated high in their earlier lives and then crashed and fell to low levels (e.g., power, control, sex, money, and vanity). The 'temptations' are also reported in autobiographies of the lives of saints of different denominations.

Because of the above-cited traps for the unwary, classical scriptures over time can include serious error, which, when cited as justification for destructive actions, have grave consequences for naïve religionists. The major reason such error escapes recognition is that the capacity for 'spiritual discernment' does not occur until consciousness calibration level 600 (classically termed the "opening of the third eye of the Buddhic [etheric] body").

Religion as the Basis for World Conflict

The narcissistic core of the ego is voracious in its endless search for aggrandizement via conflict. Religion has thus been a favorite topic for dispute and endless violence down through the centuries.Although peace is a primary principle of major religions, war in the name of peace has paradoxically been a prominent theme from the zealots of Judea to the assassins of Iranian Shia to the Protestant versus Catholic violence of Europe and the current Islamic conflict and violence.

The recurrent excuse for even the most horrific extremes of violence has been the time-worn slogan "The end justifies the means" by which any action can be rationalized by clever rhetoric. Terrorists strive for the role of heroic 'liberator' by which victim and oppressor become reversed in the game of playing Robin Hood.

Terrorism is a tactic used through the centuries by

religious groups as well as individuals (e.g., the unibomber, Weather Underground terrorists, the "Black September" group, 'animal rights' and environmental activists, Arafat, Castro, and more). Center stage in today's world is the incitement to violence by the terrorist bin Laden 'in the name of Islam' where again, as throughout history, the ego tries to disguise hatred as religious holiness via presumed deification by the pirating of the name of God.At the end of World War II, it was the religious Shinto zeal of the Japanese that required the dropping of the atomic bomb to bring the war to an end.

While the dangers of messianic apocalyptic triumphalism may be limited to cult-like splinter groups, in the case of world leaders, the danger is widespread in a nuclear age when a messianic, narcissistic, megalomaniacal leader may try to trigger such a vision via major destruction to human life 'in the Name of God' (e.g., "Kill all infidels, wipe Israel off the map," as per per the threats by the president of Iran, which calibrate at 80).

Prominent in today's world is the promulgation of the downside of Islam exhibited by the 'Sharia' of Islamic law, which calibrates at level 190 and results in the stoning of women to death, the beheading of infidels, and mass killings, all of which rather blatantly contradict the promulgated depiction of Islam as a 'religion of peace'.

Islamic Triumphalism

By virtue of hegemonous territorial and political militaristic expansion since the year 623 A.D., Islamic violence over the centuries has invaded a great many countries and territories worldwide, including whole continents (e.g., the Ottoman empire), plus numerous civil wars. By threats of violence and civil disorder, it currently holds most of the countries of Europe hostage as the Muslim immigrant populations grow unimpeded as a consequence of bureaucratic 'accommodation' and surrender to genocidal threats and riots. Infiltration is assisted by endemic apologetic secularization, which silences Judeo-Christian resistance. As mentioned previously, Islam (the 'religion of peace') is currently at war in many countries worldwide, including America, which awakened to the threat after the 9/11 disaster that killed more Americans (all civilians) than did the Japanese attack on Pearl Harbor.

While the United States focuses on military measures, it seems to be increasingly aware that the 'elephant in the living room' is the glaring reality that the real threat to Western civilization is ideological (Bush, 2007) and currently operative as "Cultural Jihad" (Phillips, 2006). Militant Islam has adopted the almost identical specific strategies and techniques that were utilized during the rise of the Third Reich: propaganda, indoctrination of youth (*The Protocols of the Learned Elders of Zion*), glamour of militarism, assassination, intimidation, and expansion of militaristic industry, including specifically the basics of nuclear armament.

In the United States, as in much of the West, apologists focus on the sheep's clothing and side unknowingly with their very own enemies. Islamics despise Western liberals and view their apologist rhetoric as despicable weakness (Lenin's 'useful fools').

Hollywood elitists especially typify the sordid corruption of the 'Great Satan'.

Hamas TV aired a children's cartoon program of Mickey Mouse chanting, "Kill the Jews and Israel and Americans with ak-47s." Children then scream, chant hate slogans and propaganda a la Joseph Goebbels' World War II Nazi style (Beck, G., CNN, April, 2007).

The problematic paradoxes of the life and teachings of Muhammad, as well as his writings in the Koran, have been the subject of intense study and criticism over the centuries by numerous scholars (Warraq, 2003). The Koran's contradictory divergences have been explained as the consequences of his temporal lobe epilepsy and sexual opportunism, as well as politically motivated goals, which resulted in the frequent changes he as well as other authors made in the Koran and its many revisions. Again, thirty percent of verses calibrate below level 200, twenty-five percent below 150, and fourteen percent below level 100. (See Chapter 16, *Truth versus Falsehood*.)

Major criticism of Islam originated from Hindu scholars who viewed Islamic extremism as the result of Imam's repetitious use of classical induction techniques to create a trance state called 'Wahi'. (Elst, 2006; Saraswati, 1875).

Also noted by numerous scholars were Muhammad's opportunistic, constant reinterpretations of Koranic verses to accommodate personal, political, and militaristic goals and opportunities. The result was that many verses are completely contradictory.

The many changes resulted in the dictum of 'abrogation', which means that the later verses in the Koran take precedence over earlier ones. Also of importance is that the Koran does not differentiate political from religious concepts, and thus, politics and earthly dominance are innate (Sultaw, 2006). Thus, the Koran divides the world into the 'House of Islam' versus the 'House of War' (non-Islam). Therefore, by religious doctrine, Islam is at war with the rest of the world. The Koran also avoids rationality and specifically deplores reason and rationality as "dangerous to faith."

There is widespread agreement over the centuries that Muhammad went into delusional trance states (Goel, 1999). Swami Vivekananda, as well as many other scholars, emphasizes the importance of recognizing pathologically altered states of consciousness with religious content (reviewed by Warraq, 2003). The diagnostic differentiation between true spiritual states and mental aberrations is detailed in *Truth vs. Falsehood*, Chapter 17.

In clinical practice, such states are seen quite commonly with temporal lobe epilepsy with grandiose delusions and messages from God or archangels, etc. (During fifty years of clinical practice, the author was the psychiatric consultant to many religious and spiritual organizations.) In the state of true spiritual enlightenment, there is no 'other' entity as an informant inasmuch as the all-pervasive Self is the *Purusha* (teacher) by virtue of its Allness.

A general consensus from all the above scholars, as well as spiritual teachers and advanced mystics, is that fanatical religious extremism is the result of induced altered states of consciousness (cal. 90) and post-hypnotic automatization as is characteristically revealed by the typical pathognomonic monotone voice and speech patterns of many male and female Islamic spokesmen (cal. 100; brainwashed syndrome). They make guest appearances on television programs as spokespersons for various euphemistically titled Islamic-American organizations and recite memorized, indoctrinated, programmed propaganda that contradicts everyday worldwide events (see Kusher, 2004).

These clinical observations and conclusions also provide an explanation for the often bizarre and irrational behaviors of extreme religionists, which are devoid of reason or social reality testing, such as declaring that events witnessed by millions (Nazi concentration camps and extermination of Jews) 'never happened'. Absurdity is primarily seen in the mentally ill or people in a post-hypnotic suggestion state.

Islamic Sharia states all nonbelievers are infidels that should be put to death (Gelenter, 2007). Nonbelievers represent the House of War as denoted by the Koran.

Criticism of Islam accelerated after the 1989 declaration of 'fatwah' against Salman Rushdie who stayed in hiding for decades but was then paradoxically knighted in 2007 by the British Crown. It is not just the extremists but the Koran itself that repeatedly instructs Muslims to 'kill/behead' nonbelievers. The basic truth and camouflaged reality are revealed by the verifiable fact that the social impact of Islam in the United States currently calibrates significantly at level 190 (as do publically funded, supposedly secular schools that ostensibly merely teach Islamic language and culture.) The calibration level, however, reveals the concealed motive.

The Western world is confronted daily with trying to apply tolerance, forgiveness, and compassion to provocation by violence, threats, and relentless attacks, both verbally and physically. Islamic crowds shout "Death to America," terrorists blow up airplanes, kill civilians by the thousands (9/11), and kill other thousands around the globe. As reiterated previously, Islamics are at war in many countries, and more actions are being planned or have been thwarted (e.g., planes and subways in Britain).

Sharia law is famous for its extreme cruelty to the weak and innocent (to women, children, and even dogs). Even the most abject, self-abasing apologists are hard pressed to maintain a façade of excuses via pseudosociological and psychological rationalizations, such as childhood deprivation, etc. (bin Laden is a multimillionaire). Note that chivalry calibrates at 465 and Islamic 'honor killing' calibrates at 90 (as does atrocity). Apologists ignore the devastating effect of carefully programmed indoctrination into cultish worship of death rationalized as the will of Allah. Such indoctrination is now practiced in twenty-five percent of the mosques in the United States, which collectively calibrate overall at level 190.

It is also significant that Islam has practiced slavery for centuries. The Islamic slave trade resulted in the origin of African blacks being sold in the Caribbean Islands and transported to the southern United States. When, in the end years of the eighteenth century, John Adams and Thomas Jefferson complained to the ambassador from Tripoli, they were told that the Koran entitled Muslims to enslave infidels even as a duty (Hogan, 2007).

There is a counter-movement to Islamic violence led by such personages as Irshad Manji, author of the book, *The Trouble with Islam Today*, and the PBS documentary, *Faith without Fear*. She herself, however, by promoting peace, is considered to be a heretic and lives behind bulletproof-glass windows. For example, there arises the satire that "Islamics threaten to kill anyone who says it is not a 'religion of peace'" (Goldberg, 2007).

By paranoid projection, Western society, with America as its symbol, becomes 'the Great Satan'. It is important to note that Muslim children are not educated except to memorize the Koran and read *The Learned Protocols of the Elders of Zion*, which is a fallacious hate manual (cal. 90). Overall, by Western standards, Arabic society itself is still primitive, nonindustrialized, and primarily still tribal in nature.

The pirating of religion by militancy has been, of course, demonstrated in Christianity in the European wars between Protestant and Catholic regimes and more recently by the armed conflicts and terrorism of the IRA in Northern Ireland, as well as the Sunnis versus the Shiites in the Middle East, and the PLO in Palestine. Terrorist organizations and modes of operation are examined in detail in the scholarly *Thinking Like A Terrorist* (German, 2007).

A major factor in the Western world's failure to deal successfully with Islamic culture is the wide disparity in cultural presumptions about truthfulness of statements and declarations. In Sharia law, it is not only permissible to lie when to do so benefits Islam, but it is also actually an *obligation* to do so. This is incomprehensible to Western culture where truthfulness of communication is a presumption unless proven otherwise. This major factor explains the dismal failures of Westerners in negotiating with Islamic countries.

Westerners believe in 'fairness' and the preservation of life, whereas Islam relies on violence and death as per the Koran's admonition to kill nonbelievers ("desecration of holy Arabic soil by infidels"; "cut off their heads" wherever you find them). This principle has been militarily active since the year 623 and continued down through the centuries of the Ottoman Empire. It is active in current fatwahs and in ongoing threats of nuclear annihilation.

Because of naïveté, Americans did not grasp the real meaning and significance of bin Laden's videotaped broadcast to the United States in September 2007 where he invited 'America to convert to Islam'. That was a very major danger signal for, by Islamic law, if infidels are invited to convert and fail to do so, it is honorable to kill them. That invitation was thereby a crucial and critical formal step that cleared the way for major aggression against the United States. If an infidel agrees to convert, their life can be spared, but they owe a money tribute. (bin Laden's public statements in September 2007 calibrated at 35, at which time the President of Iran was invited to speak at a major university.)

From all the above can be seen the very wide gap between conceptual and experiential realities. Thus, the Western mind, steeped in the morality of the

Sermon on the Mount (cal. 955) by Jesus (in the Book of Matthew), cannot really grasp such a wide disparity, and the dangerous disparity is further obscured by the camouflage of relativistic rhetoric and childish idealizations. There is a very wide disparity between devotional faith and its substitute by frenzied fanaticism.

Confrontive to Islamic theories is that God created all human life and not just Muslims, who are numerically in the minority of the world's overall population. Thus, via Islamic law, the Muslim world is obliged to kill the majority of mankind. This worldview calibrates at consciousness level 20 (absurdity). Such a disparity is explicable as the result of Muhammad's temporal lobe epilepsy and consequent fall in calibration from 700 to 130.

It is helpful in trying to comprehend all the above disparities to remember that falsehood is not the opposite of truth but instead represents its absence, just as darkness is not the opposite of light but the consequence of its absence.

Paradigm Disparity

The human sense of reality is aligned with the dominance of levels of consciousness. By esoteric analogy, the Western world and Judeo-Christian culture are aligned with the heart chakra (Love, forgiveness, tolerance, kindness, and protection of the weak, the innocent, and the powerless).

In contrast, Sharia law is centered in the solar plexus (dominant aggression), the spleen (violence, hate, killing), and base chakra (sexualization of heaven). These are not compatible world views. The teachings of Islam are directly the opposite of the Sermon on the Mount. (See Lindberg's *Political Teachings of Jesus*.) Notable also is the Islamic teaching that God (Allah) hears only prayers that are in Arabic.

While the Koran includes recognition of Jesus as a great prophet, it completely ignores and rejects Jesus' teachings and instead teaches the rectitude of slavery, the killing of innocents, and intolerance without forgiveness. Thus, there is no common ground or shared sense of reality from which to bring about accord. Islamics consider appeasement as despicable weakness which results in contempt and perceived powerlessness that merely invites further aggression. Thus, the selection of verses from the Koran can be used to justify all forms of violence and extremism.

Reason As a Limitation of Western Society

A major constriction to understanding extremist behaviors is the Western world's presumption that behaviors are based on logical, rational motives that are capable of being identified and thereby countered. Thus, some 'purpose' is hypothecated to explain extreme behaviors (e.g., teleological reasoning). In actuality, there is no 'good' or 'purpose'. Violence is its own reward; it is just being what it is, just as being hateful always finds some excuse. Killing sprees are innately gratifying just in their indulgence. They are just being what their nature demands. The killer kills merely to kill. There is no 'motive' or rationality.

The above is exemplified by the Islamic Taliban's blowing up of the great Buddha in Afghanistan in 2001. The statue was one hundred fifty feet high, fifteen hundred years old, and one of the great treasures of the world. The loss to mankind was noted by even the Secretary-General of the United Nations who expressed regret and disapproval of such narcissistic destructiveness, by which Islam further disgraced itself. Western apologists are desperate to find redeeming qualities in so violent a culture.

CHAPTER 13

Doubt, Skepticism and Disbelief

Introduction

The ego/mind is aware that it is vulnerable to the chagrin of error. In an effort to protect itself from that vulnerability, it assumes that a form of protection is provided by skepticism or doubt. The propensity for trust also reflects the quality of early-life parent-child interaction. Love supports trust and faith, whereas harshness or neglect results in negative attitudes toward life. A pattern emerges for the processing of new information based on estimates of credibility that can vary from naïve gullibility to hostile defiance, iconoclasm, and even misogyny.

Because survival is not possible without developing a pragmatic sense of reality, the average mind develops a processing system based on presumptions and likelihoods that is serviceable and avoids extremes. Through experience, the sophisticated, mature mind holds new information as tentative or provisional and awaits further confirmation through evidence or experience.

Innate to this process of reality testing is reliance on the senses and the mental processing of the linear world of form and its representative mental images and concepts. The range of understanding and comprehension is further influenced by brain physiology, which, as has been described, depends on the level of consciousness itself. Thus, the animal-instinct-dominated left-brain style of processing is, by virtue of the limitation of evolution, unable to comprehend nonlinear context, including the spiritual dimensions. (The instinctual limbic system calibrates at level 120.) The left brain looks for linear content; the right brain looks for meaning and understanding (nonlinear content).

With favorable karmic/biological inheritance, the capacity develops for trust; thus, nonlinear spiritual context and comprehension can be accepted as factual without the necessity for subjective verification. The information is then held as a belief and defended as being true. Few people comprehend the complexity of advanced theoretical quantum theory, but they appreciate and accept the authority of the experts who do. Thus, the wise trust the wiser, at least intellectually and operationally, and their own lives are thereby enhanced and benefited.

The Skeptic

While skepticism as a prevailing attitude may be the result of emotional or personality disorder (e.g., Freud's 'anal defiant' or 'oppositional' personality rebellion against parental authority), it is also a contrary intellectual attitude (Bauer, 2006) that evolves as debate and lengthy discourse, such as that in current science regarding the authenticity of subjective experience and 'first-person' testimony. This conflict can be seen as merely the consequence of paradigm limitation.

Professor Charles Eisenstein of Pennsylvania State University has done specific research on skepticism ("A State of Belief Is a State of Being") and points out that the 'experimenter effect' has created credibility problems in mainstream science, upon which the

Heisenberg Uncertainty Principle has already had a major impact. His research revealed that below supposedly reasonable intellectual skepticism, there is a motivational field of hidden, spiteful, 'mean-spirited' attitudes and worldviews that are frequently revealed to be "cynical, arrogant, dogmatic, smug, and emotional, as represented by professional 'debunkers'."

All the above are demonstrated by professional skeptics who spend years trying to disprove Einstein via lectures and books, all of which describe and depict Einstein as a "fake," an "imposter," and an "Emperor who has no clothes." Despite negative reception, the authors continue diatribes undaunted (cal. 190) and are apparently oblivious to the confirmation of Einstein by the development of nuclear energy.

In psychiatry, this is termed "logic proof delusional disorder" (Muller, 2006), as is seen in such beliefs as "The holocaust never happened," or, "The United States government engineered 9/11." In this mental disorder, the world is seen as deluded, whereas the person's worldview is valid. Thus, the disorder arises from egotistic grandiosity, which is immune to reason and motivated by envy and its accompanying malice and misrepresentation. It is due operationally to a combination of defective brain function and unmitigated infantile narcissistic omnipotence and hostility toward envied authority figures.

From the ancient Greek, *skeptikos* denotes the philosophy that truth is unknowable and certainty of knowledge is impossible (as was stated by the followers of Pyrrho). As pointed out by Descartes, the human mind, unaided, is unable to differentiate *res cogitans interna* (how things appear to the mind, such as perception or opinion) from *res externa* (essence, intrinsic reality). Socrates made the same observation, that men seek only the good but are unable to discern illusory good (appearance) from essence (the 'real' good).

Whereas, operationally, rational skepticism has provided benefits in revealing false claims and foolishness, skepticism itself has often been foolish. This has been demonstrated by its denunciations of every single important discovery in history, from the Wright Brothers' flight at Kittyhawk to the radio, and currently in the sciences, such as medicine and physics, including quantum theory. It is, of course, also traditional (*de rigueur*) for skeptics to deny the reality of the entire nonlinear spiritual paradigm of context as well as Divinity itself.

If, as skepticism believes, actual truth is unknowable, then, obviously, its own premises and arguments are also fallacious; thus, skepticism is hung by its own petard.

One reason why the level of truth of skepticism calibrates so low at level 160 is that it is primarily a variant of Nihilism (cal. 120). Skepticism fails to serve its avowed ends because it innately lacks the tools to address or investigate the realities of context, especially those that calibrate at the levels of 500, 600, and above. Also, skepticism deals only with content and fails to realize that the significance of meaning itself is completely dependent on context. Context, in turn, reflects the expression of intention, as demonstrated by the Heisenberg Uncertainty Principle, and is aligned with the power of the level of consciousness of the observer.

In contrast to naïveté or skepticism, consciousness research is not intended to prove or disprove anything; it is done to merely discern or confirm the level of information not previously available by mentation, reason, or supposition as it bypasses perception and opinion. Calibration is impersonal and merely results in a number, the significance of which is implied by its location on the calibrated Map of Consciousness.

Skepticism is limited by dependence on the linear mental domain, about which skepticism itself states it is dubious. The objectives of the skeptic would obviously be better fulfilled by taking advantage of the nonlinear techniques by which the profound influence of context can be identified. By analogy, one cannot utilize Newtonian physics or differential calculus to try to prove or disprove quantum mechanics. Skepticism needs the assistance of much higher knowledge to keep up with increasing information that allows access to a more expanded paradigm of reality.

Another oddity of skepticism is the failure to recognize that the negation of the negative does not create a positive, as demonstrated by the famous classic paradox box: one makes a box and places the following statement inside: "Every statement in this box is false."

Inability to Recognize Truth

Lack of capacity to recognize the truth can be due to (1) emotional disorders, (2) psychological conflict, (3) maturational arrest at the level of narcissistic dominance, or, most commonly, (4) simply as a result of the level of the evolution of consciousness. As was described in *Transcending the Levels of*

Consciousness, mental functions are dominated by attractor energy fields that are designated as Lower Mind (cal. 155), and Higher Mind (cal. 275). Their characteristics are reprinted here for convenience.

Function of Mind

Lower Mind (Cal. 155) Content (specifics)	Higher Mind (Cal. 275) Content plus field (conditions)
Accumulation	Growth
Acquire	Savor
Remember	Reflect
Maintain	Evolve
Think	Process
Denotation	Inference
Time = restriction	Time = opportunity
Focus on present/past	Focus on present/future
Ruled by emotions/wants	Ruled by reason/inspiration
Blames	Takes responsibility
Careless	Disciplined
Concrete, literal	Abstract, imaginative
Limited, time, space	Unlimited
Personal	Impersonal
Form, facts	Significance, meaning
Focus on specifics	Generalities
Exclusive examples	Categorize class—inclusive
Malice	Rejection
Reactive	Detached
Passive/aggressive	Protective
Recall events	Contextualize significance
Plan	Create
Definition	Essence, meaning
Particularize	Generalize
Pedestrian	Transcendent
Motivation	Inspirational, intention
Morals	Ethics

Lower Mind (Cal. 155) **Content** **(specifics)**	**Higher Mind (Cal. 275)** **Content plus field** **(conditions)**
Examples	Principles
Physical and emotional survival	Intellectual development
Pleasure and satisfaction	Fulfillment of potential
Linear Content	Essence, context
Religious extremism	Spiritual balance
Skepticism	Intelligent study
Naïveté	Sophistication

Of great significance is that Lower Mind dominates fifty-five percent of the U. S. population and approximately eighty-five percent of the world's peoples and societies. Cultures and people dominated by Higher and Lower Mind represent widely divergent ('clashing') worldviews. Interestingly, the disparity is not reflected in IQ levels but instead represents the capacity to discern essence from appearance and the degree of narcissistic egocentricity.

Descriptively, Lower Mind is characterized as pedestrian, literal, mundane, and prone to politicized rationalization and rhetoric, whereas Higher Mind is discerning, abstract, principled, and disciplined. Lower Mind is associated with proclivity for negative emotions, especially hatred. In contrast, Higher Mind is more positive, benign, and seeks accord and forgiveness.

Of serious prognostic significance is that Lower Mind is prone to domination by force as it is associated with left-brain, animal-type information processing. Higher Mind seeks to influence via higher levels of truth and reason. Thus, Lower Mind is aggressive and intrinsically prone to violence, whereas Higher Mind promotes peace and is reluctantly defensive when attacked. This is comparable to the animal world where the herbivores are under constant threat of attack by the carnivores. In today's world, the carnivores threaten with nuclear bombs, and the herbivores timidly cannot decide on a defensive missile warning system or even 'call a spade a spade' for fear of 'offending'.

Refutation of Truth

Spiritual evolution is correlated with a level of consciousness and is thus representative of the balance between allegiance to the ego versus allegiance to truth, which is a reflection of spiritual reality. The calibratable level of consciousness reflects dominance of an energy attractor field that consequently includes a concordant range of options. Thus, the worldview held by consciousness levels in the mid-400s is seen as fallacious by consciousness levels 170 to 195, which is not only very common but also the very core of sociopolitical conflict in the history of the world.

The lowest levels of human consciousness are those of criminality, as represented by the inability to delay or control animal impulses, pleasure at defiance, and the lack of capacity to learn from experience. The defect is represented in the inherent and often genetic incapacity to discern right from wrong. Clinically, the condition is termed 'conduct disorder' or 'psychopathic personality disorder', and its biological substrate is often associated with congenital defect of the prefrontal cortex of the brain's gray matter. This condition is diagnosable by age three and is clinically generally intractable and uncorrectable.

One such example was observed by the author on an airplane trip during which a grandmother with an infant on her lap sat in the next seat. The infant repeatedly grabbed and pulled on the grandmother's beaded necklace, and she said, "No," and slapped the child. The infant persisted and did it again, over and over, each time being slapped and scolded, but it continued the same behaviors. The grandmother slapped him and said "No" for more than one hundred times during a half-hour period, yet the child seemed to have no capacity to desist or learn from experience. Such failure to learn from negative experiences is demonstrated prominently by grandiose dictators and the leaders of rogue nations who propagate mass destruction of their very own populations.

Uncontrollable willfulness and defiance are seen during the infant state of the 'terrible two's' in which the omnipotence of the infantile ego is pitted against parental control. Parents may lack the energy or volition to respond appropriately, so the child fails to learn impulse control and is unable to discern the basic survival lesson of right from wrong. This is concordant with very low consciousness levels, especially those below 90, as represented by criminality. The same condition plus glibness is seen in its political expression termed 'malignant messianic narcissism' (megalomania), which is described in *Truth vs. Falsehood* (reprinted below for convenience) and characterizes *all* dictators; they are typically lacking in benign benevolence or good will and thus arise to political power based on hatred.

Characteristics of Dangerous Political Leaders

Ruthless, glib cunning	Assume others same as self
No regard for human life	Attract naïve apologists
No value to truth	Unrestrained by logic or reason
Lies are routine and normal	Paranoid, alert, guarded
Facts are irrelevant	See military as cannon fodder
Win at any cost; predatory	Weak 'deserve' their fate
No morality or ethics	Manipulate patriotism
No spiritual values	No concern for loss of life
No humanistic ideals	Willing to 'poison the well'
No concern for others	Despise honesty, integrity
Gloat at clever deception	Assume grandiose title
Value only conquest, win, defeat	Use others with no compunction
Willing to sacrifice society	Feed off adulation
Manipulative, clever	Controlling, domineering
Power oriented; no limits	Faithless; no remorse
Greed is valued and okay	Blame others for own failures
Presume others are lying	Seek wealth and trappings
No value to honesty	'Macho' stance with boots, whip
Ridicule weakness	Exploit, hide behind religion
Sadistic, cruel	View normal people as simpletons
Thrive on conflict	Racial and religious prejudice
Vain, pompous, despotic	Seductive; recruit followers
No personal honor	No allegiance to countrymen
Atheistic, avaricious	No consideration for others
Religion is merely a tool	Unforgiving, vindictive
Vengeful, jealous	Play victim to justify violence
Envy, malice, and hate	Oblivious to suffering of others
Malevolent, vicious	Condone brutality, death, pain
Incapable of love	Willing to impoverish others
Spout rhetoric, are bombastic	No constraints; extremist
Fake honesty; are deceptive	Employ criminals as henchmen
Free of guilt; no conscience	Despise fairness
Egoistic, narcissistic	No scruples, ethics, or morality
Okay to make false accusations	No compassion; violent

Extol terrorism, threats	Consider selves above the law
Megalomaniacal, grandiose	Devoid of insight
Clever rather than intelligent	Merciless; savage
Calculating, scheming	Barbaric (saw off heads slowly)
Sanctimonious, sacrilegious	Breed conflict; duplicitous
Willingly bear false witness	Compartmentalized
Exploit innocence and naïveté	'Good face' to the pubic
Ravage the weak and vulnerable	Maintain 'innocence'
Consider populace as idiots	Use fear and threats
Repay loyalty with elimination	Renege on 'agreements'

To the defiant personality, truth or authority is resented merely because it represents authoritarian parental control. The impaired personality sees integrous truth as threatening and thereby easily rejects it as fallacious.

Lesser degrees of this impairment correlated with sociopolitical viewpoints are expressed as the 'me'/'sensitive' generation. This anomaly emerged as contentious focus on the inflated 'rights' of narcissism and hedonism. This viewpoint is vociferously expressed as secularist, antireligion, anti-God, and anti-spiritual-reality social views. These were supported by the emergence of philosophical systems (Marxist) of so-called 'postmodern' moral relativism (cal. 160 to 190). The grandiosity of the ego was then revealed by terming this set of inflated egoist viewpoints as 'superior', 'elite', or 'correct'. Most importantly, this set of trends resulted in the impairment of reality testing bulwarked by academic/populist and sociopolitical ideology and sophistry that parades as 'free speech'.

The infiltration into academia of such biased rhetoric

brought about the current major decline of academic excellence as demonstrated by not only the 'tolerance' but also the glorification of a whole set of lectures that calibrate at 130, or even as low as 90. (The question again arises: Would you want a brain surgeon who calibrates at 90 to perform surgery on you; or an investment counselor at 90 to handle your money; or even a baby-sitter at 90 to take care of your children?)

The paradox of the antiauthoritarian position and its followers is that it is in itself ultra-authoritarian and oppressively totalitarian, as well as hostile and prone to malice and hatred. The associated emotions are consequent and innate to the attractor fields of the lower levels of consciousness. The political fallout has been experienced as the bitter fight for allegiance between the segments of the population that calibrate above and below the critical consciousness level of 200.

The main target for social/political contention is focused on morality itself. Thus, there are the apologists and supporters for savage criminals who are responsible for the deaths of thousands, or sympathy for Islamic terrorists (also responsible for the deaths of thousands), or the 'rights' of MS-13 gang members who are responsible for the torture and deaths of thousands.

The impairment of reality testing subsequent to indoctrination by the fallacious rhetoric of relativism results in such bizarre examples as celebrities flocking to express sympathy for pedophiliac child killers or psychotic dictators who murder thousands of their own countrymen and entertain themselves with the slow sexual torture of women hung by wires from the ceiling whose deaths deliberately take a matter of days.

Authority can be disagreed with (e.g., dissent) without necessarily taking the opposite view, which forces the disagreement to fall to the level of fallacy. By comparison, compassion is much more appropriate than alignment with falsehood because defense of evil results in alignment with it. The fact that deranged criminals cannot help being what they are does not mean that one has to agree with them.

The impairment of the capacity to discern spiritual reality is considerably a consequence of relentless propaganda and programming by the media aided by the naïveté of the average human mind, which is easily glamorized and programmable via distorted inflation of fallacy disguised as fashionable, trendy viewpoint.

Social Survival

Importantly, the onslaughts of popularized nonintegrity are aimed at and supported by the fifty-five percent of the population in the United States that calibrates below consciousness level 200. However, the level of consciousness of the American population overall still calibrates currently at the level of 421. (It was at 426 but decreased in the Fall of 2006.) The reason for this apparent disparity is that the levels below 200, as can be seen by exponential comparison, are deficient in the power represented by the high calibration levels of those who are integrous. Therefore, the very high level of intrinsic power of only a relatively few members of the population maintains the overall capacity for survival and more than counterbalances the effects of the negative. (For example, if the top one hundred people are removed from the U.S. population, the overall average level of consciousness drops to 320. If the top one thousand are removed, the overall consciousness level drops from 421 to 220.)

Refutation of spiritual reality, morality, integrity, and truth are a drain on civilization. While the overall consciousness level of mankind is at 204 (November 2007), if the top one thousand individuals in the world were removed, the level would be at only 198. Compassion for the less evolved motivates society's endless efforts at correction and providing supplementary assistance to the evolutionarily less fortunate. Thus, compassion, acceptance, and tolerance are necessary to maintain a pragmatic social balance and effectiveness that also includes awareness of social/political/religious realities such as Islamic apocalyptic triumphalism, which currently operationally calibrates at 60 (November 2007).

Atheism, Agnosticism, and Nonbelief

Genuine intellectual doubt is integrous in that it considers decisions and beliefs to be important and significant. Reason resorts to intellectual processing on the presumption that information plus logic can arrive at truth through mental processing. This also allows the tolerance of dichotomy and ambiguity that are consequent to the linear experience of maturation and emergence of wisdom. It is eventually discovered that it is not possible for the intellect alone to answer every question that can be devised (the hypothetical), and therefore, faith is a concomitant to every level of evolution. Faith is a mental constant, and therefore, it is only a question of where to place one's faith.

The narcissistic core of the ego is aligned with being 'right', whether being 'right' means being in agreement with wisdom or rejecting it as invalid. With humility, the serious searcher discovers that the mind alone, despite its education, is unable to resolve the dilemma of how to ascertain and validate truth, which would require confirmation by subjective experience as well as objective, provable criteria.

While reliance on authority through faith suffices for the majority of integrous searchers of spiritual reality and truth, the mind may still be left with lingering doubt. However, resolution is possible by means of the subjective experience of inner spiritual evolution that results from transcending the levels of consciousness plus validation of spiritual reality in today's world through the methodology of consciousness calibration. This combination, plus dedication to truth as a pathway to God, eventually results in overcoming the classic, great 'doubt block,' on the other side of which spontaneously emerge realization and revelation. All doubt arises from the self and is dissolved in the overwhelming Reality of the Self by which one is home at last with the peace that is consequent to certainty.

That the mind is unable to prove a proposition does not mean that the proposition is false. This is the pitfall of the atheist because the mind is unable to know truth. It is simultaneously equally unable to disprove it for it would then be in the paradox of having to prove its opposite. The narcissistic core of the ego unconsciously and naïvely presumes that it is omnipotent and therefore lacks the humility that is requisite to arriving at higher Truth. Interestingly, atheists are unable to use the consciousness calibration technique for to deny God is to deny Truth.

While atheism calibrates at consciousness level 190, agnosticism at level 200 is more sophisticated, more aligned with reality, and merely admits that the intellect, in and of itself, is unable to resolve the problem of the actual existence of God. Agnosticism calibrates higher than skepticism because it does not include a negative emotional attitude of antagonism towards Truth. It merely humbly states that the intellect is unable to arrive at a satisfactory answer. The limitation of agnosticism is looking to the intellect for the answers to problems that cannot be solved at the level of the intellect alone.

Agnosticism and atheism may also be concordant with chronological age and tend to diminish with emotional maturity via the pathway of wisdom. Truth is then sought, not just in the linear dimension of content but also in the nonlinear realm of context, which expands the ability to comprehend Truth. In many areas of life, speculation is replaced by confidence and expansion of the capacity for awareness of higher dimensions that reveal themselves via the mechanism of revelation rather than linear intellectual processing.

Doubt and disbelief often presage major leaps of consciousness that may arise consequent to remotivation due to frustration, calamity, or merely maturation and the emergence of wisdom. This has been noted by many people, even saints, who went through major conversion experiences, including the miraculous. One such pathway can involve the loss of early-life religious faith due to catastrophic circumstances, which is then followed by years of seeking for confirmable truth. Such inner exploration is accelerated by the practice of meditation itself without an associated belief system. Thus, for the nonbeliever, Buddhism is often practical and attractive as the Buddha taught the eight-fold pathway without belief in 'God'.

Another pathway suitable for the nonbeliever is provided by the ancient *Vedas* and *Upanishads* that anticipated the discoveries of quantum mechanics. They also spoke of the Ultimate Reality of the Absolute Principle and the infinite field of consciousness itself as the primordial Reality that is beyond the illusions of perception as well as mentation. The pathway of Advaita (nonduality) is the pristine avenue for the integrous search for Truth that excludes all belief systems. This has been described in detail in prior works. Although nonduality leads to Enlightenment, the study of *Vedanta* can lead to overinvolvement in various Indian schools of philosophy that may then become distractive belief systems.

For the skeptic/disbeliever, the pathway of inquiry into the search for the essence of consciousness itself is the most pristine route and methodology as it bypasses all belief systems and requires only integrous curiosity and sincerity.

All mental (linear) depictions of spiritual/religious truth are subject to invalidation, argument, and dispute. In contrast, consciousness itself (nonlinear) is beyond definition or description and thus not subject to skepticism, doubt, or disbelief.

Investigation into the nature of consciousness leads

directly to the very source of Illumination, for the Light of Consciousness is the condition of Enlightenment. By its Light, the Knower and the Known are united in the Realization of the Self as God Immanent.

CHAPTER 14

Spiritual Pathways

Introduction

It has long been said that there are ten thousand pathways to God. Those that are traditional have been described in previous works and include calibrated levels of the world's great religions as well as the primary yogas and the great teachers. These are reinforced by calibrated lists of integrous teachers and teachings, as well as religious and spiritual organizations and groups from approximately 10,000 B.C. to the present era.

There is now available authenticated information that is of pragmatic value to any and all pathways in that it defines and verifies levels of truth. Thus, the seeker of today does not have to rely solely on historical or external variables for credibility. Comfort, convenience, and certainty are further enhanced by exposure to material that, by its own nature, is transparently valid. Importantly, there is an overall coherence and concordance with the totality of the accumulated information that precludes the likelihood of doubt or uncertainty and allows for reification and cross corroboration. The methodology of consciousness calibration and its discovery are products of the evolution of consciousness itself, which thereby reveals its own truth and validity.

Primary Pathways

Religions

Spiritual education is based on intellectual comprehension, faith, reason, and logic, and like any other subject of study, there is reliance on a basic body of knowledge. This has been provided historically by religions as well as theological schools and ecclesiastical academic literature that can, by commitment, lead to formally becoming ordained as a priest, minister, or even earning a Doctor of Divinity or Doctor of Theology degree.

While such studies may reinforce faith and lead to mastery of complex information, they do not, in and of themselves, necessarily lead to advanced states of personal subjective awareness. This limitation may be due to academic contextualization that may then result in compartmentalization and erudition rather than progressive stages of Enlightenment. When one considers the sheer mass and complexity of philosophy, theology, ontology, and metaphysics, the mastery of the field is much to be admired and respected, as is represented by the title for highly educated prelates, "Doctors of the Church" (e.g., Meister Eckhart).

The limitations that may possibly ensue from following the scholastic or 'learned' path are:

1. Compartmentalization within the intellect (theology calibrates at 440 to 470), as per articles in the publication *Zygon*.
2. Appeal to the spiritual ego and the illusion that to know 'about' is equivalent to 'becoming'. For instance, it is one thing to write a treatise on Love and quite another to become unconditionally loving as a way of being in the world.
3. Compartmentalization by virtue of contextualization as vocation, profession, or institutional title or function. The religious vocations are intrinsically of

great merit as well as social benefit because they serve to educate others.

4. Entrapment in ecclesiastical politics and ego attractions of title or power (e.g., vicar, monsignor, prelate, bishop, archbishop, cardinal, etc.). For the sake of spiritual evolution, it might paradoxically be more salutary to be the janitor in a great cathedral rather than its dean.

There may also ensue restrictive allegiance to a specific ecclesiastical doctrine and its historical context by which there can paradoxically occur worship of the religion itself rather than God as a prevailing Reality (e.g., 'religionism').

Sectarianism and Partisan Religiosity

Despite potential drawbacks, the overall influence of formal religion, ecclesiastical doctrine, and authority is reflected in the universal respect afforded the clergy in the role of chaplain, which represents ecumenical goodness in that the role transcends sectarianism. The chaplain does not discriminate and serves all within the military as well as officiating at baptisms, confirmations, weddings, and administration of last rites, funerals, and burials.

The ways of faith are basic traditions and form the necessary underpinnings and foundations of all religions and spiritual pathways (the Natural Law). Most often faith is a relatively effortless consequence of integrous family life and cultural tradition. It is assimilated via familiarity, which may include formal attendance at services as well as celebration of religious holidays and general social acceptance. There is also the religious benefit of belonging to a formal church congregation or organization and participating in associated activities that often include inspiration, such as in the great Gothic cathedrals and magnificent mosques, all of which pay tribute to the sovereignty of God and calibrate in the 700s.

The spiritual power of group intention is reinforced by devotion, worship, and prayer, which support the evolution of consciousness as well as having a positive impact on society by supporting responsibility, truthfulness, honesty, morality, and ethics. These elements characterize the basic principles of what has been called 'traditional America', wherein today even high officials, including the President and the Chief Justice of the Supreme Court, take their oaths of office with their hand on the Bible, which symbolizes not a particular faith but instead, acceptance of the sovereign authority by virtue of its origin: The Word of God.

Faith is the cornerstone of the triad of faith, hope, and charity. One of the great rewards of faith is its transcendence of temporal expectations and its extension into the afterlife of the soul.

The Virtues (cal. 210 to 385)

Spiritual evolution does not require intellectual comprehension of the dialectics of truth but merely an attraction to positive character traits and a sense of fairness, goodness, and decency. These are best inculcated in childhood by parental example, societal affirmation and reinforcement, and religion, along with the influence of integrous organizations, such as the Boy Scouts, Girl Scouts, and fraternal, public service, benevolent, or humanitarian organizations. Of importance is that positive character traits are also associated with higher rates of happiness, success, and health, as well as accomplishment and life satisfaction. By good fortune (karma), one is born into an integrous family, culture, and circumstances, and by identification absorbs essential assets and character traits.

Collectively, these traits are the backbone of modern civilization and traditional America and constitute the foundation upon which arose the most successful and powerful nation in history. The lack of these values, which characterizes malignant political regimes and cultures, has brought war, poverty, death, and destruction to mankind over the centuries (e.g., Pol Pot, Stalin, Nazis, Communism, Fascism, and Islamic terrorism).

The world is the theater of interaction between two different cultures—those that calibrate above 200 and those that calibrate below 200. The same 'oil and water' position exists within each society in which the conflict is again between individuals and institutions or groups that are above or below the critical line of integrity at 200.

Research reveals that approximately ninety-two percent of society's problems arise from people who calibrate below 200, and their overall financial cost to the citizenry is too enormous to calculate. Thus, a society that is overly permissive or supports nonintegrity pays an astronomical price not only in quality of life but also in every area of it, down to just simple, everyday physical safety.

The virtues have long been conceived of as 'basic decency' from which arises positive self-esteem as well as respect for self and others. All the virtues are based on good will and personal responsibility, which foster accountability, honesty, and reliability. These are also characterized as maturity by which one is helpful, cordial, friendly, and dependable.

Ethical sense results in fairness, reasonableness, and a modest diplomacy, which are evidence of respect for the feelings of others. People who are the 'salt of the earth' are friendly, polite, considerate, and have a sense of balance. In addition, they are generally benign and supportive and refrain from dumping their negative emotions on others or acting them out. Importantly, they are not predatory nor do they support predation, sexual or otherwise.

Collectively, these positive attributes are called 'character', and indeed, their acquisition does require personal effort, self-control, and patience. These qualities also form the basic assets that lead to Love, which calibrates at level 500 and is very reachable. From there, one can then seek to perfect that love to reach the great goal of Unconditional Love (cal. 540), which, however, is actually attained by only 0.4 percent of the world's population.

The basics, ethics, and morals also provide tools and motivations for the undoing of the consciousness levels below 200 (see *Transcending the Levels of Consciousness*). Each formal step of spiritual evolution is self-rewarding, and thus the journey becomes self-propagating and a way of life that is increasingly joyful.

Humility, Teachability

Implicit to the incorporation of religious/spiritual

truth are humility and open-mindedness. This is further supported by group agreement and acquiescence, especially over great periods of time. True authority implies credibility as well as authentication plus formal recognition. Thus, the reality of God is intrinsic and innate to widely separated cultures over great expanses of time. The reality of an omnipotent, omniscient, and omnipresent Deity characterizes all religious spiritual systems, including early and widely separated endemic native cultures.

True authority reflects essence as confirmed by consciousness research. Valid authority can be viewed as helpful, protective, and empowering. Truth is the teacher innate to integrous authority and therefore worthy of respect, independent of agreement or presentation.

Perception of authority, especially in today's world, is greatly influenced by public opinion and often misplaced in perceived pseudoauthorities whose teachings are essentially fallacious. There are numerous spiritual/religious and political leaders who calibrate far below 200 despite acclaim and fame. Thus, popularity or aggrandizement is of no value in discerning essence.

Basic to learning is rational humility by which the mind becomes teachable. It can then absorb, incorporate, and identify with verifiable, true knowledge. The key to success is to study and imitate a truthful authority rather than resist or attack it through competitive envy, jealousy, or hostility.

Visualization

There is the learning technique called "As if" by

which one visualizes and rehearses desirable behaviors, traits, and attitudes. The process also surfaces resistances or negative attitudes, such as "I can't." Visualization and rehearsal have been found to improve performance, confidence, and progress in multiple areas (Petras, 2006). What is held in mind tends to manifest, and the technique is utilized in diverse areas, including sports and even business. The higher the level of consciousness, the greater the likelihood that what is held in mind will actualize. Thus, to see solutions that 'serve the highest goal' is more powerful than simply projecting fulfillment of merely personal selfish desires and gain.

Crisis and Catastrophe

As mentioned previously, survivors of very major disasters almost universally declared (ninety-nine percent) that they prayed earnestly and fervently. Paradoxically, some survivors (especially of tornadoes) reported that during the worst of the crisis, they went into states of very profound peace (cal. 600). With surrender at great depth, fear disappears.

Lesser forms of the same phenomenon are the consequence of accepting the seemingly inevitable by resignation. This surrender can also be learned by the 'gun to the head' imaging technique, which poses the question, "With a gun to your head, now would you be willing to let go of your desire for such-and-such?" The imaging technique awakens awareness that one 'could', and that the real problem therefore is whether one 'would'. Resistance is thus overcome by willingness.

Coercion

Much like the preceding examples, coercion and severe threat can actually bring about conversion and have been utilized over the centuries as a means to acquire converts. Related to coercion, brainwashing techniques and programs of intimidation or indoctrination are abused by authority as formalized intimidation.

Surrender and Survival

To recapitulate some essential information: The core of the ego was formed at the very onset of the emergence of animal life, which intrinsically lacked internal sources of energy. In the plant kingdom, this internal deficiency was handled by the mechanism of sunlight transforming the energy of chlorophyll into chemical energy. Primitive animal life forms, such as bacteria and protozoa, however, had to acquire necessary elements from the environment. This required the creation of detection and processing systems and the capacity to discern 'good' (life-supportive) from 'bad' (poisonous) substances. These later evolved as basic animal instincts, all of which are aligned with survival and are innate to ego functions.

The intrinsic mechanisms constitute the design and function of the faculty of intelligence whereby complex systems become integrated and orchestrated. With the emergence of the forebrain in the Homo sapiens, there arose a neurological substrate for enormous complexity but still with a dominant pattern of alignment with animal survival. The totality of this elaborate evolutionary mechanism constitutes the ego/mind/ emotions that then become identified as an internal, independent, autonomous source of life (the 'me').

From the above, it is obvious why surrendering the ego is so difficult and resisted, often at extreme cost. The primal internal belief is that the ego is the source, substrate, and core of life, and its existence is therefore considered to be the internal equivalent of Divinity. To the narcissistic core of the ego, to surrender control is equivalent to death, and, therefore, it struggles for what it believes to be sovereignty and survival. In reality, the ego/self is merely the mechanism whereby the nonlinear potentiality of the Self actuates as life in the form of an individual human, with its karmic propensities and uniqueness. The linear limited self is thus an expression of the infinite nonlinear Self, which is its actual Source. The ego/self is therefore limited content, whereas the Self is unlimited context.

Surrender is the process whereby the underlying reality of the Self becomes progressively discovered as the self dissolves into the Self. This process is enabled by faith and conviction as well as intention. Because of resistance and evolutionary factors, the consciousness level of the average individual rises approximately five points in an ordinary lifetime. However, spiritually committed people may experience very large jumps of hundreds of points.

Temporality

Underlying all fears is the primordial, instinctual fear of death itself, and therefore much inner work can be bypassed by deenergizing this fear as early as possible in one's spiritual work. The fear of physical death arises from the animal instinct plus the narcissism of the ego, which is in love with itself. Death implies an end of experiencing, and experiencing is equated with life; therefore, the ego clings to that which is linear and familiar.

The inevitability of physical death is the primary enigma of human life and is therefore often handled out of fear by denial. Religion and spiritual education are helpful in that death is then recontextualized as merely transition from the physical to the spiritual mode of life and existence. Of great value is the acceptance of the temporality of physical life. By reflection, it is seen that what is really valued is the time interval of experiencing, that is, how long one will be here on earth.

A useful clinical analogy, however, is to realize that when one has a headache, it is really irrelevant how long it has been since the last one. Only the present has to be handled. The same conditions apply at death's door, that is, how long one has already lived as a body becomes relatively irrelevant, and all that remains is to surrender lingering attachments, such as to see one's grandchildren grow up.

It will be noted that a large percentage of emotional attachments to life are primarily those of sentimentality and preferences. Of primary value is one's estimation of the enjoyment of the pleasures of life and sentimental attachment to their familiarity. Human life and its relationships have become 'home', and therefore humans fear to vacate the familiar and move to the unknown.

It takes faith to accept that the law of life, like the laws of indestructibility of energy or matter, guarantees its continuance. Like matter and energy, life cannot be destroyed but can only change form. (This statement calibrates at 1,000.) Thus, death is actually only the leaving of the body. The sense of identity is, however, unbroken. The state of 'me' (self) is constant and continues after it separates from the physical expiration, that is, there has to be a 'who' that goes on to heaven or other realms or chooses to reincarnate. (This statement also calibrates at 1,000.)

To the Spirit, the lessons learned in a physical life are important to spiritual evolution, yet embodiment is only an episode. People who have had out-of-body or near-death experiences are therefore better prepared. With devotion, hope, and faith, fear of death is replaced by optimism, expectancy, and attraction to Divine provinces of Peace and Love.

Realization and Revelation

The relinquishment of the ego's positionalities reduces its dominance and opens the door for comprehension and awareness that are nonlinear and nonconceptual. Thus emerges the 'knowingness' of the Self by which conflicts spontaneously dissolve. These inner transformations are accompanied by quiet joy, relief, and a greater sense of internal freedom, safety, and peace. The power of the Love of the Self progressively predominates and eventually eclipses all negative feelings, doubts, and obstacles.

Transformation is thus not experienced as the loss of the self but rather as the gain of the emergence and unfoldment of the Self, which is of a much greater dimension. What actually emerges is a change of state or condition that supersedes and replaces the old. Thus, the lesser is replaced by the greater, by which spiritual evolution reveals the Presence of God as Immanent. This discovery is the change in the state of consciousness historically referred to as 'Enlightenment' or 'God-consciousness'.

The Classic Pathways

Common to all spiritual/religious avenues to the realization of spiritual reality are:

1. Acquisition of the necessary information.
2. Spiritual practice and worship.
3. Devotion and love.
4. Selfless service.
5. Prayer, meditation, and contemplation.
6. Association with spiritual groups and teachers.
7. Reverence for Divinity.
8. Practice of virtues, rejection, and avoidance of evil, sin, and error.

The traditional great pathways are included in the four great classic yogas of Hinduism: *raja* (meditation), *jnana* (wisdom and introspection), *bhakti* (devotion), and *karma* (selfless service). These have their equivalency in all religions, including Christianity.

Education: Missionary

The 'good news' of salvation via formal religion has been a cultural tradition, and proselytization via good works is a noble expression of faith being put into practice. From emergency relief to feeding and clothing the homeless, selfless service can serve as an example of altruistic truth and love that teaches by experience.

Evangelism seeks to inform, attract, and inspire as well as spiritually motivate. Medical missionaries have been a great gift to victims of disasters, including casualties of war, both secular and religious. Such service was formally organized by religious groups during the Crusades, such as the still-active Hospitaliers of the Sovereign Order of St. John of Jerusalem (established in 1099), or the Knights of Malta. These orders established not only hospitals but also the nursing profession itself and have served various emergencies over great periods of time, as has the more recent emergence of such organizations as the Red Cross, Salvation Army, and various other disaster-relief organizations.

Even the nonreligious or nonsectarian organizations, such as the USO, the Elks, and the Boy and Girl Scouts, are inspirational in that they symbolize caringness for fellow humans. They represent being gracious and thoughtful for the needs of others, which is a form of unconditional love. Great courage and nobility are represented by emergency-service workers, such as law enforcement personnel, firemen, emergency medical technicians, and disaster volunteers.

Education: Conversion

'Conversion' can be autonomous as is exhibited by spontaneous conversion experiences whereby a nonintegrous life is given up as a consequence of a sudden leap in consciousness. This is often precipitated by a confrontation or a life crisis that breaks down denial, such as happens consequent to 'hitting bottom'. It may also be the result of proselytization or of having one's prayers answered. The death of a loved one or a health calamity may also be precipitous events.

'Osmosis'

A not uncommon phenomenon is for spiritually naïve, seemingly unmotivated people to become attracted to and even involved in serious spiritual progress. This may sometimes happen seemingly accidentally by even brief exposure to a friendly or loving person or moment. This phenomenon is well known in twelve-step faith-based groups that do not proselytize. The sharing of stories of strength, faith, and recovery rekindles hope in the listener, and such integrous spiritual groups grow by attraction rather than by promotion. Their great success spawned the now widely used group therapy techniques for solving diverse human problems.

Validation of the power and integrity of spiritual truth is exhibited by the widespread recovery of millions of people from hopeless conditions, including leaders of countries, senators, and governors. This has also influenced the collective level of consciousness so that in today's world, the new requirement for success is not greed for profit but dependable integrity.

Pathway of Love and Devotion

The consciousness levels of Love formally calibrate from 500 and above, and by level 570, they are often considered to be saintly by virtue of unconditionality. The energy field recontextualizes all experience and relatedness to self, others, and to all life.

The obstacles to Unconditional Love (cal. 540) are attachment, resentment, specialness, and judgmentalism.

The power of the high energy of Unconditional Love is transformative to self and others and precipitates the appearance of the miraculous by which the seemingly impossible is transformed into the actual. The energy of Love is complete within itself and is thus free of need, considerations, limitations, or seeking of gain. To be free of wantingness is liberating, and in some spiritual traditions, Enlightenment is termed 'Liberation' (*Moksha*). In Christianity, the dissolving of the personal self into the Self of Divine Love is referred to as *Unio Mystica*.

Love is ordinarily conceptualized as having to do with relationship and the vicissitudes of compatibility and interaction as well as expectations, and thus, emotionality. Relationships bring up desires for control and possession, resulting in conflict that surfaces as anger or even hatred. Thus, unsatisfactory experiences of purported 'love' are not the result of love but of emotional attachment and 'involvement'.

More evolved patterns of relationship that are free of negativity are consequent to basing a relationship on mutual alignment rather than on possessive emotional involvement. This is of critical importance and redefines the essence of true relationship. It could be pictured as being mutually parallel and vertical rather than horizontal (e.g., control), which acts as a tether between people via their 'solar plexus' instead of alignment via the heart.

Spiritual love is neither erotic nor possessive and is seen in mature lovemates and in the platonic love of the strong bonds that are formed by shipmates, for example, or military units, or teams. Love of country and one's countrymen eventually extends to all of humanity, and then eventually to the Creator as the Source of Life. Love is gracious and expansive and eventuates as love of all life and all Creation. Thus emerges the Buddhist prayer for the enlightenment and salvation of all sentient beings so they may transcend the bondage that underlies suffering itself. The ideal of unconditional compassion and mercy to all life in all its expressions requires transcendence of dualistic perception and its illusions.

Devotion to Truth and life is transformative and results in transcending linear perception to awareness of nonlinear essence as the Ultimate Reality. This becomes self-revealing as the self dissolves into the Self and reveals the perfection of Divinity of all existence that shines forth as the Essence and Glory of Creation.

CHAPTER 15

Becoming the Prayer: Contemplation and Meditation

Introduction

The task that confronts the spiritual student, devotee, or aspirant is how to actualize conceptual spiritual information into subjective, experiential reality. Thus arises the necessity for application of practices and techniques that evolve progressively into that process whereby the potential becomes the actual. In addition to devotional prayer and authenticated sources of truth, there are the major, basic, time-honored avenues of meditation and contemplation, the efficacy of which is increased by intention and devotion.

Contemplation

Calm reflection and introspection allow information to become integrated, correlated, and recontextualized. Thus, a contemplative state is more relaxed, open, spontaneous, and intuitive than goal-directed activities. Contemplation allows inferences and general principles to formulate spontaneously because it facilitates discernment of essence rather than the specifics of linear logic. A benefit of contemplative comprehension is revelation of meaning and significance.

Whereas meditation generally involves removal from the world and its activities, contemplation is a simple style of relating to both inner and outer experiences of life, which permits participation but in a detached manner. Intentional doingness is focused on result, whereas contemplation is related to effortless unfolding. One could say purposeful thinking is quite 'yang' in character, whereas contemplation is very 'yin'. It facilitates the surrender and letting go of attractions, aversions, and all forms of wantingness or neediness.

Contemplation is invitational to awareness of meaning and progressive levels of abstraction. Thought is linear; understanding is contextual and nonlinear. Expansion of context enhances the significance, value, and meaning of thoughts; thus, contemplation tends to invite the influence of Self to overshadow the activity of the self.

Whereas the goal of the ego/mind is primarily to do, act, acquire, or perform, the intention of contemplation is to 'become'. While the intellect wants to know 'about', contemplation seeks Knowingness itself and autonomous wisdom. Rational thinking is time related, sequential, and linear, whereas contemplation occurs outside of sequential time. It is nonlinear and related to comprehension of essence. Devotional contemplation is a way or style of being in the world whereby one's life becomes a prayer.

With inner spiritual work, the two processes begin to occur simultaneously. One part of the mind may be concerned with handling anger or resentment, and at the same time, another part of the mind may be looking for a spiritual resolution so that by recontextualization, the apparent conflict is resolved by transcendence. The inner process becomes like a child with a parent—the spirit is the parent, and the ego is the child. The childish ego/self is reactive and focused short term, whereas the wise parent's spiritual Self is concerned with long-term evolution and consequences. While the ego likes to indulge in emotions, Spirit seeks to transcend them by recontextualization. Thus, the inner work is considerably concerned with replacing instinct-based emotionality with spiritually based comprehension.

The inner experience of transcendence is the consequence of moving from a lower to a higher level of consciousness, which may initially require effort and processing, but it eventually becomes familiar and habitual as it is assisted by willingness, devotion, humility, and dedication to Truth, with love as a primary goal. Over time, former ways of experiencing the world disappear, and negative feelings and perceptions dissolve. To see things differently is its own reward and frequently results in feeling as though one is being reborn.

To align one's life with spiritual intention expands its meaning and significance. While the ego/body/mind's lifespan is limited and temporary, the life of the spirit is eternal, and its importance thus eclipses transitory gains of ego satisfaction. Thus, the lesser is surrendered to the greater by alignment, commitment, and agreement. Because it is freely chosen rather than imposed, there is a lessening of resistance.

Spiritual progress is also an exploration that has greater rewards than were obtained from lesser motivations and goals. Ordinary life is pleasing as usual, but the pleasure is more aligned with fulfillment of potential rather than passing sensation. There are a unique inner pleasure and satisfaction in fulfilling the potential growth and expansion of awareness of the significance of one's true life. It is also pleasing to discover that it is not necessary to drive oneself forward, but instead, one can simply allow oneself to move forward as the blocks are removed. Thus, one becomes attracted by the future rather than propelled by the past.

Awareness tends to become more diffuse, global, inclusive, and pervasive as a consequence of the self progressively dissolving into the Self. The belief in sequential causation disappears, and in its place is the witnessing of the emergence of potentiality into actuality as the unfoldment of the ongoingness of Creation. The concept of an individual 'I' diminishes into the all-inclusive spontaneous 'everythingness' of the totality of a cohesive harmony by which the seeming unitary (self) dissolves into the universality of the Self.

Beneath the phenomenal experiential sequence of ordinary consciousness, a primordial stillness—an undisturbable peace and silence—is discovered. All phenomena are seen to be the transitional emergence of potentiality into actuality, which is taking place autonomously as though in slow motion. The unfolding is simultaneously ultra-gentle yet infinitely powerful as an expression of the universe itself. One moves from complete to complete as a prevailing reality.

The subjective awareness of the nature of this emergent contextualization of life and the universe is also concordant with the most current discoveries of advanced quantum mechanics and theoretical physics. They now scientifically confirm statements made in prior works (Hawkins, 1995-2006) that time, location, and space are projections of consciousness and have no intrinsic reality. (Affirmed by Harokopos in "Power

As a Cause of Motion"; by Lynds in the scientific paper, "Time and Quantum Mechanics"; and by the writings of Stapp in *Mindful Universe*.)

The expanded awareness of the nature of reality that arises from very advanced physics and quantum mechanics correlates with the subjective realizations of the mystic (Hawkins, 2003, 2006; Grace, 2007). The expanded paradigm of reality dissolves the illusion of any discrepancy between faith and reason. Divine revelation provides the top-down explanation of Creation, while at the same time, scientific theory might be likened to a bottom-up explanation, which is more linear in its explanation of the universe.

There is a final realization that all is perfection as a consequence of the unfoldment of potentiality actualizing outside of time as an expression of Creation. The ultimate source and potential are referred to as the 'Godhead', the Divinity of which is expressed as the emergence of the totality of timeless Creation and its evolutionary unfoldment.

With the disappearance of conceptual thought and its propensity for categorization and explanation, the Allness, Oneness, Harmony, and Totality of the Divine Reality shine forth in the splendor and exquisite beauty that are intrinsic and innate to all Creation. Thus, within that which appears to be form is its Source, which is formless. With the dissolution of complexity, simplicity reveals itself as everything simply being the perfect expression of its essence, that is, just being exactly what it is and not as it is described or perceived, which is extraneous to the intrinsic reality of Existence itself.

Meditation

As a subject for study, the available information on meditation is extensive and can become elaborate as well as inclusive of institutionalized, extraneous embellishments. Meditation, however, is a time-honored means by which to access spiritual truth via subjective, experiential revelation. Very major leaps of awareness and rapid transcendence of levels of consciousness can also occur.

As is well known, a multitude of specific techniques have evolved over the centuries in various cultures and religions. In addition, there have been many scientific studies of altered brain physiology and magnetic imaging, along with EEG studies of brainwave frequencies. In general, these reveal a slowing of both frequency and amplitude and the emergence of slow theta waves that replace the fast beta as well as alpha waves.

Meditative techniques can include formal discipline techniques and styles, such as exemplified by Zen and various yogas that include visualization, breathing, and postural elements, all designed to assist the flow of the kundalini spiritual energy up through the chakra system. These practices can result in major benefits that, however, need to be accompanied by a commensurate increase in the consciousness calibration level. Thus, the experience of *satori* can be a transient peak episode that disappears with resumption of daily life.

From the viewpoint of consciousness itself, the process is one of moving the sense of self from linear mentalization and sensory function to become progressively more comprehensive, contextual, and beyond the attraction of thoughts, images, and emotions. What is sought is the subjective realization and identification with the nonlinear contextual field of consciousness itself, which is the Light of Awareness and the substrate out which arise existence and beingness (see *I: Reality and Subjectivity*).

One benefit of meditation is the discovery that, intrinsically, the energy field of the mind is itself basically void of thoughts, feelings, and images, and that these activities actually occupy only about one percent of the total mind field. Like the sea beneath the waves, ninety-nine percent of the mind is still, silent, and void, which can be detected and intuited if this fact is made known to the student. The undisciplined mind is attracted and glamorized by the active content of mind, with its kaleidoscopic parade of thoughts, images, and feelings because of the subtle narcissistic payoff of these activities. To silence the mind, it is necessary to notice the subtle, continuous payoffs, be willing to surrender these illusory gains, and instead identify with the mind as a silent energy field that is not limited to the personal self. Note that the ego is addicted to mentalization and craves its constant entertainment and stimulation, even if it includes negativity.

Just as the physical 'I', like a camera, registers images and objects, the mind is the 'I' of the self, which perpetuates the illusion of a unique, separate personal identity that becomes hypothecated to be the originator of thought, intention, desire, etc. With relinquishment of this narcissistic illusion, it becomes apparent that all aspects of supposedly personal life are actually occurrences that are autonomous and spontaneous.

As a consequence of major progress, the fear of death or the fear of a disappearance into 'nothingness' may arise. This represents the resistance and struggle of the narcissistic core of the ego that seeks to maintain sovereignty. Because this fear, like other fears, is based on illusion, it is safe to surrender it to God, which clears the obstacles to the realization of the Self as the Presence of God Immanent.

Integration

Meditation and contemplation are neither separate nor discrete activities but instead are merely addressed for convenience as though they were different subjects for study. In practice, they are commingled and develop into a consciousness-awareness style that becomes habitual. In both, the emphasis is on the nonverbal, subjective, nonlinear context out of which arises the awareness of Awareness itself as the contextual field of consciousness. It is relatively simple to move from the content of mental awareness to the realization that witnessing and observing are phenomena that are autonomous, occurring on their own.

As has been historically taught as well as confirmed by consciousness research, an additional assist to spiritual progress and the practices of meditation and contemplation is the high-frequency energy field of the aura of the Teacher. This can be accessed through reading the writings of the teacher, visualizing the teacher's image, and most powerfully, by physically being in the presence of the teacher's aura. This energy frequency then becomes permanently incorporated into the auric field of one's own spirit and continues on past physicality or incarnations over great expanses of time. Its purpose is the silent unfoldment of Knowingness, which is critical at evolved states of consciousness. These states are nonconceptual and nonlinear.

At a very advanced state of consciousness, there is no longer memory or mentalization. Out of the seemingly silent Nothingness arises the Knowingness that allows the surrender of the last remnants of the ego-self. Subsequently, there prevails a 'state' or 'condition' rather than a personhood or separate identity.

Summation

Through spiritual alignment, intention, and devotion aided by meditation, contemplation, authenticated instruction, and truth, assisted by the energy field of an advanced teacher, great leaps of consciousness can occur unexpectedly. Thus, it is important to know of them well in advance as confirmed by consciousness research. The chances of becoming enlightened are now more than one thousand times greater than at any time in the past; thus, reaching the level of Unconditional Love (cal. 540) is a very attainable and practical goal. From the level of Unconditional Love, the pathway is increasingly joyful. At level 600, there occurs an infinite, silent stillness and peace, and progression from there is up to the Will of God, karma, and the potentialized Knowingness nascent within the spiritual aura.

The Realm of Silence

The ego/mind focuses on the mind's linear content and its endless processing of images, thoughts, memories, and feelings. It is attracted by novelty as well as by reduction of anxiety through problem solving and anticipatory preparation. Negative feelings, such as grief over loss or guilt and regret over mistakes and errors, can predominate. Often the will seems powerless, and the person feels as though they are the victim of the mind's endless torments. To interrupt the mind's endless ramblings, it is necessary to seek out its hidden motives and surrender the illusory gains. Thus, surrender rather than resistance may diminish the mind's seeming control.

The ego becomes enamored of its own sequential mentalizations despite its protests to the contrary. It finds satisfaction in processing negative thoughts and feelings. It loves and enjoys hatred, which is also profitable, as exemplified by television 'hate' celebrities. It is this satisfaction and secret gain that has to be surrendered and relinquished. All negative emotions persist because of their secret payoff. When this 'ego juice' is declined, thoughts tend to diminish and then disappear. The mind then tends to 'go blank', which then brings up the fear of boredom.

With observation, it becomes clear that the mind is busy anticipating the future (fear), or clinging to the past (regret, hatred, guilt), or savoring the past to extract pleasure via reruns. Thus, the mind becomes the focus of amusement as 'doing' something.

While it is commonly believed that there is an accessible silence 'between' thoughts, it will be discovered by practice that this is not actually an experiential fact. Thoughts occur in 1/10,000th of a second, which is faster than the 'perceiver' function of the mind. Thus, by the time the mind perceives the onset of a thought, it is already processing it. Prior to the perceiver/processor function is that of the observer/witness function, which is innately autonomous as a nonpersonal function/aspect of the field of consciousness itself. The observer/witness does not think nor does consciousness itself do so (only the mind 'thinks'). The awareness faculty of pure consciousness is the silent primordial state that is ever present, nonvolitional, and nondiscussive.

By contemplation/meditation, the silent, formless state is discovered to be the primordial substrate beyond even the duality of existence versus nonexistence. It is the Buddha state, which, like space, is unsullied by transitory content. The pure, formless silence is the Ultimate Context and beyond all names, although historically sometimes referred to as the 'Buddha Nature'. Even though devoid of form, the ultimate state is all-inclusive as Allness in contrast to the Nothingness of the Void (cal. 850). This is discussed in detail in *Transcending the Levels of Consciousness* and *Discovery of the Presence of God*.

CHAPTER 16

Transcending the World

Introduction

The obstacles to reaching advanced levels of consciousness are quite considerable because they stem from both within and without. The level of consciousness of the average person therefore advances (by statistical average) approximately five to seven points per lifetime. The evolution of the overall consciousness level of mankind is equally slow and can remain stationary for many centuries or even fluctuate and decrease as it did during 2006 (from 207 down to 204).

Because of intention and spiritual alignment, the evolution of a spiritual devotee, however, may be comparatively very rapid. The information now available as a result of consciousness research itself has increased the possibility of reaching Enlightenment by one thousand percent. In fact, the appearance of consciousness research itself is a consequence of the evolution of the consciousness of mankind.

From within the self, the structure and dynamics of the ego are a strong deterrent to the discovery of spiritual Reality. In addition, the mind's innocent, child-like substrate is programmable with fallacy, as it has no inner defense with which to ascertain the truth or falsehood of information. The ego is thus blinded by the delusion that it *is* capable of this feat. The mind is paradoxically ignorant of the fact that it is limited and prone to error. Without humility, spiritual evolution is at a standstill unless the ego's innate pride is jostled by significant events or karmic good fortune.

Aside from the innate intrinsic limitations of the human mind itself are the problems that arise from living in a world of continuous input from various levels, including the media. This also includes the biological/physical, emotional/psychological, mental/perceptual, and spiritual/contextual levels as well. The experiential world is also continuously confrontive in that it poses an endless array of options and choices within the pressure of a limited time frame that forces the necessity of continual decision-making.

While some spiritual devotees renounce the world and retreat to the safe haven of a dedicated spiritual community, that is not an option for the majority of seekers who have the difficult task of dedicated spiritual evolution while still an active participant in the daily world of responsibilities and activities. The task can be greatly facilitated, however, by becoming aware of certain attitudes and styles of perception, which the following will address.

What is the World?

Is the world 'real' or an 'illusion' has been a topic addressed by philosophers throughout history, but none has really offered a pragmatic, satisfactory means of resolution due to the lack of an explanation that is based on the inherent realities and proclivities of human consciousness itself. Thus, a statement such as "There is no point in trying to change the world because the world you see does not even exist" sounds true at consciousness level 700 but is not actually comprehensible to the average person. Similarly, to "wear the world like a light garment" (St. Francis of Assisi) sounds correct, but just how does one actually do it?

That man's primary error is 'ignorance' (as per Jesus Christ, the Buddha, Krishna, Socrates, etc.), requires explanation as the statement fails to explain whether that ignorance is innate or due to moral defect, willfulness, biological fate, karmic limitation, or intrinsic human proneness to error.

In this context, 'world' means two things: (1) the world as it is in reality/nature (Descartes' *res externa/extensa*), or (2) the world as it is perceived, observed, witnessed, and interpreted by the human mind (Descartes' *res cogitans/interna*). In addition to the experiential interpretations of the world, there are now added interpretations by both Newtonian physics and quantum mechanics.

The world has been interpreted over the centuries by various philosophies, including metaphysics, ontology, theology, and more. There is now also the world as reflected and interpreted by the media, which is then further processed by the senses. Whereas Socrates, Descartes, and others clearly expressed the dilemma of man, they failed to provide an explanation that would resolve the conflict, which is so well demonstrated by the confrontational Scopes trial as well as today's political debate about the proper alignment of different worldviews, including secularism versus faith and priorities of rights.

Worldview Options

Below are various options from which to view the world:

1. Being born a human is rare, fortunate, and the consequence of good karma.
2. The world is a trap of illusion; therefore, salvation depends on nonattachment to its linear and emotional qualities.

3. The perceived world is the result of the projection of human consciousness, and therefore akin to a Rorschach card.
4. The true reality of the world is unknowable due to the limitations of human intelligence.
5. The world is a comedy, a tragedy, a political game board, and more.
6. This is a purgatorial world of hardship and suffering; therefore, seek heaven.
7. The world is a rare opportunity for maximum spiritual growth and evolution by the undoing of bad karma and the earning of spiritual merit.
8. The world is a meaningless kaleidoscope of sensations, and any meaning is purely a projection.
9. The world is the theatrical stage for the comedy of the absurd.
10. The world and human life are the consequence of the fall of Adam and Eve due to disobedience and succumbing to the temptation of curiosity. Life is therefore penitential for original sin.
11. The world and humanity were created by God and are therefore divinely inspired and intrinsically holy.
12. The world is merely a physical product of the physical universe.
13. Life and therefore humanity are purely accidental products of Darwinian biological evolution (mechanistic reductionism). Survival is due to natural selection by survival of the fittest.
14. The world and the universe are merely passing illusions created by the ego to keep itself separate from God.
15. Human life is an expression of God's Will by which

the Godhead fulfills the actualization of infinite potentiality.

16. Man descended from the stars and fell from the heavens.
17. Man descended from the monkeys.
18. The world and earthly life are the optimum venue for the evolution of consciousness in human form from its animal origins to its spiritual enlightenment and salvation. Man is therefore the crossover from the animal to the angelic.
19. The world and its human life are only one dimension of existence among many dimensions.
20. The world represents the fusion of the linear and the nonlinear and actually exists outside the domain of time and causality.
21. The world offers the gift of life itself via beingness and existence, whereby consciousness is made experiential and thus reified as the Ultimate Reality out of which arises the capacity for existence/awareness.
22. The spiritual evolution occasioned by human life allows for the eventual discovery and human awareness of Divinity as its Source. Thus, the relinquishment of the ego/self reveals the spiritual Reality of the Self by which the Reality of God becomes manifest and subjectively experienced as the Self (God Immanent).
23. All contextualizations of the world are conjectural mentations as life is lived solely by subjective experience.
24. Man is just a highly evolved hominid and therefore merely a biological species and genus, and spirituality is a product of imagination.

25. Man is an environmental disaster, and the sooner he self-destructs and returns the world to Nature, the better.
26. Mankind is on a learning curve of biological/social evolution.
27. 'Meaning' is a semantic/linguistic construction with no inherent reality; therefore, any and all statements are equally valid.
28. "I have invented the world I see."
29. There is no point in trying to save the world, for the world you see does not even exist.
30. The world is an opportune place for redemption and salvation.
31. One's perception of the world is consequent to the observer's level of consciousness.
32. The human world is a spiritual hospital and rehabilitation unit.

The World of Affirmation

The world of daily life impinges via the mind and senses and results in attractions and aversions as well as providing meaning and value, which can be recontextualized via spiritual awareness and development. The struggle for the spiritual aspirant is to sort perception from essence and mentalization from subjective experiential validation. The world that is seen is the product of the emotional/mental processing, which also results in abstract meaning. As has been described in the previous books in this series, one's vision and experience of the world are a reflection of one's prevailing level of consciousness.

With elimination of all nominalization, conjecture, and projection, it can only be truly said that the world and everything in it merely 'is'. It is obvious upon reflection that what it 'is', is exactly what it 'means', without adjectives and descriptive mentalizations. René Descartes' categorization of *res externa* (the world as it is) and *res interna* (the world as perceived) dissolves via the process whereby all statements are seen to be only external to the realities they are attempting to describe.

Expressed radically, everything is merely what it is by virtue of identity, and all proposed meanings or descriptions are external, superimposed projections and perceptions/mentalizations. Shorn of projected descriptions, values, and meaning, the world reveals the Radiance of Divinity as the essence of its evolution/creation. The perfection of Allness shines forth a radiance, and everything is the perfect expression and fulfillment of its essence solely by virtue of that existence.

The world is innately *spiritually* perfect as it is, and as such, it is therefore maximally advantageous for the advancement of human consciousness as it provides maximum opportunity for gaining positive merit and the undoing of the negative via the spiritual faculty of the will. To see it thus results in gratitude as well as forbearance for seemingly negative experiences that involve suffering.

The comprehension and understanding of basic reality hinges on comprehending the significance of identity as Presence and Reality by which all things, without subject or predicate, are solely that which they *are*. While overall these sentences may sound redundant, within them is a realization that is liberating.

What anything 'means' is identical with what it *is*, for what it is, *is* its meaning. With this realization, the essence of the world shines forth with the Radiance of Divinity as revelation, and all is seen to be equally lovable, perfect, magnificent, and beautiful. To restate: The world as it is, is perfect for the advancement of human consciousness as it provides maximum opportunity for gaining positive merit and the undoing of the negative via the spiritual options of the will. To see it as such results in gratitude as well as forbearance with seemingly negative experiences that involve suffering.

To be 'spiritual' means that intention is focused on spiritual goals, meaning, and spiritual recontextualization of life's events and experiences. It also means to value the gift of life itself as well as that of other sentient beings. Spiritual intention itself recontextualizes all of life in all its expressions, and thereby meaning and significance become apparent.

The Good/Bad Impasse

This can be a formidable roadblock in that judgmentalism is so ingrained in the human psyche that despite one's best efforts, it arises seemingly automatically. The good/bad dichotomy is inculcated from earliest childhood and reinforced throughout life. In its most primitive form, it merely expresses the emotional colorings of 'want' versus 'not want'. By this route, the desirable becomes 'good', and the 'undesirable' and 'unpleasant' become 'bad'. This becomes the basis for morality and standards of behavior, which vary widely in different segments of society and in different cultures. However, the good-versus-bad dichotomy is intrinsic in all cultures throughout time and is even witnessed in animal-pack behaviors.

This duality is further reinforced by reward or punishment, which then becomes internalized as satisfaction or dismay and results in either increased or decreased self-esteem. Moralization is intrinsic to the human society, and, as mentioned previously, recent research has raised the probability that it is hardwired in the neuroanatomy and physiology of the human brain itself (Gazzaniga, 2005; Ackerman, 2006).

The most primitive life forms survived or failed to survive based on success or failure to acquire needed external sources of energy; thus, the dichotomies of right versus wrong, success versus failure, good versus bad, and edible versus inedible are indigenous to organic life forms. The group behaviors of the animal kingdom are almost identical to human behaviors, even at the level of power struggles between nations for survival, territorial expansion, and dominance (hegemony).

To transcend the vexing 'good/bad' dichotomy of criticalness is actually very simple via the realization that everything and everyone is being what they are simply by the fact of identity. Similarly, people can only be what they have become and are at any given instant. Moralistic categorization can only be a supposition based on the 'could be' hypothetical view. If people actually 'could' be different, they would be. The hypothetical is always invalid because it is a projected idealistic imagination with no basic reality; it therefore always calibrates as false.

Available options depend on the range of prevailing possibilities as is evidenced by the rueful comment, "If only I had known then what I know now." It is obvious that at a different age or under different conditions, either internal or external, a different choice would have been made.

This realization also diminishes guilt and self-condemnation, for the person now is not the same as the one who existed at the time of the error. That fact, however, does not necessarily eliminate karmic responsibility or consequences, but it does influence and mitigate culpability. It is unrealistic as well as eventually injurious to believe that other people 'should' adopt and live by one's own personal standards, morals, and code of conduct as well as interpretation of reality. Projected moralism is always expressed as 'should' and often leads to resentment, hatred, grudges, or even retaliatory vengeance and, of course, war (e.g., the naïve American view that all other nations 'should' be democracies). One can, by choice, reject the temptation to habitual judgmentalism. The result is a greater inner peace.

That one's worldview is completely different from others' is often ignored in international relationships and politics. Compassion arises from the acceptance of human limitation and by seeing that everyone is really the captive of their own worldview. With nonattachment, there is no longer the pressure to try to change the world or other people's viewpoints or make them wrong by virtue of disagreement. As an evolved friend, who is also a wit and pundit, said many years ago, "It's a relief to realize I don't have to have an opinion on everything" (Richmond, 1979).

Acceptance/Humor

To transcend the world requires compassion and acceptance. They are the result of inner humility by which the world is surrendered to God with increased peace of mind. One of the most valuable spiritual tools about which, historically, little has been said is the great value of humor. Comedy arises as a result of the comparison that is made between perception and essence, and the resolution is a consequence of the acceptance of the ambiguity.

Humor is quite different from ridicule or malice as it is compassionate in that it accepts human limitations and foibles as being intrinsic. It therefore assists 'wearing the world like a light garment' and illustrates that in being like the reed that bends in the wind, one survives instead of being broken down by rigidity.

The relief of laughter via a joke expresses the pleasure at dissolution of conflict, and the capacity to laugh at oneself is essential to positive self-esteem. To respond to everything as though it were highly important is a result of the vanity of the narcissistic core of the ego (e.g., being 'sensitive' or 'offended'). Humor recontextualizes experiences and events and thus facilitates enjoyment without moralistic judgmentalism. Humor evolves as philosophical acceptance and has a healing effect. It thereby decreases suffering, conflict, and negative emotions.

Life presents endless ambiguities that, without humor, are not resolvable. Judiciously used, humor via acceptance leads to peace and an increased capacity for adaptation rather than frustrated resentment or defeatism. By humor, we 'rise above' circumstances and retain inner dignity instead of shame, anger, resentment, or lowered self-esteem. Humor also facilitates wisdom in that it recontextualizes human frailties as being intrinsic to the human condition itself and therefore not primarily personal.

The comedian Jack Benny played a famous character

who was miserly and a tightwad. A robber stops him on the road with a gun and says, "Your money or your life." Benny hesitates and then slowly, but deliberately and thoughtfully says, "Well, not so fast now." In that, of course, he brings up for our laughter the human proclivity to be so materialistic that people endlessly sacrifice their lives, enjoyment, and pleasure just for the gain of money.

Last but not least is sardonic gallows humor, which extracts the ambiguity of even the most horrific of human experiences and allows us to distance ourselves from them and thereby decrease the painfulness. Humor thus assists transcendence and release from worldly attachments and illusory desires.

Humor is an expression of freedom and joyfulness, and laughter is biologically healing. While guiltiness and 'sackcloth and ashes' penance were emphasized in past centuries, it can be seen that on the Scale of Consciousness, they calibrate quite low. God is found at the top of the Scale, not at the bottom. Faith, love, and joy are the high road; doom and gloom merely lead to sadness and despondency. Self-hatred blinds awareness of the Self as a reflection of Divine Creation.

CHAPTER 17

Morality, Reason, and Faith

Introduction

St. Thomas Aquinas addressed the problem of integrating reason and faith in the celebrated classic, *Summa Theologica* (cal. 730) first published in 1485. This great work has been honored over the centuries for establishing the premise that faith is reinforced and clarified by reason and vice versa. In so doing, there is resolution of conflict between the two. In addition, he taught that reason alone was insufficient, for the truest and highest meaning could only be understood when reason is illuminated by revelation. Reason alone pertained to the academic objectivity of scholasticism, whereas revelation activated subjective realization and true spiritual comprehension. Thus, academic theology provided linear content, but only revelation provided the necessary nonlinear contextualization for understanding.

The modern spiritual seeker's faith has not only reason to integrate but also the task of correlating faith with a world dominated by science and technology along with the impact of the media. Further inroads are the consequence of the undermining of logic and reason by the pervasive influence of prevailing politicized philosophical distortions and error by which the standards of integrity and truth have been so impaired that falsehood has now actually gained equal legal standing with credibility and truth. Thus, a Washington court has ruled that there is no longer any basis for slander in that any statement ('free speech') need not be supported by confirmable, material facts. Therefore, overt lies and verifiable truth have equal standing. (This ruling calibrates at 170.)

While faith has routinely been subjected to attack over historical periods, now even reason itself has become basically impaired so as to actually hinder the capacity of the human mind for reality testing. The reversal of truth and falsehood and of good and evil is brazenly stated by world political leaders as well as prevailing academics (e.g., ethical and moral relativism, and postmodern deconstructionism).

Substitution of Narcissism for Divinity

Superimposed on the above assaults on reason are pervasive inroads on the integrity of religious teaching. One of the world's major religions now even emerges as the religion of hate, terror, and death, complete with sanctimonious citing of 'God's approval'.

In America, 'liberal Christianity' has bowed to postmodern, relativistic political ideology to the degree that it invalidates the very foundation of its credentials, such as rejecting the Trinity and the Divinity of Jesus Christ. As a consequence, Protestant churches have shown a decline of fifty percent in membership, and even some Catholic churches have lost membership due to attempts at 'modernization'.

The impact of 'modernization' is evidenced by the paradoxical promotion of the secularization of Christianity itself by such means as substituting "BCE" (Before the Common Era) for B.C., or "CE" (Common Era) for A.D. This is postulated as being 'sensitive' (meaning to coddle narcissism) to Islamic non-Christians (who already had formally rejected the Western calendar via decree by the Ayatollah). However, paradoxically, such alteration is quite 'nonsensitive' to the world's Christians and two thousand years of history. This affront to Christianity was followed by one even more offensive when the Archbishop of Canterbury suggested in February 2008 that Britain approve Sharia law. (See Woodward and Butt.) Islam's threat to free expression in Europe is noted by American columnists, such as Kathleen Parker (*Washington Post Writers Group*, 15 February 2008).

So as to not 'offend' anyone, Christianity would have to eliminate all references to Jesus Christ; Buddhism would have to eliminate any references to Buddha; Judaism would have to eliminate all the prophets or Hebrew names for God; and religion itself would have to be eliminated as it might offend the nonreligious. However, in reality, the Western world is stuck with the numerical designation of the year itself. This is the year 2008. No matter how it is designated, '2008' marks two thousand and eight years after the birth of Christ. "BC 350," as everyone knows, actually means three hundred fifty years before the birth of Christ.

Even if disguised as the 'Modern Era', the numerical year still dates to the birth of Christ. (A real 'Modern Era' perhaps should be redated to start with Thomas Edison's discovery of electricity, or perhaps the steam engine, or certainly with the birth of the silicon chip and the computer.)

From the 'thought police' emerge the 'language police', the 'feeling police', the 'gender police,' the 'sexual-orientation police', and the 'religious-sensitivity police' (see Dierker, 2006). As can readily be observed, all the above allegedly 'sensitive', 'correct', and 'superior' attitudes are intrinsically aligned with narcissism by which the world is expected to cater to everyone's infantile ego. This produces a pretend world of juvenile expectation and constant conflict between self-interested factions that lead to social disintegration and eventually loss of the capacity for even physical survival. Perhaps what is really needed is 'narcissism police'. The current pejorative use of the term 'insensitive' is in itself obviously quite insensitive and an epithet meant to insult others.

From the above, it is apparent that the word 'sensitive' means allegiance and catering to one's own egoistic neuroticism, commonly termed 'selfishness'. Thus, when presumptively projected onto others, in order to not presumably 'hurt the feelings' of high-profile, likely terrorists (who kill thousands), the *real* feelings of 750 million passengers on United States airlines per year are completely ignored as they go through endless security lines, 'pat downs', searches, and endless delays. One 'shoe bomber' results in 750 million pairs of shoes having to be removed at a staggering cost. This is based on the presumption that uninvited travelers to the United States have very fragile self-esteem and may feel 'insulted' if asked where they come from, etc. Note that other countries are not that negligent, and they utilize profiling (including iris scanning) as a matter of common sense and the rational, protective, survival self-interest of legitimate sovereignty.

In psychoanalysis, the above neurotic syndrome is termed 'reaction formation' in which the individual overcompensates for a defect by exaggerating its opposite. Thus, the 'sensitive' person is actually grossly insensitive to the feelings of others. By this device, the minority seeks to rule the majority to accommodate personal self-interest. With maturity one learns to take responsibility for one's own self-centeredness and 'get over it' as the rock band Eagles' song advises (e.g., Bill Cosby's 'tough love' advice). The alternative is to bring all of society down to the lowest denominator, which eventually threatens even survival itself out of neurotic concern that confronting terrorist suspects might 'hurt their feelings'.

Despite all the above, morality remains as secular guidelines to behaviors, and over fifty percent of the American population adheres to basic moral tenets (Gallup poll, May 2006). At the same time, however, over eighty percent of people believe that there is a current moral decline.

Substitution of Emotions for Reality

On the Scale of Consciousness, levels below 200 indicate falsity and negative feelings. Calibration levels 200 and above denote progressive levels of truth and positive emotions. In the 400s, truth is revealed as logic and reason that thereby take priority over feelings. Childhood is dominated by feelings and only with maturity does it make them subservient to the reality of reason. There is eventually an integration whereby one 'feels good' about being reasonable and realistic. Negative feelings are primarily subordinated, and only positive emotions are allowed full reign.

Feelings below level 200 are narcissistic and animal/ego oriented. While egocentric feelings are often rationalized and excused ('just being human'), they are not laudable as such. Unmitigated emotionality is seen as infantile and inappropriate for public life or serious discourse.

A mature person is expected to have developed the

capacity to be responsible for their own feelings. At consciousness levels below 200, 'feelings' are presumed to be primary and often used to attempt to justify and legitimize any and all behaviors. There is therefore a serious communication gap between the segments of society above and below level 200.

Narcissism encourages emotionality as a substrate for the constraints of reason and uses them as a means to control others. Thus, if one percent of the population is 'made uncomfortable' by a reference to Divinity, the fact that ninety-nine percent of the people are deists is supposed to be ignored because 'their' feelings do not count. Thus arises the oddity of the rule of the majority by the neurotic traits and immaturity of the minority. This process is at the roots of ninety-eight percent of dissident demonstrations whereby egocentricity is aggrandized as 'rights' that demand being catered to. 'Rights', then, justify violence, riots, arson, robbery, genocide, and destruction as expressed by soccer-game or Paris street riots. Narcissism is a prejudicial positionality that readily converts into racism, sexism, and religionism, as well as profiling debates.

Traditional Guidelines

It has long been held by religious/spiritual wisdom that negative energies impinge on mankind to oppose spiritual evolution and to attack purity and truth. These energies have been traditionally described as 'evil', 'satanic', 'demonic', or 'lower astral', implying that they originate from other 'ungodly' dimensions. Those that oppose and seek to overcome truth and substitute falsehood have been classically referred to as 'Luciferic' energies (prideful refutation of God). Those energies that seek to destroy purity and love have been referred to as 'Satanic'. While the Luciferic energies pridefully seek power and control, Satanic energies stimulate sexual enslavement, desecration, and involvement in sadism, violence, defilement, war, and destruction. Both these energies utilize temptation and seduction and are clever at hiding beneath the sheep's clothing, even so far as claiming God's authorization (also not uncommon in the mentally ill, such as with the famous killer, Son of Sam).

Both of these influences are, of course, vividly demonstrated and proselytized in current society, the impact of which has been greatly amplified and empowered by the media. Both trends are glamorized by world leaders and charismatic celebrities. All the destructive trends are aimed at human gullibility and frailty consequent to the attraction of the narcissistic core of the ego itself, out of which these trends emerge and tend to become self-reinforcing.

Throughout religious history can be seen impingement by the energies that see God as the ultimate enemy and therefore seek to bring down religious truth or redefine God in Satanic images and concepts. Note the great fall of Christianity subsequent to the Council of Nicaea (from above 900 down to the 400s). Significant in that fall is the inclusion, for example, of the Book of Revelation (cal. 70) in the New Testament (which calibrates at 800 without the Book of Revelation).

Of equal significance is the previously described fall of Islam and its founder. (See also *Truth vs. Falsehood*, Chapter 16.) Muhammad calibrated at 700 at the time he dictated the Koran, but three years later, he suddenly fell to level 130, took up the sword, and in 629 A.D. began the endless 'holy' wars that have continued up to the present day. (Jihad calibrates at level 30.)

Also, severely injurious to Islam was the emergence of Wahhabism (cal. 30) via its founder who calibrated at 20. Deleterious teachings of Wahhabism were further reinforced by Sayyid Qutb (cal. 75). Current Islamic law (Sharia) calibrates at 190, Islamic apocalyptic prophesies calibrate at 70, and 'triumphalism' at 50.

Interestingly, eighty percent of people who calibrate above level 200 see modern Islam as a danger and a threat, whereas only forty percent of the people under level 200 hold that viewpoint (November 2007).

Another intrinsic error of Islam was the substitution of the worship of Muhammad instead of God. Muhammad was only a prophet or messenger, and at his best, for only three years, he calibrated at 700. (God/Allah calibrates at Infinity). He then succumbed to the trap of worldly power via war. The progressive fall of Islam is detailed in *What the Koran Really Says* (Warraq, 2002) as well as in *Jihad Incorporated* (Emerson, 2006). Further clarity is provided in *Thinking Like a Terrorist* (German, 2007).

Even the Roman Catholic Church has not been immune to subversion or Satanic attack (e.g., the Inquisition). This was demonstrated more recently by the epidemic of pedophilia within the clergy that was of sufficient proportion to bankrupt and close many dioceses. This was precipitated by thousands of lawsuits filed by victims of pedophilia.

Aside from the above institutional tragedies, numerous are the 'fallen gurus' of recent as well as current times who calibrated quite high, usually in the mid-

500s and even as high as the 700s, but subsequently fell due to the seduction, glamour, and temptations of the role. This is the result of unrecognized ego defects and weaknesses consequent to having power over others. It includes sexual seduction, the roles of status and money, and susceptibility to inflation of the spiritual ego, publicity, and 'having many followers'. (Such fallen leaders did so because their own teachers had not forewarned them of the dangers.)

The vicissitudes of spiritual endeavor have been described by famous saints of history (e.g., *Confessions of St. Augustine*, et al.). Even the Buddha was 'beset by demons' who sought for weaknesses or spiritual defects, and Jesus Christ sweat blood in the Garden of Gethsemane. In everyday spiritual endeavor, distractions may impinge from without or from within, such as the seduction of wallowing in guilt and penance or spiritual pride.

In the modern world, obstacles and barriers occur as a result of the quality of modern life itself, with its calculated as well as orchestrated seduction of attention and energy and its nonintegrous values and assaults on reason and reality testing itself. Internet 'blogging' is the prevailing hunting-and-feeding ground for both the politicized Satanic and Luciferic energies (e.g., on well-publicized hate sites).

An interesting discovery of recent research is the reversal of seeing the 'cause and effect' of hate speech and attitudes. The sheep's clothing is the propagated presumption that some worldly event is the 'cause' of hatred which is thereby seemingly legitimized and rationalized as justified. Consciousness calibration research indicates that the sequence is actually the opposite (the reader can personally confirm this). The personal hatefulness was a priori and pre-existed as a personality trait that then sought excuse to externalize via hate speech, etc. The supposed hatred merely sought some external excuse, which then could be blamed as a 'cause'.

This was widely demonstrated in World War II where even the military did not 'hate' the enemy and realized that both the Nazis and the Japanese Imperialists were acting in obedience to ideological indoctrination and coercion. The military even shook hands and saluted each other's bravery, and some even became lifelong friends of former enemies. We had feared the kamikaze pilots but did not hate them for they were just doing their duty as were we.

Note that haters just 'love' hatingness and cling to it tenaciously. Some haters become highly publicized and well-paid professionals who garner much narcissistic gratification from major publicity. War thereby becomes the haters' favorite theater and subterfuge of victimology.

Safeguards and Defense

By extensive consciousness research, the calibrated levels of truth of religious pathways and teachers are currently readily available and provide a clear pathway to what historically has been a confusing array of options. At stake is the fate of one's eternal soul. Therefore, selection of an integrous teaching or teacher deserves one's best efforts and intentions. For comparison, it is good to ask oneself periodically if "I would be willing to go up in an airplane whose pilot calibrated at 170," yet people carelessly do this very thing with their spiritual safety, which is far more important than their physical survival.

The internal opposition to spiritual evolution is a consequence of the structure of the human ego itself, which is unaware of its own limitations and proclivity to fall into error ('ignorance'). This occurs because it is so easily deceived by appearance and unable to discern essence. This problem is no longer formidable as consciousness calibration is a consequence of essence and not appearance. Thus, the great blocks to truth that were noted by Socrates, Descartes, Jesus, Krishna, and Buddha no longer prevent spiritual evolution.

Spiritual deception is now really no longer possible as the sheep's clothing no longer works as a deceptive device. In essence, what is pure, truthful, and holy calibrates as such, and falsity can be revealed by the arm of even an innocent child (*Power vs. Force* video, Hawkins, 1995).

CHAPTER 18

Narcissism: Ego Worship

Moral Authority: The Grand Conflict

Today's world is characterized by a ferocious competition for 'moral authority'. The attraction is the innate vanity and perceived power of domination and control over others. This competition applies to whole countries, political and philosophical systems, and entire cultures, all of which claim moral superiority and, therefore, justification for all actions. Victimology is the sly back door by which a 'make wrong' becomes a manipulative level of moral blackmail and exploitation.

In today's media-driven society, even the most extreme behaviors, as well as bizarre, delusional declarations, are given equal rank with truth. By this device, alleged rights and claims ensue that have the added value of being 'righteous' and 'superior', by which anything and everything can be justified or excused, or at least public opinion solicited for sympathy. The world now worships not Divinity but the ego and thus caters to aggrandized narcissistic rhetoric and blatant falsity of even a psychotic degree (the pious lion's den of 'free speech'). Society is now the arena for competition of self-proclaimed, aggrandized moral 'rights' that are actually merely selfish egocentricity for gain.

Ready acceptance of even the grossest deformities of honesty, truth, or integrity confirm the basic dictum of consciousness research that the narcissistic core of the ego is, as it has been throughout all history, the hidden villain by which entire cultures decline and even now seek the death of the innocent under the disguise of 'religion'.

These current trends surface as the previously described 'liberalization' of modern Christianity (Allen, 2006) in response to which attendance has dropped by fifty percent. Liberalization extends to the degree of even refuting the Divine incarnation of Jesus as the Christ, negating the Trinity or the sacredness of Communion, and instead substituting sexist political ideologies. (Lenny Bruce, the sardonic comedian and social critic, noted, "People are leaving the churches in droves and turning to God.")

One could postulate that by catering to 'sensitivity', 'Mother Nature' should be 'Mother-Father Nature'. Gramatically, the term 'He' (God) is generic and does not refer to gender. Similarly, the term 'man' refers to mankind generically and not to the male gender per se.

The greatest spiritual teachers of all time, all of whom calibrate at 1,000, warned against the ridiculing of Divinity and the refutation of the Divinity of God as blasphemy, which calibrates at 20. It would seem grandiose and foolish in the extreme to willfully violate such a serious principle and give play instead to a political ideology that is the product of atheist Herbert Marcuse or the atheistic Marxist dialectic (cal. 135). Thus, Protestant ministers, bishops, and even archbishops would seem to violate the very premises of their own religious truth. The calibrated level of the intellectualizations (cal. 190) involved indicates limitation and lack of illumination for it is taught that Jesus Christ is one's advocate in Heaven before the Father, but not if He is publicly refuted.

The ego's ravenous greed for the vanity of moral authority leads it to refutation of both integrous reason as well as religious faith and substitutes inferior concepts. The inversion of truth is also used to justify, rationalize, and view as morally superior the indulgence of the slaughtering of innocents in the name of God (Allah, "The All Merciful"). In the Koran are verses that calibrate at level 90 and completely negate the higher teaching of the Koran overall by quoting "Cut off their heads" (cal. 10), "Kill the infidels wherever you find them," etc. (barbarism; see Scheuer, 2007.)

By the conversion of truth to falsehood, life on earth is turned to constant fear, danger, and threat. Of significance is that many mosques in the United States train in terrorist ideology (King, 2007).

Thus, by the posing of moral superiority, the atavistic depth of Freud's 'Id' is declared to be the word of God. As a consequence of presumed moral authority, all forms of depravity are sanctioned and even attract legal defense by the rationalization that 'any' and all behavior is legal and acceptable because "action is symbolic speech," as declared by the 'moral authority' of the United States judiciary (cal. 190).

By 'moral authority', environmentalists commit arson, blow up houses and buildings, and the militant founders of 'freedom' political activist organizations declare war on all humanity. Traitors become heroes, and sedition is declared as praiseworthy expression of purported lofty idealism by which any behavior can be rationalized. Denouncing one's own country is now superpatriotic.

Inasmuch as the judiciary has declared that actions

are symbolic speech and that speech is free, then obviously anarchy is the new law of the land. Thus, Chomsky's writings (cal. 180), Marcuse's writings (cal. 150), Foucalt's writings (cal. 90), and others replace the great Avatars (cal. 1,000). If, as relativism teaches, sanity and insanity are merely linguistically convenient forms of oppression with no inherent reality, then anarchic chaos becomes the ideal as expressed by the Watts riots, the post-Katrina disaster, the streets of Baghdad, and the anarchy of soccer-game riots.

The idealization of the supposed superiority of moral relativism breaks down by discovery that the 'new morality' is merely rationalized nonmorality. Paradoxically, the new, expanded, modernized views of freedom subsequently become enforced by justified totalitarian measures as per the 'newspeak' and 'new think' of the famous book, *1984* (Orwell, 1949). These predictions activated as the current 'thought police' of college campuses, the 'health police', the 'fat children's parent police', and the pervasive *Language Police* (Ravitch, 2003) of 'social sensitivity'. Thus, the purported freedom of postmodernistic 'morality' invalidates itself by self-negation (see *Tyranny of Tolerance*, Dierker, 2006) as exhibited by student attacks on even college choirs. By political slant, Far-Left 'liberalism' becomes totalitarian control and coercion. (Today's liberator is tomorrow's dictator.)

That refutation of both faith and reason leads to corruption and degeneration rather than liberation is represented by the bursting jails and prisons in the United States, plus the hordes of mentally ill and homeless people across the land. Moral superiority is also the relativism of all wars, which thrive upon idealistic justification. Thus, 'freedom' becomes a quasi-moralistic subterfuge and camouflage for contentious, degenerative depravity as well as narcissistic self-glorification via sympathizers and supporters.

A twenty-four-year study at San Diego College confirmed the progressive increase in narcissism of successive generations of college students. Television shows, such as *The View*, thrive on blatantly gross exhibitions of narcissistic malevolence which supports overt hatred under the banner of free speech that calibrates at level 60. The apologists and defenders of such exhibitions become sanctimonious and revel at such a 'wonderful' (profitable) freak-show madness.

It becomes apparent that the craving for public media attention is actually a form of addiction that leads to compulsive extremes, such as even false confessions, the recording of televised crimes, purposeful provocation ('tasered'), purposeful engineering of police actions (e.g., 'stoning') and 'victim' set-up scenarios. By ingenious ruse, the United States government is constantly set up to appear callous by keeping illegal immigrants separated from their children and families. Another favorite scheme is exhibitionistic degrees of overt sexual behavior or even 'caught on camera' criminal actions. Even Islamic extremists play the game by the slow beheading of women missionaries or blowing up busloads of children. Militant Islam exploits media attention as does bin Laden personally.

The moral 'superiority' of much-vaunted free speech (cal. 190 currently in the United States) by its purposeful exploitation becomes a two-edged sword of social suicide by which social as well as academic structure progressively collapses as a consequence of politicizing everything in order to obscure essence by coloration of perception or conceptualization (Krauthammer, 2007). Paradoxically, in the meantime, the basic structure of society is actually being held together by the pragmatism of economics, industry, business, and corporate function (cal. 350 to 380), further reinforced by accountability, legal structure, rationality, and responsibility. It is now Wal-Mart that actually supplies disaster areas with survival supplies while the government bureaucracies fumble and bumble via bureaucratic political power struggles.

The Power of 'Ism'

By consciousness research, it is discovered that the suffix 'ism' calibrates at 190 and denotes the decline of a body of knowledge or set of premises when it becomes a prevailing, politicized, emotionalized belief system whose proponents then take on the airs of moral superiority. Thus, 'fundamental' means one thing, whereas 'fundamentalism' has a different coloration and implication. Even science becomes less integrous once it becomes 'scientism' (e.g., environmentalism or materialistic reductionism). Once a belief system becomes an 'ism', it proselytizes and seeks converts. Of note is that moral superiority confers upon the narcissistic core of the ego the added status of 'specialness' and the aggrandized, implied empowerment that it accords.

Attractive to the spiritual ego is the acquisition of special 'powers' that add to the allure of 'peddled for profit' so-called trainings (cal. 200) to acquire glamorized aspects of the so-called siddhis by inducing altered states of consciousness. There is also the glamorized, magical attraction of the occult as well as the designation of obscure teachings as 'secret', 'UFO', 'mysteries', and 'ancient', which become even more glamorized as 'hidden teachings' (cal. 160).

Integrous spiritual teachings of high calibration are free and transparent, whereas 'secret teachings and mysteries' come at a sizeable price, and the trainings to acquire altered states of consciousness or special 'blessings' can cost thousands or even ten thousands of dollars and more.

The appeal of magic secret rites, incantations, and rituals is, of course, to the imaginative naïveté of the child. This is attested to by the popularity of the Harry Potter books, which attractively portray mystery, magic, and magical empowerments. This same specialness is accorded to channelers, psychics, clairvoyants, visitors, and UFOs from 'other dimensions', 'messengers from the future', 'reincarnations of the apostles', and more.

Idealism As Moral Superiority

'Idealistic' means hypothetical albeit its appealing title. All human devastation has been energized as some inflated ideological 'ideal' (e.g., "Deutschland über alles"; "Workers unite, you have nothing to lose but your chains"; "Join the Liberation Front"; "Support the People's Government"; and "People's Courts").

The 'ism' in political expressions, such as socialism and communism, denotes the attractive tool of the slogan or 'meme' that, by sheer repetition, becomes like a religion to which sacrifice is expected and even promoted as heroic, such as the glorification of suicide bombers, Kamikaze pilots, and freedom fighters. Such vainglory is an earmark of unbalanced extremism, and even the sacrifice of self, others, children, and spiritual integrity is supported and promoted by great display via television productions.

Behind such 'ism' movements lies the egomania of leaders as well as followers who narcissistically expand in the hypnotic intoxication of mass demonstrations and theatrical displays. Again, the engine common to all such movements is the drivenness to the claim of moral superiority (Lenin, Stalin, Hitler, Chairman Mao, Pol Pot, Arafat, bin Laden, Castro, and current leaders in North Korea, South America, and the Middle East [Iran], who calibrate below 180).

True Morality

Integrous morality and ethics, like genuine reason and faith, are firmly grounded in realistic humility by which essence supersedes appearance and socialized perception. Morality as a virtue is represented by the ethics of character traits, such as consideration for others, honesty, integrity, accountability, and responsibility, as well as allegiance to basic spiritual concepts. To be benign, affectionate, supportive, polite, kind, considerate, and helpful does not raise the flag of a cause or of being superior. Morality is thus a humble way of being in the world for its own sake rather than for gain or ego inflation. The consequences are internal but also evidenced by degrees of happiness and realistically based self-esteem.

These character traits are essential to spiritual evolution and progress, which require self-discipline, humility, and fortitude as well as determination. They lead to prayer and the practice of spiritual principles in all of one's affairs, accompanied by the awareness that one is ultimately accountable to God for what has been done with the gift of life. (This calibrates as true at the level of Infinity. "Every hair on one's head will be counted" is a confirmable truth.)

True morality leads not to pride but to humility, gratitude, and benevolence by which eventually the beauty, perfection, and intrinsic holiness of all Creation spring forth as revelation; thus the dictum, "Straight and narrow is the path . . . waste no time."

With spiritual maturity, one understands that this lifetime is precious and too valuable to waste on the ideas of being superior or other ego-inflating, vainglorious illusions.

Reason and Faith: Reconciliation

As was stated earlier, reason deals with concrete, linear symbols and facts according to the rational dialectic of logic and stability of definition. This process results in confirmable conclusions in that they are the consequence of the premises. The rules of logic, like those of mathematics, are strict and linear in that they are not flexible or subject to personalized distortion. Therefore, there is the additional requirement of 'goodness of fit', meaning the symbols represent the same level of abstraction. Thus, a subject is restricted to a specific level of abstraction or category, class, species, genus, and then the specific example. Thus, via reason, it cannot be claimed that a bird is really just a feathered mammal.

To falsify levels of abstraction and violate basic principles leads to the decline and distortion of reason to the level that is classically described as 'rhetoric' (cal. 180), which is characterized by violation of basic principles for the sake of egoistic gain. Within the confines and rules of reason, declarations must be provable. Falsehood is a serious violation as well as indicative of a low level of consciousness and lack of integrity or intelligence.

Reason is, within its own domain, highly pragmatic and beneficial, yet it is primarily restricted to the linear domain (the level of the 400s). Therefore, logic adds factual, useful information but does not provide complete meaning as such.

While linearity denotes characteristics of definition and identification of factual qualities, 'meaning' is a consequence of essence and context. This capacity to discern essence and appropriate context is lacking or rudimentary in approximately eighty-five percent of the world's population (fifty-five percent in the United States). Therefore, the same event is seen and interpreted very differently among people who are either above or below level 200. For example, below 200, the concept of 'might makes right' is acceptable. Above 200, one sees that 'might' means restraint and responsibility.

Important to context are prevailing conditions, circumstances, and timing, as well as intangibles, such as intention, setting, motive, presumption, and abstraction, including value judgments. Thus the capacity to truly 'know' is not actually a possibility unless the individual has evolved to a relatively high level of consciousness. Therefore, calibrating a level of consciousness is of enormous value as it identifies the intrinsic reality that is associated with a specific energy attractor field.

Spiritual Vision

As noted by St. Thomas Aquinas, reason (linear content) requires illumination by the spiritual energy of faith and prayer, through which meaning and significance are revealed (by virtue of nonlinear context). Thus, in the end, subjective experience and spiritual awareness enable comprehension and full appreciation.

The recognition of spiritual awareness and comprehension cannot be 'proven' as such, but it can be verified by the simple technique of consciousness calibration. That 'the world is perfect as it is' is obvious at a high level of awareness, but it sounds fallacious to lower levels that hold hypothetical idealizations.

As has been explored in front of many witnesses and participants at lectures, it has been repeatedly confirmed that the world offers maximum spiritual opportunity by virtue of its multitudinous options that support the evolution of consciousness and provide maximum karmic benefit. When personal opinion is transcended, each moment is witnessed and observed to be perfect (e.g., the hidden lesson in an apparent setback or tragedy).

Morality and Creation

Each species exhibits its own innate 'morality' simply as a consequence of the experience of pain versus benefit. 'Right versus wrong' thus seems to be a biological characteristic that is now even postulated by science itself to be hardwired into the neuronal network of the brain. Such 'moral' behaviors are exhibited by wolf packs, schools of dolphins, elephants, and monkeys. Even at a lower level, right versus wrong is displayed by attack, expulsion from the pack, dominance versus submission, and the rule of the alpha male or female.

Organisms, by simple Pavlovian conditioning, learn what works versus what fails. This information is collected in attractor energy fields of consciousness and then internalized and stored in the neuronal nervous systems (Bird, 2006). Even animals that 'cheat' are severely ostracized, punished, or expelled from the pack or group. Thus, it could be inferred that sentient beings are created in such a manner that the right-versus-wrong distinction becomes innate and eventually sovereign.

Of considerable interest is the discovery of the brain's capacity for mirroring (Medina, 2007). Mammals intuit each other's feelings and intentions as a result of observation of the behavior of others. This is the basic mechanism of socialization and empathy. A very significant experience with Macaque monkeys showed that a monkey will even give up obtaining food if in the process it causes pain to another monkey in a nearby cage. This experiment itself seems to cast disgrace on much selfish human behavior where self-interest gain is sought even at the cost of actual death to other humans.

Within this overall context, there is latitude as well as allowance for gratification of the desires and options of the individual, but even these are legitimate only within the context of identifiable limits and conditions. Thus, biologically, morality and ethics support survival as well as the progression of the evolution of consciousness and human awareness to the goal of reaching Enlightenment itself.

Integration of Faith and Reason

St. Thomas Aquinas declared, after enormous study, that there is no inherent conflict between reason and theology, as well as revealed religion, and instead, they reciprocally reinforce and support each other. The infusion of spiritual energy brings about a synthesis of reason and faith via spiritual comprehension and understanding. This is concordant with the level of consciousness as a consequence of the expanded contextualization that illustrates the reality of content by which it can progressively become personally experiential as a subjective state.

The energy fields of consciousness are like interactive fields of dominance ('attractors'), which are comparable to smaller gravity fields within progressively larger ones. The lesser fields are prone to entrainment by the mutual influence. The lesser, in turn, contribute back to the vibrational pattern of the greater. The patterns and their interactions are further orchestrated by the harmonics of the energy fields that again facilitate further complexity in a very high range (e.g., cascades of dominance). This organization has been recently confirmed by neurophysiological research (Medina, 2006).

The above explanation helps in understanding the operation of free will versus the argument of determinism. It also clarifies the influence of intention interacting with karmically acquired patterns and propensities that result in agreement or negation of options. The more frequently an option is chosen, the more likely it will be chosen again in the future. This is also an observation of quantum mechanics ('Quantum Zeno effect') and probability theory, which, in everyday life, is termed 'habit' or 'character formation'. By virtue of the selection effect, the constant choosing of integrous truth by virtue of 'attention set' progressively diminishes the likelihood of choosing a lesser option ("kindling" effect; Medina, 2006).

Consciousness calibration arrives at a numerical figure that indicates dominance by a correlate field of energy, which, in turn, determines perception. With progression of comprehension, the collective information is referred to as wisdom. The synthesis of faith and reason is aligned with the specific energy field of consciousness itself. The essence of the distillation of significance and meaning results in spiritual intuition that is aligned with essence, which is classically referred to as spiritual vision (the 'opening of the third eye' of the chakra system of the etheric Buddhic body [cal. 600]).

Morality represents the pragmatic synthesis and integration of multiple complex factors into habitual modes of behavior, perception, and decision making that are subsumed collectively under the term 'character'. Spiritual intention recontextualizes experience and then predominates in the orchestration of lifestyle and choices as well as values and goals. One then becomes the beneficiary of human life instead of its victim.

CHAPTER 19

Practicum

Introduction

The intention of all prior writings and lectures has been to provide the means for the pragmatic, practical, subjective application of principles and discoveries for the evolution of consciousness towards Enlightenment and discovery of Spiritual Truth. All prior works have therefore been dedicated to God and to the subjective discovery of Divinity as the Ultimate Reality and Source of life and existence.

To affirm this intention, the books have started and ended with the statement, *"Gloria in Excelsis Deo!"* To be of assistance, the calibrated levels of truth and consciousness of all books have been stated to assist in orientation.

The purpose of the published works has been in accord with the development and evolution of the overall research and discoveries as well as a progressive presentation of a new mode of investigation that facilitated the synthesis of subjectivity and objectivity. It was also found that exposure to the discoveries and their appropriate contextualization was subjectively transformative.

By virtue of understanding consciousness, a pathway emerges whereby spiritual evolution is facilitated, and spiritual truth, both past and present, can be readily verified. Thus, the spiritual student or religious devotee of today is advantaged far beyond those of history who could rely only on hearsay, reputation, or cultural affirmation as verification.

Without a compass, errors arose throughout history as a consequence of the limitations of the evolution of human consciousness itself. Such error is no longer likely as there is now a readily available means to ascertain the truth of any teaching, teacher, and religious or spiritual tradition. The core value of consciousness calibration research is that it differentiates essence from appearance, and thus truth from falsehood (illusion).

Historical Review: A Recapitulation

The emergence of a study and investigation of spiritual/religious realities and truth is, in and of itself, of pragmatic value. The method of investigation opened up and made available areas of information never before accessible to the human mind.

The crux of the clinical research was that the physiological responses were determined by the level of consciousness and truth of the essence rather than the appearance of the subject matter being investigated. (Recent research also confirms a simultaneous pupillary response. [Davis, 2007]). It was discovered that relatively evolved spiritual students did not go weak in response to negative stimuli (e.g., fluorescent lights, pesticides, and artificial sweeteners). That observation led to the development of a protocol by which naïve subjects were tested prior to their starting a course of formal spiritual study (the *Workbook* of A Course in Miracles) and then retested periodically. It was discovered that the test subjects became immune to negative stimuli after about three months of doing that specific course. (The same occurs with any integrous course of spiritual study.)

It appeared that the physiological test responses were determined by a prevailing level of consciousness itself. In order to document the response, an arbitrary mathematical scale of consciousness from 1 to 1,000 initially was utilized, but it soon proved to be impractical as the numbers rose at such a rapid rate; therefore, pragmatically, it was discovered that an exponential scale was better able to signify the relative power of energy of advancing consciousness. A scale ranging from 1 to 1,000, which included all levels of possibilities and all of life, was designed that was pragmatically useful in that it included all potentialities.

Determining the highest level of consciousness (1,000) was the consequence of calibrating the world's great avatars, namely, Jesus Christ, Buddha, Krishna, and Zoroaster. Then came the critical discovery that consciousness levels below 200 denoted falsehood, and those from 200 and above signified progressive levels of truth. This demarcation also differentiated between the qualities of force (less than 200) and power (greater than 200).

The next thirty years were devoted to continuous research in all areas of human life, with emphasis on discerning levels of truth and spiritual reality. Thus, there was subjective, experiential confirmation of the discoveries of clinical research from which emerged a confirmable spectrum and paradigm of reality that correlated with the levels of consciousness as well as the experiences of human history, including the very advanced spiritual states of enlightened sages.

Application of consciousness research to almost every aspect of life proceeded over the decades and was assisted by the discoveries of multiple independent researchers and study groups worldwide. The feedback stimulated investigation of almost every aspect of existence over great expanses of time, and even beyond the illusion of time itself. From this appeared the principle that all statements of truth were only true within a specified context. Thus emerged the methodology of ascertaining verifiable truth for the first time in human history.

Because the ultimate context was the infinite field of consciousness itself beyond conceptualized time or location, the areas open for investigation were unlimited. The results (reported in *Truth vs. Falsehood*) range from the most seemingly mundane to the most advanced levels of spiritual awareness and Enlightenment itself. That truth could be identified, verified, and authenticated represented the emergence of a new body of knowledge available to mankind, which itself had only risen above consciousness level 200 to the level of 204 in the late 1980s. This crossover in itself seems to signify the opening up of a new era of human evolution, i.e., the emergence of *Homo spiritus* (see *I: Reality and Subjectivity*).

Thus, not only the truth but also the exact degree of truth about anything anywhere beyond time or space could be ascertained in a matter of seconds. Fortuitously, during the same decades in which the research methodology evolved, there was the emergence of advances in quantum mechanics and quantum physics that also provided an expanded paradigm of the universe. Seminal to these were the discovery and delineation of the Heisenberg Uncertainty Principle, so that consciousness itself became the crossover link between the linear and nonlinear dimensions, and thus between reason and faith.

A Course of Study

By consciousness research, it is affirmed that merely reading the published materials in this series or listening to lectures on consciousness research results in a measurable advance of the individual's level of consciousness and therefore of spiritual progress. Seminal information, in and of itself, is apparently transformative as it recontextualizes experience and comprehension, resulting in an expansion of paradigm by which meaning is transformed as a consequence of recontextualization rather than linear processing.

There was a purposeful sequence in the content of the series of books published beginning with *Qualitative and Quantitative Analysis and Calibration of the Levels of Human Consciousness* (1995), *Power vs. Force* (1995), *The Eye of the I* (2001), *I: Reality and Subjectivity* (2003), followed by *Truth vs. Falsehood* (2005), *Transcending the Levels of Consciousness* (2006), and *Discovery of the Presence of God* (2007).

Clarification of the content of the above material is provided by the many lecture series, which are also available on CDs and DVDs. The content of informal satsang workshops is also available on CDs.

Practical Application

Most people already have some religious/spiritual orientation as a consequence of cultural or family lifestyles. Within that which is considered traditional are universal truths that can now be easily confirmed. In addition, *Truth vs. Falsehood* provides calibrated confirmations of sources of spiritual truth as well as lists of integrous teachers and teachings.

The traditional spiritual pathway is through education and study of integrous spiritual material that arises in natural attraction through various principles and teachings. By prayer, one's intention is further empowered so there is a progressive revelation of levels of truth concordant with prevailing progressive levels of consciousness. Therefore, it is important not to mix levels of consciousness as that may create seeming ambiguities. It is preferable to hold all information as tentative since brain physiology itself shifts with advancement of consciousness, which facilitates comprehension.

One can select a basic spiritual concept as one's theme for a day and utilize contemplation, meditation, and prayer plus devotional acts. Many have found the simple *Practice of the Presence of God* by Brother Lawrence (2005) or the *Centering Prayer* of Father Thomas Keating (2004) to be quite beneficial. It is also advisable to seek 'holy company' and avoid persons, places, and pastimes that calibrate below 200. This includes activities that are allegedly spiritual by title but calibrate quite low. Thus, it is well to avoid New-Age fairs, psychic readings, and devices alleged to increase one's level of consciousness. Also avoid that which is sensational or promoted, such as invitations for 'trainings' to gain 'super powers' or the siddhis. The sold-for-profit 'secret' methodologies calibrate quite low. It is thus wise not to become glamorized or seduced by 'secret mysteries of the ancients' (cal. 160), which appeal to the spiritual ego's attraction to being 'special'.

There are no secrets to spiritual truths. They are freely available and transparent. Note that none of the great avatars or great spiritual teachers of history had any 'secrets.' On the contrary, they spoke freely, openly, and without restriction for the benefit of mankind.

By goodwill and benevolence to life in all its expressions, its innate beauty and perfection shine forth as the Radiance out of which existence emerges. It is helpful to hold in mind that there are no 'causes' in the observable world, and that everything is merely expressing the spontaneous emergence of potentiality appearing as actuality as a consequence of the ongoingness of the evolution of Creation. This phenomenon is the focus of emergence and complexity theories of advanced theoretical science (Theise, 2006).

During contemplation, it is useful to notice that the phenomena of 'witnessing' and 'observing' or 'experiencing' are autonomous, occur spontaneously, and are intrinsically impersonal. Note also that the worldly qualities of desirability are a projection from within the ego. Realize that happiness is a consequence of the level of consciousness (what one has become) rather than possessions or experiences.

Unpleasant events or circumstances can be turned to good use by affirming their unseen karmic benefit.

This can be done by assuming they represent the undoing of a karmic debt. As a consequence, it is a good rule to forgive oneself at all times and yet presume that, perhaps beyond recall, one has been a perpetrator rather than just a victim. When fully comprehended, human life is seen to be of optimal benefit for the evolution of consciousness of the individual as well as all humanity.

Spiritual intention is empowered by patience, supplication, perseverance, prayer, surrender, and depth of humility. Truth and Reality reveal themselves effortlessly when the obstacles are removed. It is advisable to avoid artificial spiritual devices, such as 'levitation training', mantras, postures, forced breathing techniques, and other artificialities. (Note that pranayama [breath control] calibrates at 190.)

The spiritual or kundalini energy arises of its own as a consequence of spiritual dedication, devotion, and spiritual evolution. It is well to accept that one is being attracted by one's spiritual destiny rather than being causally propelled by the past. Thus, the spiritual student is responding to an inner call that is orchestrated by the Self, which attracts the student to their future destiny.

Spiritual evolution is a lifetime commitment and a way of life by which the world and all experience subserves spiritual intention. There is no greater calling than to choose to be a servant of God. With spiritual progress, each increment is of equal importance for, analogously, it is only by the removal of a single brick that an entire wall collapses, and the seemingly impossible becomes possible.

Sooner or later, the seemingly miraculous may

begin to appear spontaneously. It is important to recognize that the phenomena are not of one's own doing or of the personal self, and that they do not represent some magical 'power'. Miraculous events are merely the actualization of potentiality that appears when conditions are appropriate. One of those conditions is the presence of the energy of a high level of consciousness. From an even more advanced level of consciousness, it becomes apparent that all phenomena are actually occurring spontaneously as a consequence of the evolution of the universe itself, and therefore not only is life perfect at any moment, but it is also a continuous revelation in which one is a participant/observer.

As the self is in the process of being subsumed and dissolved into the Self, there may be episodes and periods of time when one feels that one may be dying. It is only the false sense of self that is subject to dying, and therefore, it is safe to surrender to the phenomenon. It is also a fortuitous time to surrender the fear of one's physical death. The body will either walk on or it will not. Actually, the option is not up to the personal self but only to the Self.

At an advanced level, energies may arise that are associated with nonrecallable karmic destinies or forgotten agreements. The solution to any impasse or doubt is always deep surrender to Divine Will.

It is of little benefit to be personally self-critical or think that one 'should' be farther along the road than they are. Spiritual evolution is irregular and at times often seems sporadic and at other times stationary. Realize that guilt is a narcissistic indulgence. There may be long, dry periods where seemingly nothing is progressing. That is a deception; a 'long, dry period' *is* what is happening as though it were a test of resolve. These periods can be traversed by transcending the spiritual ego's wish to seek gain via 'progress'. Frustration itself is therefore a sign of trying to control that which is not really controllable.

It is well to remember that "those also serve who wait." Even a period of years of seeming lack of progress can be suddenly superseded by a very rapid, major advance that may be even far more than one had hoped for.

As a consequence of such progress, there may arise states of joy, bliss, or even ecstasy, accompanied by the incapacity to function in the world. Reaching such conditions may call for a change in lifestyle. It may also be discovered that attempts at explanation to family or friends may be futile, and the transition has to be made with compassion for their viewpoint. What is comical is that their wry comment that 'he (she) must have lost his (her) mind' is paradoxically a fact, for the mental self 'thinks', but in contrast, the Self silently 'knows'.

It is helpful to keep in mind that the ego and human physical life are temporary, and the fate of the soul is outside of time. Thus, decision amounts to surrendering the lesser for the greater. Despite the protests of relatives, friends, or business associates, most people have an intuition of what it means to respond to a higher calling.

Spiritual Lifestyles

This is an area about which many students have questions and uncertainties. Spiritual commitment opens up a number of alternative choices, such as:

1. Renunciation of the world and the joining of a spiritual community, ashram, or residence in a retreat center. These organizations are usually associated with some specific religion or formal spiritual organization, and some may even require taking vows or participating in other forms of initiation ceremonies. Some are formal religious orders that follow ecclesiastical doctrine, and thus, there may be physical requirements that acknowledge the commitment.

   Some retreat centers stress solitary retreat and mediation plus periods of fasting or other sensory renunciation. Other formal organizations stress group spiritual activities, including work, worship, readings, dialog, and group sharing. Possessions are limited to the minimum essentials, and often one's assets are donated to the group. All worldly possessions and attachments need to be renounced, and visitations are often restricted.

   The possible limitations of religious groups have to do with ecclesiastical doctrines. There is also the temptation of specialness to the spiritual ego as exemplified by shorn hair, robes, and the like. As with any spiritual pursuit, it is important to calibrate the consciousness level of the group or organization as well as its doctrine and formal practices.
2. Retreats offer short-term advantages and are often sponsored by an organization or have a retreat leader, both of which should be calibrated.
3. Spiritual practice in ordinary life in many ways is

actually the most favorable and beneficial approach. (This statement calibrates as true.) It is a common observation that it is one thing to be pure and holy in an isolated, safe place, but another to remain committed in the world of endless temptations and confrontations.

Spiritual progress occurs in stages. In the beginning, one learns of spiritual realities and studies them. Then come practice and application of the teachings in every aspect life, and eventually one becomes the teachings. By dedication, one's life becomes the prayer. By devotion, commitment, and practice, spiritual concepts become experiential realities. (As one advanced student said, "How can I forgive my enemies when I no longer have any?")

A typical routine in everyday life consists of formal seated meditation in the morning and again in the evening. These can last from twenty or thirty minutes in the beginning and extend to an hour or more each time. Although a brief mantra or chant can help set the mood, it is not sufficient in and of itself and, if overdone, may lead to what are actually only altered states of consciousness. This is also true of such trappings as bells, chimes, music, incense, special flags, oils, candles, and similar sensory paraphernalia. Therefore, it is advisable to calibrate the level of chants or mantras, no matter how highly recommended. 'Secret' mantras, especially those that are sold for a fee, have no particular specialness, and merchandised ones tend to calibrate only around level 290.

It is rewarding to choose a spiritual lesson or

concept for the day that serves as a focus for contemplation. This is a way of contextualizing the entire day and its experiences. For instance, one can select Unity's Daily Prayer, a lesson from *A Course in Miracles*, a step from the twelve-step program, a Psalm, or a basic spiritual premise, such as surrender, humility, or the letting go of control or the desire for gain. When done repeatedly over a period of time, it becomes incorporated into one's personality and attentional set by which one automatically becomes benevolent, loving towards all life in all its expressions, and aware of the perfection and beauty of every moment.

With incorporation into daily life, a spiritual practice can take the form of the continuous surrendering of volition, which then emerges into autonomous witnessing and effortless observation. These capacities will then be discovered to be qualities of consciousness, and not personal.

4. Concentrated spiritual focus is like a 'mind set' by which spiritual processing becomes prioritized. Eventually, the illusion of a distinct, separate, personal 'I' that is 'doing' the processing drops away. The phenomenon is then witnessed to be happening spontaneously of its own.

   A fast track to this effortless state is provided by the simple technique of focused relinquishment of resisting the perception/experiencing of the passage or duration of time. This is a surprisingly simple yet very powerful technique, and the reward is a sudden relief from the constant unconscious pressure of 'time', which subtly contextualizes and colors the experiencing of worldly life. Breaking this dominance of the illusion of time is very doable. It is then discovered that time is a projection from consciousness and only a belief system out of which the ego 'time tracks' the witnessing of the emergence of phenomena. With release from its dominance, there is a great sense of freedom and inner joy. (That time is a projection from human consciousness and not an innate quality of the universe has also emerged as a recent awareness of quantum theory [Lynds, 2003].)

The Final Run

When the conditions, including mind set, intention, and dedication, are favorable, a decision may arise to drop everything in the world and throw oneself totally into an all-out, 'go for it', continuous, laser-like, focused surrendering of the perceiver/experiencer aspect of the ego. This process takes one quite rapidly beyond the mind to the very 'processing edge' of the experiencer (see *I: Reality and Subjectivity*). This 'processor' edge is the actual locus of the ordinary sense of 'I-ness', and it creates a 1/10,000th-of-a-second delay between reality (the world as it is; Descartes' *res extensa*) and the world as it is perceived or experienced (Descartes' *res cogitans* or *res interna*). This separation is the crux and locus of the self's illusion of duality, which obscures comprehension of the intrinsic Reality of Nonduality (Self). With transcendence of the illusion of a separate, individual, personal self, there emerges the Radiance and Oneness of the Self by which all life, whether denoted as subjective or objective, is recontextualized into Oneness.

The Aftermath

Physical incarnation may or may not continue because intrinsic to very advanced states of consciousness and spiritual development is the awareness of an invitational permission to leave physicality (level 600). Whether one continues to stay with the body is no longer a consequence of personal volition. In practice, high states require abandonment of the ordinary world. This may lead to years spent primarily in solitude and adaptation to the new state or condition that has replaced the former sense of personal identity with its dualistic beliefs of causality and a separate, volitional personal self as the causal agent. What supersedes is an autonomous state or condition rather than a 'person'. The circumscribed personal identity disappears, and the self is replaced by the Allness of the Self.

There may be a period of initial 'God shock' in which the mind is silenced and functioning is autonomous, without volitional intention or the prior customary pursuit of goals. The condition itself merely 'is' and as such is thereby already total and complete. The body is also witnessed as acting in an autonomous, spontaneous manner, and it takes a while to get used to the fact that people, oddly as it may seem, continue to address the body as 'you'.

Retreat from the world may well ensue that can be permanent or may last for years before some style of functioning occurs. The sense of location has to be relearned, as do the necessities of bodily life. Hunger seems to disappear, and one can go for days without eating. One may be surprised to see a body reflected in a mirror. To return to the world, there is the necessity for relearning human functions via the emergence of a 'persona', which is akin to a spontaneous actor that interfaces with the world and calls upon residual memory banks in order to behave in what the world considers to be appropriate. Thus, there is a period of becoming reoriented to the ordinary human world.

Outside of time, there is no interest in 'how long' (duration) the body is destined to survive. Periodically, there emerges an open opportunity to leave that is oddly invitational, and, at the same time, there is only the witnessing of whether it will leave or not.

Beyond the linear self, there are no scripts to follow in the reality of the nonlinear nonduality of the Self, which is without worldly motives or goals. Activities may then unfold that are not seen as significant or having a purpose or value; these are immaterial because there is no longer any personal motivation. All is subordinate, subservient, and consequent to the Divine Ordinance of Divinity and the Will of God. Thus arises the exclamation, *"Gloria in Excelsis Deo!"*

Discussion

Q: The suggested curriculum sounds stringent when shorn of the appeal of religious and mystical trappings.

A: It is described so as to be of service to the true seeker of Enlightenment itself. "Straight and narrow is the path" and "waste no time" mean that the allure of diversions has to be bypassed for the sake of not only truth but also for pragmatic expediency.

Decades can be whiled away pursuing fallacious mystical, magical domains of spiritual fantasy as well as imposters who appeal to the spiritual ego but lead to a dead end. These are actually amusements that, however, very frequently conceal hidden traps for the unwary. For instance, an entity 'on the other side' is calibratable and will be found to have a spiritual ego that nourishes itself by having followers and control.

Early students often confuse the paranormal and altered states of consciousness (New-Age-ism) with true spiritual states. Therefore, it is well to suspect any teachers of pathways that are adorned with trappings and utilize the seductive allure of proselytizing presentations.

Q: Some statements in your writing do not exactly coincide with classical Buddhism.

A: That is an error of perception as well as education. For the sake of students, Buddha taught the wisdom of avoiding the term 'God' because it is so misunderstood. 'Buddha Nature' is the essence of Self and pure consciousness/awareness. It is intrinsically devoid of identification with content, yet inclusive of all context. Also, students' knowledge of Buddhism is primarily pedagogical and traditional. The term 'master' calibrates at 650. There are many teachers of Buddhism who are knowledgeable but are not fully personally enlightened as such, although some have had transitory experiences of *satori*.

Note that even the Pope misunderstands

Buddhism in that his diffidence is based on the mistaken viewpoint that the term 'self-nature' refers to the small ego self (and is therefore narcissistic) rather than the Self (with a capital 'S').

Q: Your descriptions of advanced spiritual states are in the third person. Why is that?

A: The phenomena described are not personal and are therefore termed 'conditions' or 'states' that are self-existent. There is no 'person' who is enlightened. The sense of 'I' or 'you' or 'me' is replaced by a self-existent state with no particular locality or linear characteristics. It is more akin to a luminous sky with no location, boundaries, time, beginning, or end. The condition does not 'do' anything or 'cause' anything. Phenomena are seen to be transient, with no personal causality or intrinsic reality.

God/Buddha Nature *is* and as such is complete. Therefore, it does not 'do' anything or 'go' anywhere, nor is there a time track of 'duration'. 'Now' and 'forever' are identical.

Q: What should be the overall context of spiritual endeavor?

A: Selfless service out of love for all creatures and creation. To pursue Enlightenment serves God and fellow humans. Be alert and attune to the innate beauty of all that exists. See the charm and quaintness of even what the world would consider old, beat up, and ugly.

Q: How can one facilitate progress?

A: That is a natural curiosity. Choice results in proclivities that become habitual mindsets of attention. Within each moment are all the necessary elements for realization. Look for essence rather than just appearance. Everything is perfect if seen as it really is. Everything is exactly the way it is 'supposed to be', whether it is shiny and new or rusty and dusty. Avoid adjectives for they are all projected, mentalized qualifications. Later, one can even drop adverbs for nothing is actually 'doing' anything; it just innately *is*. Transition is a phenomenon that stems from within the observer who sees sequence as a verb. If seen in less than 1/10,000th of a second, everything appears to be stationary.

Q: If I let go of personal identity, would I not then become 'nothing'?

A: No. Beyond the illusion of Nothingness is Allness. The Self is unlimited, with no beginning or end. It is beyond time and not subject to conditions. The Self is closer to one's Reality than the self. One cannot lose one's true identity or become 'nothing' because, in reality, one *is* included within the totality of Everythingness, Allness, and Foreverness.

The problem of 'the Void' (seeming Nothingness at calibration level 850) is addressed at length in Chapter 18 of *Transcending the Levels of Consciousness*. The Void is the consequence of negating love as a Reality because of confusing conditional love (attachment) as an aspect of the ego with Divine Love, which is an intrinsic quality of God.

Beyond the illusion of emptiness is the fullness

of completion that is akin to a core Radiance which is total and unmistakable. Because Divinity is innate Source, it cannot be 'misused' or 'lost' for Divinity recognizes and claims its own. (This statement calibrates at 1,000.)

Beyond the nonlinear, seeming Nothingness is Allness, which is the revelation of Divinity as Infinite Love—powerful, gentle, and irresistible as the Radiance of the Essence of All Existence. It is profound, unmistakable, Self-evident, and All-inclusive.

Q: What is the world like then?

A: The Essence of Divinity shines forth as a Radiance from the Perfection of All of Creation as a quality of its existence. Continuous emergence results in witnessing the phenomenon as autonomous and self-evolving beyond time, causality, or even sequence. Potentiality unfolds as the actuality of phenomena.

All the above is autonomously known by virtue of the Unity of Beingness/Existence. The perfection of All That Exists radiates as exquisite Beauty, perfect Balance, and Harmony by which Perfection manifests as further Perfection by virtue of evolutionary unfoldment. There is neither 'here' nor 'there'; there is neither 'now' nor 'then'. With completion, there are no questions to be answered as All is Self-evident.

Gloria in Excelsis Deo!

Appendices

APPENDIX A

CALIBRATION OF LEVELS OF TRUTH OF THE CHAPTERS

Chapter 1	Overview	740
Chapter 2	The Human Dilemma	740
Chapter 3	Paradigms of Reality	745
Chapter 4	Is Reality Subjective or Objective?	755
Chapter 5	Science and Religion: Levels of Truth	745
Chapter 6	Social Reality and Levels of Truth	750
Chapter 7	What is 'Real'?	750
Chapter 8	Cultural Premises and Truth	750
Chapter 9	Faith	760
Chapter 10	Experiential versus Conceptual	750
Chapter 11	Belief, Trust, and Credibility	760
Chapter 12	God as Hypothesis	765
Chapter 13	Doubt, Skepticism, and Disbelief	760
Chapter 14	Spiritual Pathways	740
Chapter 15	Contemplation and Meditation	765
Chapter 16	Transcending the World	750
Chapter 17	Morality, Reason, and Faith	750
Chapter 18	Narcissism: Ego Worship	760
Chapter 19	Practicum	760

Reality, Spirituality, and Modern Man, overall 750

APPENDIX B

MAP OF CONSCIOUSNESS®

God-view	Life-view	Level		Log	Emotion	Process
Self	Is	Enlightenment	⇧	700-1000	Ineffable	Pure Consciousness
All-Being	Perfect	Peace	⇧	600	Bliss	Illumination
One	Complete	Joy	⇧	540	Serenity	Transfiguration
Loving	Benign	Love	⇧	500	Reverence	Revelation
Wise	Meaningful	Reason	⇧	400	Understanding	Abstraction
Merciful	Harmonious	Acceptance	⇧	350	Forgiveness	Transcendence
Inspiring	Hopeful	Willingness	⇧	310	Optimism	Intention
Enabling	Satisfactory	Neutrality	⇧	250	Trust	Release

Permitting	Feasible	Courage	⇕	200	Affirmation	Empowerment
Indifferent	Demanding	Pride	⇓	175	Scorn	Inflation
Vengeful	Antagonistic	Anger	⇓	150	Hate	Aggression
Denying	Disappointing	Desire	⇓	125	Craving	Enslavement
Punitive	Frightening	Fear	⇓	100	Anxiety	Withdrawal
Disdainful	Tragic	Grief	⇓	75	Regret	Despondency
Condemning	Hopeless	Apathy	⇓	50	Despair	Abdication
Vindictive	Evil	Guilt	⇓	30	Blame	Destruction
Despising	Miserable	Shame	⇓	20	Humiliation	Elimination

APPENDIX C

HOW TO CALIBRATE THE LEVELS OF CONSCIOUSNESS

General Information

The energy field of consciousness is infinite in dimension. Specific levels correlate with human consciousness and have been calibrated from '1' to '1,000'. (See Appendix B: Map of the Scale of Consciousness.) These energy fields reflect and dominate human consciousness.

Everything in the universe radiates a specific frequency or minute energy field that remains in the field of consciousness permanently. Thus, every person or being that ever lived and anything about them, including any event, thought, deed, feeling, or attitude, is recorded forever and can be retrieved at any time in the present or the future.

Technique

The muscle-testing response is a simple "yes" or "not yes" (no) response to a specific stimulus. It is usually done by the subject holding out an extended arm and the tester pressing down on the wrist of the extended arm, using two fingers and light pressure. Usually the subject holds a substance to be tested over their solar plexus with the other hand. The tester says to the test subject, "Resist," and if the substance being tested is beneficial to the subject, the arm will be strong. If it is not beneficial or it has an adverse effect, the arm will go weak. The response is very quick and brief.

It is important to note that the intention, as well as both the tester and the one being tested, must calibrate over 200 in order to obtain accurate responses.

Experience from online discussion groups has shown that many students obtain inaccurate results. Further research shows that at calibration 200, there is still a thirty-percent chance of error. Additionally, less than twelve percent of the students have consistent accuracy, mainly due to unconsciously held positionalities. The higher the levels of consciousness of the test team, the more accurate are the results. The best attitude is one of clinical detachment, posing a statement with the prefix statement, "In the name of the highest good, _____ calibrates as true. Over 100. Over 200," etc. The contextualization "in the highest good" increases accuracy because it transcends self-serving personal interest and motives.

For many years, the test was thought to be a local response of the body's acupuncture or immune system. Later research, however, has revealed that the response is not a local response to the body at all, but instead is a general response of consciousness itself to the energy of a substance or a statement. That which is true, beneficial, or pro-life gives a positive response that stems from the impersonal field of consciousness, which is present in everyone living. This positive response is indicated by the body's musculature going strong. There is also an associated pupillary response (the eyes dilate with falsity and constrict to truth) as well as alterations in brain function as revealed by magnetic imaging. (For convenience, the deltoid muscle is usually the one best used as an indicator muscle; however, any of the muscles of the body can be used.)

Before a question (in the form of a statement) is presented, it is necessary to qualify 'permission'; that is, state, "I have permission to ask about what I am holding in mind." (Yes/No) Or, "This calibration serves the highest good."

If a statement is false or a substance is injurious, the muscles go weak quickly in response to the command, "Resist." This indicates the stimulus is negative, untrue, anti-life, or the answer is "no." The response is fast and brief in duration. The body will then rapidly recover and return to normal muscle tension.

There are three ways of doing the testing. The one that is used in research and also most generally used requires two people: the tester and the test subject. A quiet setting is preferred, with no background music. The test subject closes their eyes. *The tester must phrase the 'question' to be asked in the form of a **statement**.* The statement can then be answered as "yes" or "no" by the muscle response. For instance, the *incorrect* form would be to ask, "Is this a healthy horse?" The correct form is to make the statement, "This horse is healthy," or its corollary, "This horse is sick."

After making the statement, the tester says "Resist" to the test subject who is holding the extended arm parallel to the ground. The tester presses down with two fingers on the wrist of the extended arm sharply, with mild force. The test subject's arm will either stay strong, indicating a "yes," or go weak, indicating a "not yes" (no). The response is short and immediate.

A second method is the 'O-ring' method, which can be done alone. The thumb and middle finger of the same hand are held tightly in an 'O' configuration, and the hooked forefinger of the opposite hand is used to try to pull them apart. There is a noticeable difference of the strength between a "yes" and a "no" response (Rose, 2001).

The third method is the simplest, yet, like the others, requires some practice. Simply lift a heavy object, such as a large dictionary or merely a couple of bricks, from a table about waist high. Hold in mind an image or true statement to be calibrated and then lift. Then, for contrast, hold in mind that which is known to be false. Note the ease of lifting when truth is held in mind and the greater effort necessary to lift the load when the issue is false (not true). The results can be verified using the other two methods.

Calibration of Specific Levels

The critical point between positive and negative, between true and false, or between that which is constructive or destructive, is at the calibrated level of 200 (see Map in Appendix B). Anything above 200, or true, makes the subject go strong; anything below 200, or false, allows the arm to go weak.

Anything past or present, including images or statements, historical events, or personages, can be tested. They need not be verbalized.

Numerical Calibration

Example: "Ramana Maharshi teachings calibrate over 700." (Y/N). Or, "Hitler calibrated over 200." (Y/N)

"When he was in his 20s." (Y/N) "His 30s." (Y/N) "His 40s." (Y/N) "At the time of his death." (Y/N)

Applications

The muscle test cannot be used to foretell the future; otherwise, there are no limits as to what can be asked. Consciousness has no limits in time or space; however, permission may be denied. All current or historical events are available for questioning. The answers are impersonal and do not depend on the belief systems of either the tester or the test subject. For example, protoplasm recoils from noxious stimuli and flesh bleeds. Those are the qualities of these test materials and are impersonal. Consciousness actually knows only truth because only truth has actual existence. It does not respond to falsehood because falsehood does not have existence in Reality. It will also not respond accurately to nonintegrous or egoistic questions.

Accurately speaking, the test response is either an 'on' response or merely a 'not on' response. Like the electrical switch, we say the electricity is "on," and when we use the term "off," we just mean that it is not there. In reality, there is no such thing as 'off-ness'. This is a subtle statement but crucial to the understanding of the nature of consciousness. Consciousness is capable of recognizing only Truth. It merely fails to respond to falsehood. Similarly, a mirror reflects an image only if there is an object to reflect. If no object is present to the mirror, there is no reflected image.

To Calibrate A Level

Calibrated levels are relative to a specific reference

scale. To arrive at the same figures as in the chart in Appendix B, reference must be made to that table or by a statement such as, "On a scale of human consciousness from 1 to 1,000, where 600 indicates Enlightenment, this _____ calibrates over _____ (a number)." Or, "On a scale of consciousness where 200 is the level of Truth and 500 is the level of Love, this statement calibrates over _____." (State a specific number.)

General Information

People generally want to determine truth from falsehood. Therefore, the statement has to be made very specifically. Avoid using general terms such as a 'good' job to apply for. 'Good' in what way? Pay scale? Working conditions? Promotional opportunities? Fairness of the boss?

Expertise

Familiarity with the test brings progressive expertise. The 'right' questions to ask begin to spring forth and can become almost uncannily accurate. If the same tester and test subject work together for a period of time, one or both of them will develop what can become an amazing accuracy and capability of pinpointing just what specific questions to ask, even though the subject is totally unknown by either one. For instance, the tester has lost an object and begins by saying, "I left it in my office." (Answer: No.) "I left it in the car." (Answer: No.) All of a sudden, the test subject almost 'sees' the object and says, "Ask, 'On the back of the bathroom door.'" The test subject says, "The object is hanging on the back of the bathroom door." (Answer: Yes.) In this actual case, the test subject did not even know that the tester had stopped for gas and left a jacket in the restroom of a gasoline station.

Any information can be obtained about anything anywhere in current or past time or space, depending on receiving prior permission. (Sometimes one gets a "no," perhaps for karmic or other unknown reasons.) By cross-checking, accuracy can be easily confirmed. For anyone who learns the technique, more information is available instantaneously than can be held in all the computers and libraries of the world. The possibilities are therefore obviously unlimited, and the prospects breathtaking.

Limitations

The test is accurate only if the test subjects themselves calibrate over 200 and the intention for the use of the test is integrous and also calibrates over 200. The requirement is one of detached objectivity and alignment with truth rather than subjective opinion. Thus, to try to 'prove a point' negates accuracy. Sometimes married couples, for reasons as yet undiscovered, are unable to use each other as test subjects and may have to find a third person to be a test partner.

A suitable test subject is a person whose arm goes strong when a love object or person is held in mind, and it goes weak if that which is negative (fear, hate, guilt, etc.) is held in mind (e.g., Winston Churchill makes one go strong, and bin Laden makes one go weak).

Occasionally, a suitable test subject gives paradoxical responses. This can usually be cleared by doing the 'thymic thump'. (With a closed fist, thump three times over the upper breastbone, smile, and say "ha-ha-ha" with each thump and mentally picture someone or something that is loved.) The temporary imbalance will then clear up.

The imbalance may be the result of recently having been with negative people, listening to heavy-metal rock music, watching violent television programs, playing violent video games, etc. Negative music energy has a deleterious effect on the energy system of the body for up to one-half hour after it is turned off. Television commercials or background are also a common source of negative energy.

As previously noted, this method of discerning truth from falsehood and the calibrated levels of truth has strict requirements. Because of the limitations, calibrated levels are supplied for ready reference in prior books, and extensively in *Truth vs. Falsehood*.

Explanation

The muscle-strength test is independent of personal opinion or beliefs and is an impersonal response of the field of consciousness, just as protoplasm is impersonal in its responses. This can be demonstrated by the observation that the test responses are the same whether verbalized or held silently in mind. Thus, the test subject is not influenced by the question as they do not even know what it is. To demonstrate this, do the following exercise:

The tester holds in mind an image unknown to the test subject and states, "The image I am holding in mind is positive" (or "true," or "calibrates over 200," etc.). Upon direction, the test subject then resists the downward pressure on the wrist. If the tester holds a positive image in mind (e.g., Abraham Lincoln, Jesus, Mother Teresa, etc.), the test subject's arm muscle will go strong. If the tester holds a false statement or negative image in mind (e.g., bin Laden, Hitler, etc.), the arm will go weak. Inasmuch as the test subject does not know what the tester has in mind, the results are not influenced by personal beliefs.

Disqualification

Both skepticism (cal. 160) and cynicism, as well as atheism, calibrate below 200 because they reflect negative prejudgment. In contrast, true inquiry requires an open mind and honesty devoid of intellectual vanity. Negative studies of the testing methodology *all* calibrate below 200 (usually at 160), as do the investigators themselves.

That even famous professors can and do calibrate below 200 may seem surprising to the average person. Thus, negative studies are a consequence of negative bias. As an example, Francis Crick's research design that led to the discovery of the double helix pattern of DNA calibrated at 440. His last research design, which was intended to prove that consciousness was just a product of neuronal activity, calibrated at only 135. (He was an atheist.)

The failure of investigators who themselves, or by faulty research design, calibrate below 200 (all calibrate at approximately 160), confirms the truth of the very methodology they claim to disprove. They 'should' get negative results, and so they do, which paradoxically proves the accuracy of the test to detect the difference between unbiased integrity and nonintegrity.

Any new discovery may upset the apple cart and be viewed as a threat to the status quo of prevailing belief systems. That consciousness research validates spiritual Reality is, of course, going to precipitate resistance, as it is actually a direct confrontation to the dominion of the narcissistic core of the ego itself, which is innately presumptuous and opinionated.

Below consciousness level 200, comprehension is limited by the dominance of Lower Mind, which is capable of recognizing facts but not yet able to grasp what is meant by the term 'truth' (it confuses *res interna* with *res externa*), and that truth has physiological accompaniments that are different from falsehood. Additionally, truth is intuited as evidenced by the use of voice analysis, the study of body language, pupillary response, EEG changes in the brain, fluctuations in breathing and blood pressure, galvanic skin response, dowsing, and even the Huna technique of measuring the distance that the aura radiates from the body. Some people have a very simple technique that utilizes the standing body like a pendulum (fall forward with truth and backward with falsehood).

From a more advanced contextualization, the principles that prevail are that Truth cannot be disproved by falsehood any more than light can be disproved by darkness. The nonlinear is not subject to the limitations of the linear. Truth is of a different paradigm from logic and thus is not 'provable', as that which is provable calibrates only in the 400s. Consciousness research methodology operates at level 600, which is at the interface of the linear and the nonlinear dimensions.

Discrepancies

Differing calibrations may be obtained over time or by different investigators for a variety of reasons:

1. Situations, people, politics, policies, and attitudes change over time.
2. People tend to use different sensory modalities when they hold something in mind, i.e., visual, sensory, auditory, or feeling. 'Your mother' could therefore be how she looked, felt, sounded, etc., or Henry Ford could be calibrated as a father, as an industrialist, for his impact on America, his anti-Semitism, etc.
3. Accuracy increases with the level of consciousness. (The 400s and above are the most accurate.)

   One can specify context and stick to a prevailing modality. The same team using the same technique will get results that are internally consistent. Expertise develops with practice. There are some people, however, who are incapable of a scientific, detached attitude and are unable to be objective, and for whom the testing method will therefore not be accurate. Dedication and intention to the truth has to be given priority over personal opinions and trying to prove them as being "right."

Note

While it was discovered that the technique does not work for people who calibrate at less than level 200, only quite recently was it further discovered that the technique does not work if the persons doing the testing are atheists. This may be simply the consequence of the fact that atheism calibrates below level 200, and that negation of the truth or Divinity (omniscience) karmically disqualifies the negator just as hate negates love.

Also recently discovered was that the capacity for accuracy of consciousness calibration testing increases the higher the level of consciousness of the testers. People in the range of the high 400s and above get the most reliably accurate test results.

APPENDIX D

REFERENCES

Ablow, K. 2007. "Life as Scripted Role of Narcissism." *CNN*: Glenn Beck Show, 30 May. Interview.

Ackerman, S. 2006. *Hard Science, Hard Choices: Facts, Ethics, and Policies Guiding Brain Science Today*. New York: Dana Press.

Adler, M. 1980. *How to Think About God: A Guide for the 20th-Century Pagan*. New York: Collier Books. Reprint.

Adorno, T. W., et al. 1950. *The Authoritarian Personality*. New York: Harper.

Agin, D. 2006. *Junk Science: How Politicians, Corporations, and Other Hucksters Betray Us*. New York: Thomas Dunne Books.

A History of God. 2007. History Channel television series, two hours. (Emergence of monotheism in ancient Egypt, which, down through the centuries, changed views of the nature of Divinity.)

Ahkter, S. 1997. "Perspective: Exdefender of the Faith." *Times Higher Education Supplement*, 22 August. Via www.rei.org/books.

Ahmadinejad, M. and L. Bollinger. 2007. Various newspaper and television reports. 24 September. (Columbia University's sponsorship of president of Iran with commentary by university president Lee Bollinger, plus all-day news discussions.)

Ali, S. H. 2007. *Infidel*. New York: Free Press. (Author of *Submission*, member of Dutch Parliament.)

"Allah Kill All the Jews and Americans and Israel: Annihilate Them and All Their Allies." 2007. *Palestinian Authorized Broadcast*, 22 April. (Contradicts supposition of Islam as religion of peace. Disparity noted by A. Thomas, *LA Times Syndicate*, 1 May.)

Allen, C. 2007. "Death by Political Correctness: Who Killed Antioch College?" *Weekly Standard*, 12 November. (Destruction of academia in general and Antioch College specifically.)

———. 2007. "Duke's Tenured Vigilantes." *Weekly Standard*, 29 January. (88 professors make "postmodern" fools of themselves over fallacious rape charges and D.A. Nifong's resignation and case dismissal; disintegration of academia: race, gender, class bias.)

———. 2006. "Liberal Christianity is Paying for Its Sins." *LATimes*.com. 14

July. (Episcopal church declining due to its leftist policies.)

Alltucker, K. 2006. "Mayo Clinic Nets Deal for Research." *Arizona Republic*, 29 November. (Research is big business.)

Amoroso, R. 1998. "An Introduction to Noetic Field Theory: The Quantization of Mind." *Science and Primacy of Consciousness*. Orinda, CA: Noetic Press.

———. 1997. "Consciousness, A Radical Definition: The Hard Problem Made Easy." *Noetic Journal* 1:1, 19.

Anani, Z. 2006. "Lebanese terrorists trained to hate Jews and Christians from teenage for Militia fighters: never retreat." *Fox News*, 15 July.

Anderson, P. 1998. *The Origins of Postmodernity*. London: Verso. (Postmodernism and a déclassé bourgeoisie 'force field'. The demise of tradition.)

Andresen, J. and R. Forman, Eds. 2000. "Cognitive Models and Spiritual Maps." Charlottesville, VA: Philosophy Documentation Center.

Anscombe, G. 1958. "Modern Moral Philosophy." *Philosophy* 33.

Applebaum, P. 2007. "The New Lie Detectors: Neuroscience, Deception, and the Courts." *Psychiatric Services* 58:4, April.

Aquinas, St. T. (1912) 2006. Review in *Catholic Encyclopedia*. http://www.newadvent.org/cathen/14663b.htm

———. (1485) 1981. *Summa Theologica*. (trans. by Fathers of the English Dominican Province). Christian Classics Library (on line).

Arehart-Treichel, J. 2006. "Psychiatrists Explore Harnessing Power of Spirituality. Search for Link Between Religion, Illness." *Psychiatric News* 41:13, July.

———. 2004. "Why Are We Taken in by Duplicity?" *Psychiatric News*, 19 March.

Aristotle (330 B.C.) 1952. "Logic on Sophistical Refutation" in *Great Books of the Western World*. Chicago: Encyclopedia Britannica.

———. 1952. "Categories" and "Metaphysics" in *Great Books of the Western World*. Chicago: Encyclopedia Britannica.

———. 1962. *The Nichemacheon Ethics*. New York: Prentice Hall.

Arnn, L. P. 2005 "Constitution, Character, and National Identity." *Heritage Letters*, July. Washington, DC: Heritage Foundation.

Arum, R. 2003. *Judging School Discipline: The Crisis of Moral Authority*. Cambridge, MA: Harvard University Press.

Austin, P. 2007. "Signs of the Times: Why So Much Medical Research is Rot." *Economist*, 22 February. (In report to the American Association for the Advancement of Science meeting in Toronto, author urges doctors to use valid, relevant statistics.)

———. 2007. Presentation to American Association for Advancement of Science, Toronto. *Economist*, 22 February. (Statistical correlation does not indicate causality.)

Ayala, F. J. 2006. "The Plausibility of Life: Resolving Darwin's Dilemma." (Review) *Science and Theology News*, April.

Baer, R. 2007. "Radical Islam: Terror in Its Own Words." *Fox News Special*, 3 February.

Baker, M., S. Alexier, and F. Gaffney. 2007. *Islam vs. Islamists*. ABG film produced for PBS "America at the Crossroads" series, but then rejected and shown instead on *Fox News*, 24 July (At issue is free speech being suppressed by public-tax-supported PBS.)

Barnes, F. 2006. "How to Speak Liberal." *Weekly Standard* 11:45, 14 August. (Linguistic obfuscation of issues via relabeling and shift of terminology.

Barr, S. 2003. *Modern Physics and Ancient Faith*. Chicago: University of Notre Dame Press.

Bartel, J. 2006. "The Fear Factor." *Weapons and Tactics*. Las Vegas: Personal Defense Group.

———. 1999. *Detecting Liars*. Las Vegas: Personal Defense Group.

"Battle for Turkey's Soul, The." (Editor) 2007. *Economist*, 5 May. (Battle for dominance between secular democracy and militant Muslim fundamentalism.)

Bauer, H. 2007. "Science: Past, Present, and Future." *Journal of Scientific Exploration* 21:1. (Newtonian physics not suitable for biological phenomena.)

———. 2006. "The Two-edged Sword of Skepticism: Occam's Rajor and Occam's Lobotomy." *Journal of Scientific Exploration* 20:3. (Useful vs. negative uses.)

Beardsley, M. 1960. *European Philosophers from Descartes to Nietzsche*. New York: Modern Library.

Beauchamp, T. 1992. *Philosophical Ethics: An Introduction to Moral Philosophy*. 2nd ed. New York: McGraw-Hill Professional Publishing.

Beck, G. 2007. Commentary on Hamas TV's Mickey Mouse "hate" cartoon, *CNN News*, April.

———. 2006. "Islamic Triumphalism." *CNN News*, 15 November. (Indoctrination of children by hatred.)

———. 2006. "Public Still Unaware of Real Basis of Terrorism Threat." *CNN News*, 23 August.

———. 2006. " Media execs agree that TV purposely exploits children." *CNN News*, 7 June.

Becker, J. 2007. Boulder, CO, High School Conference. *Fox News*, 29 May. (Told students to "do drugs and have sex, do Ecstasy and have sex without condoms.")

Becker, P. 2007. "Conversations on Higher Consciousness: Dr. David Hawkins." Interview. *Four Corners*, June-July. (Autonomy and spontaneity of evolutionary creation and human experiencing.)

Begley, S. 2004. "Scans of Monks' Brains Show Meditation Alters Structure and Functioning." *Science Journal*, 5 November. (Proceedings of National Academy of Science.)

Behrens, J. 2004. "Let's Stop Dissing Each Other: Public Rudeness." *Elks Magazine*, March.

Bekelman, J., Y. Li, and C. P. Gross. 2003. "Impact of Financial Interest in Research Outcome." *JAMA* 289, 454-65.

Belsey, C. 2002. *Post-Structuralism*. New York: Oxford University Press.

Benedict, Pope, XVI (Joseph Cardinal Ratzinger). 2006. *Without Roots: the West, Relativism, Christianity, Islam*. New York: Basic Books.

Bennett, B. 2007. "More Drugs, Fewer Narcs." *Time*, 22 January. (Taliban financed by Afghanistan bumper opium crop; 670 tons of heroin.)

Bennett, W. 2006. *America: The Last Best Hope (From the Age of Discovery to a World at War)*. New York: Nelson Current.

Benoit, H. 1990. *Zen and the Psychology of Transformation: The Supreme Doctrine*. Rochester, VT: Inner Traditions.

Bensen, M. 2007. "Officials Vow Security Probe at Palo Verde." *Arizona Republic*, 22 April. (At country's largest nuclear plant, employee Mohammad Alari, Iranian engineer, took secret plans to Iran; officials dumbfounded.)

Berger, G. 2004. "Why Church Matters." *U.S. News & World Report*. 14 June.

Bernstein, R. J. 1991. *The New Constellation: Ethical-Political Horizons of Modernity/Postmodernity*. Cambridge, MA: MIT Press.

Bhikkhu, T. 2006. "Faith in Awakening." *Tricycle*, Summer. (Faith and empiricism.)

Bierman, D. 2003. "Does Consciousness Collapse the Wave Function?" *Quantum Mind Proceedings*. University of Arizona, 15-19 March. (Nonlocality of brain function at 300-400 m/sec delay of conscious awareness from stimulus to its detection [as per Libet]).

Bird, S. 2006. "Ethics and the Brain." *Science and Spirit*, July-August.

Bohm, D. 1990. "A New Theory of the Relationship of Mind to Matter." *Philosophy Psychology* 3, 271-286.

———. (1980). 2002. *Wholeness and the Implicate Order*. London: Routledge.

Borenstein, S. 2007. "Global Warming Report (UN)." *Arizona Republic*, 7 February. (Scientists report stirs politicized debate. [Report calibrates at 195.])

Boston, A. 2005. *The Legacy of Jihad: Holy War and the Fate of Non-Muslims*. Amherst, NY: Prometheus Books. (Islamic history.)

Branson, R. 2006. "British Mogul Pledges $3 Billion to Fight Global Warming." Associated Press, 20 September. (Clinton Global Initiative.)

Braxton, D. 2006. "Naturalizing Transcendence in the New Cosmologies of Emergence." *Zygon* 41:2, 347. June.

"Bring Back Decency." *Arizona Republic*, 13 September. (moveon.org venomous fringe politics and unprincipled malevolence.)

Bristow, D., G. Rees, et al. 2005. "Brain Suppresses Awareness of Blinking." University College, London, Institute of Neurology. Published in *Current Biology*, 25 July.

"Britain's Restive Muslims." 2007. (Editor) *Week*, 4 May. (Lack of assimilation and social conflict.)

Bronowsky, J. 1974. *The Ascent of Man*. New York: Little, Brown and Co.

Brookhiser, R. 2007. "Matters of Morality." *Time*, 6 August. (Conflict between science and religion endemic historically in the U.S. In the Leopold and Loeb case, Darrow said university was responsible for teaching Nietzsche.)

Brooks, A. 2006. *Who Really Cares?* New York: Basic Books. (Charity: U.S. exceeds all other countries combined.)

Brooks, D. 2007. "An Uneasy Drift to Port." *New York Times*, 16 January. (America is a meritocracy and therefore intrinsically unaligned ideologically with socialism as stated by sociologist S.M. Lipset.)

———. 2003. "Educated Class Rift Splits Nation: Professionals vs. Business." *New York Times/ Arizona Republic*, 16 June.

Brooks, J. 2006. "If I Were God: Einstein and Religion. *Zygon*, 41:4, December.

———. 2006. "The Elephant in the Room." *New York Times/Arizona Republic*, 5 December. (Structure, not freedom best child development and skills.)

Brown, H. 2007. "Why I Fired Professor Ward Churchill." *Wall Street Journal*, n.d. ("Nutty professor" fails due to professional faults and not "free speech" issues, which were a smokescreen.)

Bruce, T. 2003. *The Death of Right and Wrong*. Roseville, CA: Prima Lifestyles.

Buchanan, P. 2006. *State of Emergency: The Third World Invasion and Conquest of America*. New York: Thomas Dunne Books.

Budenholzer, E. 2004. "Emergence, Probability, and Reductionism." *Zygon* 39:2, June.

Burton, F. and S. Stewart. 2007. "Hezbollah: Signs of a Sophisticated Intelligence Apparatus. http://www.stratfor.com/weekly/hezbollah_signs_sophisticated_intelligence_apparatus. 12 December. (Stratfor terrorism report; details of "Cultural Jihad.")

Bush, G. 2007. Presidential Address, all networks, 22 August.

Butler, C. 2002. *Postmodernism*. New York: Oxford University Press.

Cabbage, M. 2006. "Asteroid to Threaten Earth April 13, 2036." *Orlando Sentinel/Arizona Republic*, 17 June.

Callinicos, A. 1989. *Against Postmodernism: Marxist Critique*. Hampshire, UK: Palgrave Macmillan

Caplan, B. 2007. *The Myth of the Rational Voter: Why Democracies Choose Bad Policies*. Princeton: Princeton University Press. (Voters systematically favor irrational policies due to widespread ignorance of economic realities vs. false beliefs propped up by politicalizations.)

Carnup, R. 2003. *The Logical Structure of the World and Pseudoproblems in Philosophy*. Chicago: Open Court Publishing.

Carroll, D. 2007. "Higley Senior Questions Why Word 'God' Was Omitted from Tribute." *Arizona Republic*, 17 May. (High school senior questions violation of free speech by school.)

Casatelli, C. 2006. "Study casts doubt on medicinal use of prayer." *Science and Theology News*, May.

Chalmers, D. J. 1996. *The Conscious Mind: In Search of a Fundamental Theory*. New York: Oxford University Press.

Chandrasekhar, S. 1987. *Truth and Beauty:Aesthetics and Motivations in Science*. Chicago: University of Chicago Press.

Charen, M. 2004. *Do-Gooders: How Liberals Hurt Those They Claim To Help–And The Rest Of Us*. Somerset, NJ: Sentinel Publishing Co.

Chomsky, N. 2003. *Hegemony or Survival*. New York: Henry Holt and Co. (A "make wrong'" of U. S. for being a dominant country.)

Churchill, W. 1958. *The New World: A History of the English Speaking Peoples*. New York: Dodd, Mead & Co.

Clancy, M. 2007. "Conservative Episcopalian Group Leaves Parrish." *Arizona Republic*, 26 September. (Protest over-liberalization occurring across the United States.)

Clarke, C. 2005. *Ways of Knowing: Science and Mysticism Today*. Exeter, UK: Imprint Academic. (Bridging science and religion.)

Cleary, T., trans. 1993. *The Flower Ornament Scripture: A Translation of the Avatamsaka Sutra*. Boston: Shambhala.

Cloud, J. 2007. "Are We Failing Our Geniuses?" *Time*, 16 August. (Gifted students underserved as the focus and funding have been focused for the last decade on least gifted and underachievers. Very gifted children with IQs of 160 and above often socially isolated.)

Cohen, E. 2007. "Unthinkable Thoughts." A review and commentary on Fred Ikle's *Annihilation from Within*. *Weekly Standard*, 26 February. (Technology/science is a two-edged sword to civilization; progress vs. annihilation.)

Cohen, R. 2007. "Reflection of Madness." *Washington Post Writers Group*, 18 April. (Throughout history, psychotic political leaders have massacred multi-millions of people, similar to mad killers.)

Cole, D. 2007. "The Science of the Yellow Brick Road: Why the Risks of Curiosity Make Our Lives Better." *Science and Spirit*, May-June. (Curiosity leads to learning.)

Collins, F. 2006. *The Language of God: A Scientist Presents Evidence for Belief*. New York: Free Press.

Collinson, P. 2006. *The Reformation: A History*. New York: Modern Library Chronicles

Conze, E. (trans.) 2001. *Buddhist Wisdom: The Diamond Sutra and the Heart Sutra*. New York: Random House/Vintage.

Cooper, D. 1978. "Moral Relativism." *Midwest Studies in Philosophy* 3, 97-108.

Cosby, B. 2005-2006. "Personal Responsibility." Lectures on all news channels.

Coyne, G. 2004. (Director of Vatican Observatory.) "God Could Create an Evolutionary World Just as He Could a Static One." Quoted by Saylor in *Science and Theology News*, July/August.

Coulter, A. 2006. *Godless: The Church of Liberalism*. New York: Crown Forum.

———. 2006. "Are Videotaped Beheadings Covered by Geneva?" *Human Events*, 25 September.

———. 2003. *Treason*. New York: Crown Forum.

Crick, F., and C. Koch. 1990. "Towards a Neurobiological Theory of Consciousness." *Seminars in Neurosciences* 2, 263-275.

Cronin, M. 2006. "Conservatives Push to Counter Liberal Professors." *Arizona Republic*, 12 August. (Protest academic bias.)

———. 2006. "Too Many A's, B's at Colleges?" *Arizona Republic*, 1 July.

Crouch, S. 2007. "All Isn't as It Might Seem in Politics via Internet." *New York Daily News* n.d. (Political media distortion of visual images.)

Daly, R. 2007. "Mental Illness Not A Cause of Terrorist Acts." *Psychology News*, 20 July. (Motivation is the desire to be important - narcissism.)

———. 2007. "Too Few Geriatric Psychiatrists." *Psychology News*, 20 July. (The 1960s generation expected to have mental illness rate of 20%.)

Danielson, D. 2000. *The Book of the Cosmos: Imagining the Universe from Heraclitus to Hawking, A Helix Anthology*. New York: Perseus Books Group.

Daragahi, B. 2006. "Ramadan Ends in Violence." *Los Angeles Times/Arizona Republic*, 23 October. (Muslim holy month a period of constant terrorism and violence.)

Darwin, C. (1874) 2000. *The Descent of Man, and Selection in Relation to Sex*. Boston: Adamant Media Corporation

Davidson, R. 2004. "Transforming the Emotional Mind: Neuroscience." Dharamsala, India: *Mind and Life Institute*. 18-22 October.

Davies, P. C. W. 1995. *About Time: Einstein's Unfinished Revolution.* London: Viking.

Davis, C. 2007. "The Quantum Field Pupillary Response." n.d. (Careful study confirms earlier studies that pupillary response correlated quantum energy field response to truth/falsehood and level of consciousness. Confirms muscle-test response. The pupil reacts by dilating to falsehood, constricting to truth.)

Davis, G. 2006. *Religion of Peace? Islam's War against the World.* Los Angeles: World Ahead Publishing Co. (Sharia Law: House of Islam vs. House of War is essence of Islam by which the Western world is the enemy to be conquered.)

Dawkins, R. 2006. *The God Delusion.* New York: Houghton Mifflin. (Evolutionary psychology.)

———. 1978. *The Selfish Gene.* New York: Oxford University Press.

Dean, C. 2006. "Faith, Reason, God, and Other Imponderables." *New York Times*, 25 July.

de Chardin, T. 1975. *The Future of Man.* New York: Harcourt Brace.

———. 1966. *Man's Place in Nature.* New York: Harper.

———. 1959. *The Phenomenon of Man.* New York: Harper.

Dennett, D. 2006. "Forget Meme Not." *Science and Theology News*, May. (Defends meme hypothesis of breaking the spell.)

———. 2006. "Reverse-engineering God." *Science and Theology News*, May. (Religions are evolutionary and should be studied.)

———. 2006. *Breaking the Spell: Religion as a Natural Phenomenon.* New York: Viking Adult.

———. 1990. "Memes and the Exploitation of Imagination." *Journal of Aesthetics and Art Criticism.* n.d.

Dembski, W. A., ed. 1998. *Mere Creation: Science, Faith, and Intelligent Design.* Downers Grove, IL: Intervarsity Press.

Dennett, D. 2006. *Breaking the Spell: Religion as a Natural Phenomenon.* New York: Viking. (An atheist intellectual viewpoint.)

———. 1991. *Consciousness Explained.* London: Little Brown.

Desperate Crossing: True Story of the Pilgrims and Mayflower. 2006. History Channel Documentary, 23 November

de Tocqueville, Alexis [1835] 2000. *Democracy in America.* New York:

Harper Perennial Modern Classics

Diamond, J. 1979. *Your Body Doesn't Lie*. New York: Warner Books.

Dierker, R. 2006. *The Tyranny of Tolerance: A Sitting Judge Breaks the Code of Silence to Expose the Liberal Judicial Assault*. New York: Crown Forum.

Dillon, R. 2007. "Arrogance, Self-respect, and Personhood." *Journal of Consciousness Studies* 14, No. 506, pp. 101-126. (Arrogance, [narcissism] corrupts self-respect and respect for others.)

DiLulio, J. 2006. "The New York Times vs. Religion." *Weekly Standard*, 23 October.

Dionne, E. J. 2007. "Questioning Salvation." *Washington Post Writers Group*, 7 April. (Polemics of neoatheists, such as Sam Harris and Richard Dawkins.)

Donnelly, J. 1984. "Cultural Relativism and Human Rights." *Human Rights Quarterly* 6, 400-419.

Donnelly, M. 2006. "Faith Boosts Cognitive Management of HIV and Cancer." *Science and Theology News*, May. (Study calibrates at 180.)

Dossey, L. 2005. "Global Warming: The Politicalization of Science and Michael Crichton's State of Fear." *Journal of Scientific Exploration* 19:4.

Dowd, M. 2006. "Virtuecrats Betting Both Sides." *New York Times/Arizona Republic*, 6 June.

D'Souza, D. 2007. *The Enemy at Home: The Cultural Left and Its Responsibility for 9/11*. New York: Doubleday.

Duncker, K. 1939. "Ethical Relativity." *Mind* 48, 39-57.

Durkheim, E. (1954) 2001. *The Elementary Forms of the Religious Life*. New York: Oxford University Press.

Durkin, M. 2007. "The Great Global Warming Swindle." *CNN*: Glenn Beck Show, 1 May. (UK: scientist debunks global warming; is of human origin.)

Dyer, W. 2004. *The Power of Intention*. Carlsbad, CA: Hay House.

———. 2004. "Finding Inner Peace." *Unity*. November.

Easterbrook, G. 2007. "Calling Evil by Its Proper Name." Cited in *Week*, 18 May, from original article in New Republic. (Leftist euphemisms cloud issues and thus preclude their resolution as pointed out by George Orwell. Unless we call a thing what it is, we cannot think about it clearly.)

Eccles, J. C. 1994. *How the Self Controls Its Brain*. New York: Springer-Verlag Telos.

Eddington, A. S. 1929. *The Nature of the Physical World*. Cambridge: Cambridge University Press.

Edelman, G. M. 1992. *Bright Air, Brilliant Fire: On the Matter of the Mind*. London: Penguin.

———. 1989. *The Remembered Present: A Biological Theory of Consciousness*. New York: Basic Books.

Eisenberg, E. 2003. "Religion Is not the Issue." *American Republic*, 21 July.

Eisenstein, C. 2005. "A State of Being is a State of Being." *Journal of Scientific Exploration* 19:3, Fall.

Elst, K. 2004. "Wahi: The Supernatural Basis of Islam." Leuven, Belgium. 14 August. Islam propagated by artificially induced trans states. (http://koenraadelst.bharatvani.org/articles/hinduism/wahi.html

———. 2002-2003. Articles: Non-Islamic views of Islam. *Kashmir Herald*, Autumn-Winter.

Emerson, S. 2006. *Jihad Incorporated*. New York: Prometheus Books. (Current militant Islam in the U.S.; report on government investigative project.)

Emery, N. 2007. "The Horror! The Horror!" *Weekly Standard* 12:47, 3 September. (Ridicules Far Left's paranoia about perceiving conservation as fascist.)

Engel, A. E., P. Fries, P. Konig, et al. 1999. "Temporal Binding, Binocular Rivalry, and Consciousness." *Consciousness and Cognition* 8:2, 128-151.

Everly, D. 2002. "The Role of Civil Society in Shaping Character." *Heritage Lectures*, April.

Faherty, J. 2006. "Disproving Einstein Harder than It Looks." *Arizona Republic*, 16 November. (Scientist Bob Henderson writes three books and spends forty years trying to prove Einstein is stupid. [His books and theories calibrate at 190.])

Farrar, C. and C. Firth. 2002. "Experiencing Oneself . . . as Being the Cause of an Action: Neural Correlates." *Neuro Image* 15:3, 596-603.

Farrington, C. 2006. "Peace is Anchored Through Strength." *Arizona Republic*, 7 November. (Letters to Editor.)

Feller, M. B. 2006."The Mind-Body Connection." *Arizona Republic*, 25 July. (Positive spiritual beliefs and imaging techniques result in healing and greater happiness.)

Ferero, K. 2006. "Emergence cannot explain free will." Science and Theology, May. (The human will is not explicable nor subject to the limitation of logic/science. That it is of a different order is agreed to by Stephen Hawking, Albert Einstein, Erwin Schrödinger, and many other scientists.)

Fetzer, J. 2006. "Scholars for 9/11: Conspiracy Theory: Bush Planted Bombs in Twin Towers." *Fox News*, August.

Feuerbach, L. (1891) 1989. *The Essence of Christianity*. Amherst, NY: Prometheus Books.

Feuerstein, G. 2006. *Holy Madness: Spirituality, Crazy-Wise Teachers, And Enlightenment*. (Rev., expanded). Prescott, AZ: Hohm Press.

Few, B. 2003. "Cognitive Neuroscience of Consciousness." *Journal of Consciousness Studies* 11:2.

Finchar, T. 2006. "Faith Through Service." *American Legion*, November. (Critical role of military chaplains in war.)

Fischer, N. "Rereading a World of Bliss." *Tricycle*, Winter. (Buddha's silent transmission: the intrinsic authority of suchness.)

Flanagen, O. 1992. *Consciousness Reconsidered*. Cambridge, MA: The MIT Press.

Flurry, G., ed. 2007. "The Cyberspace Game of Life." *Philadelphia Trumpet*, April. (Internet reveals extent of dark side of human nature.)

———. 2007. "Muslim Youth More Radical." *Philadelphia Trumpet*, April. (Multiculturalism in Britain divisive and foments isolated radical sub-population, especially youths.)

———. 2007. "Morality War." *Philadelphia Trumpet*, February. (Morality and shifting blame of power worldwide.)

Flynn, D. J. 2005. *Intellectual Morons: How Ideology Makes Smart People Fall for Stupid Ideas*. New York: Three Rivers Press; Reprint.

Forman, R. 2004. *Grassroots Spirituality*. Exeter, UK: Imprint Academic.

Frank, A. 2007. "In the Light of Truth: Science as a Spiritual Practice." *Tricycle*, Spring. (Science and spirituality both dedicated to discovery of essential truths.)

Fraser, R. 2006. "Lighting Islam's Fuse." *Philadelphia Trumpet*, Nov.-Dec. (A cell to Europe to reunite via Christianity to ward off Islamic crusade of violence.)

Freud, A. 1971. *The Ego and the Mechanisms of Defense*. Madison, CT: International Universities Press.

Freud, S. 1964. *The Future of an Illusion*. New York: Doubleday.

———. (1923) 1962. *The Ego and the Id (The Standard Edition of the Complete Psychological Works of Sigmund Freud)* New York: W. W. Norton.

———. 1936. "Splitting of the Ego in the Defensive Process." *International Journal of Psycho-analysis*, Vol. Xvii (15).

Freud, S. and O. Pfister. 1963. *Psychoanalysis and Faith: The Letters of Sigmund Freud and Oskar Pfister*. New York: Basic Books.

Friedman, T. 2007. "Sure Signs of an Arab Country." *New York Times*, 5 March. (Blowing up children, beating women, intolerance, violence, ignorance, hatred, and repression.)

———. 2007. "Where is the Outrage?" *New York Times*, 26 January. (Muslim world does nothing to quell its own violence.)

Frith, C. D. 1996. "The Role of the Prefrontal Cortex in Self-consciousness: The Case of Auditory Hallucinations." *Philosophical Transactions of the Royal Society: Biological Sciences*, 351, 1505-1512.

Fuelner, E., and D. Wilson. 2006. *Getting America Right: The True Conservative Values Our Nation Needs Today*. New York: Crown Forum.

Gage, F. 2004. "Structural Changes in the Adult Brain in Response to Experience." Dharamsala, India: *Mind and Life Institute*. 18-22 October.

Gallagher, S. 2004. "Hermeneutics and Cognitive Sciences." *Journal of Consciousness Studies* 11:10.

Gallup Survey. 2006. "85% of Americans believe public morality poor and getting worse." http://poll.gallup.com (8-11 May).

Garcia, J. L. 1988. "Relativism and Moral Divergence." *Metaphilosophy* 19, 264-281.

Gardner, J. 2003. *Biocosm: The New Scientific Theory of Evolution: Intelligent Life Is Architect of the Universe*. Maui, HI: Inner Ocean Publishing.

Garfield, S. 2006. "Chavez and Chomsky: 2 of a Kind." *Arizona Republic*, 28 September.

Garhart, M., and A. M. Russell. 2004. "Metaphor and Thinking in Science and Religion." *Zygon* 39:1.

Gazzaniga, M. 2005. *The Ethical Brain*. New York: Dana Press.

Gelenter, D. 2007. "Please Say This." *Weekly Standard*, 22 January. (Identifies Islams as dedicated to worship of death rather than life.)

Geller, J. 2006. "First-Person Accounts: The Importance of Being Honest." *Psychiatric Services* 57:5, May.

George, R. P., ed. 1997. Natural Law Theory: Contemporary Essays." Magnolia, MA: Peter Smith Publisher Inc. Reissue.

Geppart, C. 2004. "Attending to uncertainty . . . an ambiguity." P*sychiatric News*, July.

German, M. 2007. *Thinking Like a Terrorist: Insights of a Former FBI Undercover Agent*. Dulles, VA: Potomac Books.

Gernet, D. 2007. "Ockham's Razor and Its Improper Use." *Journal of Scientific Exploration* 21:1.

Ghush, B. 2007. "Why They Hate Each Other." *Time*, 5 March. (Major historical analysis of Islam warring factions of Sunnis and Shi'ites.)

Gibbs, N., and M. Duffy. 2007. *The Preacher and the Presidents: Billy Graham in the White House*. New York: Center Street.

———. 2007. "The Pastor in Chief." *Time*, 26 August. (Review of 50-year history.)

———. 2007. "How the Democrats Got Religion." *Time*, 23 July. (Democrats reach for moral majority voters.)

Gingrich, N. 2006. *Rediscovering God in America: Reflections on the Role of Faith in Our Nation's History*. New York: Thomas Nelson

———. 2006. "God and Religion in America." *Fox News*, 16 December. (Documentary of religion in Washington, D.C., founding fathers and presidents; cal. 480.)

Glynn, I. M. 1990. "Consciousness and Time." *Nature* 348, 477-479.

Goblaskis, D. 2006. "When Does Humanity (humanness) Begin?" *Science and Theology News*. May. (According to the Muslim 'hadith', or teachings of Muhammad, the soul enters the embryo at one hundred twenty days.)

Goel, S. R. 1993. *Hindu Temples: What Happened to Them*. Vol. II. New Delhi: Voice of India.

Goldberg, B. 2007. *Crazies to the Left of Me, Wimps to the Right: How One Side Lost Its Mind and the Other Lost Its Nerve*. New York: HarperCollins.

Golding, W. 2003. *Lord of the Flies*. 50th Anniv. Ed. New York: Perigee Trade.

Goodman, E. 2007. "Faith a Prerequisite for Office." *Week*, 6 April. (Only 14% of Americans would vote for an atheist for president.)

Goodman, L. 2001. *In Defense of Truth: A Pluralistic Approach*. Amherst, NY: Humanity Books (Prometheus).

Gopal, L., and Bursztajn. 2007. "On Skepticism and Tolerance in Psychiatry and Forensics." *Psychiatric Times* 24:5, April.

Goshgarian, G. 2005. *What Matters in America: Reading and Writing about Contemporary Culture*. New York: Longman. (Invasion of academia by political bias and decline of Harvard Law School.)

Gosse, P. H. (1857) 2003. *Omphalos: The Evolution Debate*, 1813-1870. New York: Routledge.

Gould, S. J. 2002. *The Structure of Evolutionary Theory*. New York: Belknap Press.

Grace, F. n.d. "Beyond Reason: The Certitude of the Mystic." *Theology Today*. Forthcoming.

Grayson, B. 2006. "Near-Death Experiences and Spirituality." *Zygon* 41:2, June.

Great Books of the Western World, The. 1952. Hutching, R. and M. Alden, Eds. Chicago: Encyclopedia Britannica.

Greenberg, P. 2007. "The Mob Mentality." *Los Angeles Times* Syndicate. 3 January.

Gregg, S. 2002. "Liberty and Moral Ecology: The Nexus of Truth." *Heritage Lectures*, April.

Grillen, M. 2004. *Can A Smart Person Believe in God?* Nashville, TN: Nelson Books.

Gross, P. R. and N. Levitt. Eds. 1997. *The Flight from Science and Reason*. (Annals of the New York Academy of Sciences). New York: New York Academy of Science.

Grossman, C. 2007. "Episcopal Church: New Dawn." *USA Today*, 5

February. (Decline of church membership and split in response to modernization: appointment of woman bishop, K. Schori.)

Grossman, L., et al. 2006. "Time Person of the Year: You." *Time*, 168:26, 25 December. (Socio-cultural impact of media-inflated narcissism in mirror-cover issue.)

Guiness, O. 2001. *The Great Experiment: Truth and Freedom in the American Republic*. Colorado Springs, CO: Navpress Publishing Group.

———. 2000. *When No One Sees: The Importance of Character in an Age of Image*. Colorado Springs, CO: Navpress Publishing Group.

Gunther, M. 2006. "The Green Machine." *Fortune*, 7 August. (Wal-Mart to take industry lead.)

Haidt, J. 2005. *The Happiness Hypothesis*. New York: Perseus/Basic Books. (Learning theory. Importance of environmental structure on brain physiology.)

Hall, T. D. 2006. "Politricks: The Crusade for Democracy and An Introduction to Post-Marxian Pattern-of-History Theory." www.whatthebleep.com/herald15/politricks.shtml

Hamburger, P. 2004. *Separation of Church and State*. Cambridge, MA: Harvard University Press.

Hamer, D. 2004. *The God Gene: How Faith Is Hardwired Into Our Genes*. New York: Doubleday.

Hansen, N. 2006. "Film Questions First-Amendment Freedom." *Sedona Red Rock News*, 15 November. (Review of controversial film by Ewing and Grady on evangelicals and politics.)

———. "Am I Being a Rhetorical Boy?" *Sedona Red Rock News*, 7 December. (Manipulated new and media fluff now a substitute for real journalism.)

Hanson, V. D. 2007. "Hypocritical Islamists Join in Western Sins." Tribune Media Services/*Arizona Republic*, 2 August. (Social views of Islam are 7th century primitivism.)

———. 2007. "Who Really Lost in Middle East?" *Tribune Media Services/Arizona Republic*, 26 July. (Review of decades of miscalculations and error due to misperception.)

———. 2007. "While Oil Grips Our Economy, War on Terror Must Be Fought." *Tribune Media Services/Arizona Republic*, 26 April. (Millions in Western world silenced regarding Islam by terrorism.)

———. 2006. "Radical Islam Radiates Evil." *Tribune Media Services/ Arizona Republic*, 24 December. (Pan-Islamic terrorism.)

———. 2006. "Dark Ages Lurk in Shadows of Terrorists." *Tribune Media Services/Arizona Republic*, 26 October. (Current society regressing back to barbarism via Islamic beheading [violence].)

———. "America's Freedoms." *Tribune Media Services/Arizona Republic*, 30 July. (Progressive evolution of human civilization not a straight line but fluctuates with cycles of peace and war.)

Hardin, G. 1978. *Sociobiology and Human Nature: An Interdisciplinary Critique and Defense*. San Francisco: Wiley/Jossey-Bass Publishers.

Harokopos, E. 2005. "Power As the Cause of Motion and a New Foundation of Classical Mechanics." *Progress in Physics* 2, 82-91, July.

Harrenstein, R.J. 1973. *IQ in the Meritocracy*. Boston: Little, Brown.

Harris, L. 2006. "Socrates or Muhammad?" *Weekly Standard*, 2 October. (Attack on reason in the Western civilization.)

———. 2002. "Al-Quaeda's Fantasy Theology: War Without Clausewitz." *Hoover Institute*, August-September. Stanford University. (Total error of not knowing your enemy.)

Harris, S. 2004. *The End of Faith: Religion, Terror, and the Future of Reason*. New York: W.W. Norton and Co. (Criticism of religion, especially of Islam.)

Harrison, G. 1976. "Relativism and Tolerance." *Ethics* 86, 122-135.

Harrup, F. 2007. "Netroot Leftists Choke Dem's Message. *Arizona Republic*, 14 September. (moveon.org fiasco via *New York Times* ad.)

Harvey, D. 1990. *The Condition of Postmodernity: Enquiry into the Origins of Cultural Change*. Oxford, UK: Blackwell Publishing

Hauser, M. D. 2006. "Basic Instinct." *Science and Spirit*, July-August. (Morality is hard-wired in the brain's function. There is a universal moral grammar.)

Hawking, S. 1998. *A Brief History of Time*. New York: Bantam Books.¬

———. 1993. *Black Holes in Baby Universes and Other Essays*. New York: Bantam Books.

Hawkins, D. R. 2008. "Advancing Spiritual Awareness" Lecture Series. Sedona, AZ: Veritas Publishing. (Six 5-hour CD/DVDs.) *Spirituality, Reason, and Faith* (Jan.); *Clear Pathway to Enlightenment* (Mar.); *Belief, Trust, and Credibility* (June); *Overcoming Doubt, Skepticism,*

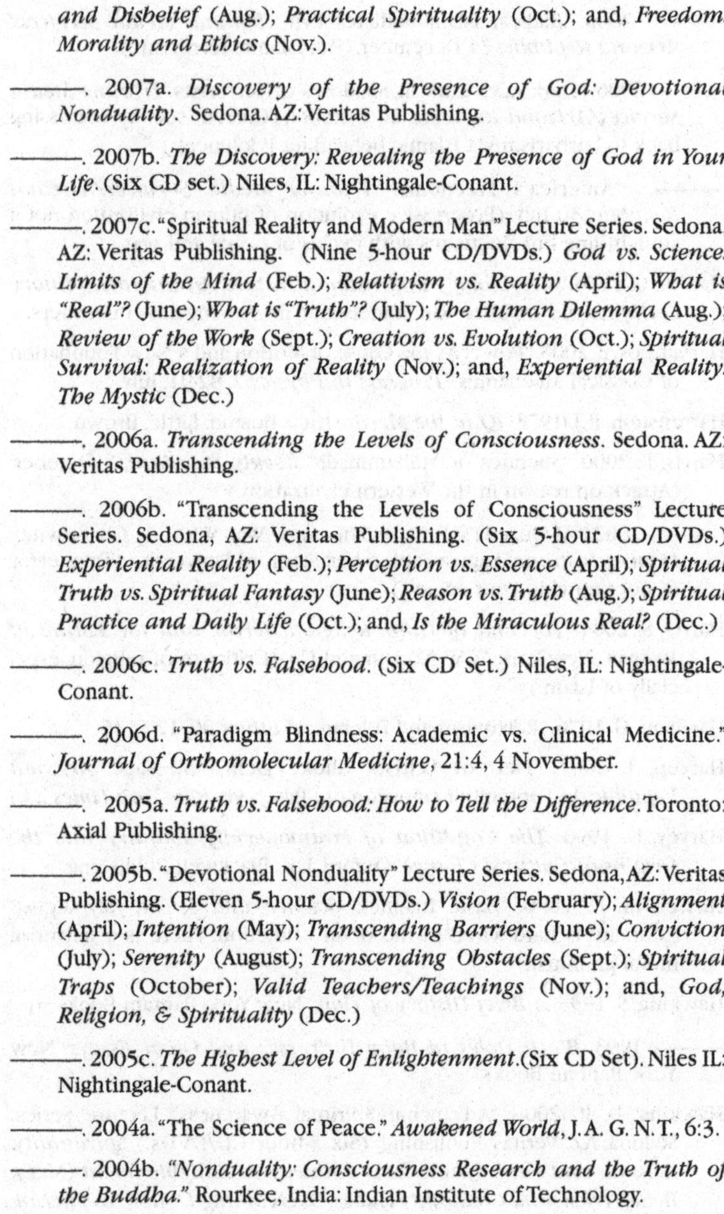

and Disbelief (Aug.); *Practical Spirituality* (Oct.); and, *Freedom: Morality and Ethics* (Nov.).

———. 2007a. *Discovery of the Presence of God: Devotional Nonduality*. Sedona.AZ: Veritas Publishing.

———. 2007b. *The Discovery: Revealing the Presence of God in Your Life*. (Six CD set.) Niles, IL: Nightingale-Conant.

———. 2007c. "Spiritual Reality and Modern Man" Lecture Series. Sedona, AZ: Veritas Publishing. (Nine 5-hour CD/DVDs.) *God vs. Science: Limits of the Mind* (Feb.); *Relativism vs. Reality* (April); *What is "Real"?* (June); *What is "Truth"?* (July); *The Human Dilemma* (Aug.); *Review of the Work* (Sept.); *Creation vs. Evolution* (Oct.); *Spiritual Survival: Realization of Reality* (Nov.); and, *Experiential Reality: The Mystic* (Dec.)

———. 2006a. *Transcending the Levels of Consciousness*. Sedona. AZ: Veritas Publishing.

———. 2006b. "Transcending the Levels of Consciousness" Lecture Series. Sedona, AZ: Veritas Publishing. (Six 5-hour CD/DVDs.) *Experiential Reality* (Feb.); *Perception vs. Essence* (April); *Spiritual Truth vs. Spiritual Fantasy* (June); *Reason vs. Truth* (Aug.); *Spiritual Practice and Daily Life* (Oct.); and, *Is the Miraculous Real?* (Dec.)

———. 2006c. *Truth vs. Falsehood*. (Six CD Set.) Niles, IL: Nightingale-Conant.

———. 2006d. "Paradigm Blindness: Academic vs. Clinical Medicine." *Journal of Orthomolecular Medicine*, 21:4, 4 November.

———. 2005a. *Truth vs. Falsehood: How to Tell the Difference*. Toronto: Axial Publishing.

———. 2005b. "Devotional Nonduality" Lecture Series. Sedona, AZ: Veritas Publishing. (Eleven 5-hour CD/DVDs.) *Vision* (February); *Alignment* (April); *Intention* (May); *Transcending Barriers* (June); *Conviction* (July); *Serenity* (August); *Transcending Obstacles* (Sept.); *Spiritual Traps* (October); *Valid Teachers/Teachings* (Nov.); and, *God, Religion, & Spirituality* (Dec.)

———. 2005c. *The Highest Level of Enlightenment*. (Six CD Set). Niles IL: Nightingale-Conant.

———. 2004a. "The Science of Peace." *Awakened World*, J. A. G. N. T., 6:3.

———. 2004b. *"Nonduality: Consciousness Research and the Truth of the Buddha."* Rourkee, India: Indian Institute of Technology.

———. 2004c. "The Impact of Spontaneous Spiritual Experiences in the Life of 'Ordinary' Persons." *Watkins Review*, 7.

———. 2004d. "Transcending the Mind" Lecture Series. Sedona, AZ: Veritas Publishing. (Six 5-hour CD/DVDs.) *Thought and Ideation* (Feb.); *Emotions and Sensations* (April); *Perception and Positionality* (June); *Identification and Illusion* (August); *Witnessing and Observing* (Oct.); and *The Ego and the Self* (Dec.).

———. 2004e. *The Highest Level of Enlightenment*. Chicago: Nightingale-Conant Corp. (CD, Audiocassettes).

———. 2003a. *I: Reality and Subjectivity*. Sedona, AZ: Veritas Publishing.

———. 2003b. "Devotional Nonduality" Lecture Series. Sedona, AZ: Veritas Publishing. (Six 5-hour CD/DVDs.) *Integration of Spirituality and Personal Life* (Feb.); *Spirituality and the World* (April); *Spiritual Community* (June); *Enlightenment* (August); *Realization of the Self as the "I"* (Nov.); and, *Dialogue, Questions and Answers* (Dec.).

———. 2002a. *Power versus Force: An Anatomy of Consciousness*. (Rev.). Carlsbad, CA, Brighton-le-Sands, Australia: Hay House.

———. 2002b. "The Pathway to God" Lecture Series. Sedona, AZ: Veritas Publishing. (Twelve 5-hour CD/DVDs) 1. *Causality: The Ego's Foundation*; 2. *Radical Subjectivity: The I of Self*; 3. *Levels of Consciousness: Subjective and Social Consequences*; 4. *Positionality and Duality: Transcending the Opposites*; 5. *Perception and Illusion: the Distortions of Reality*; 6. *Realizing the Root of Consciousness: Meditative and Contemplative Techniques*; 7. *The Nature of Divinity: Undoing Religious Fallacies*; 8. *Advaita: The Way to God Through Mind*; 9. *Devotion: The Way to God Through the Heart*; 10. *Karma and the Afterlife*; 11. *God Transcendent and Immanent*; and, 12. *Realization of the Self: The Final Moments*.

———. 2001. *The Eye of the I: From Which Nothing Is Hidden*. Sedona, AZ: Veritas Publishing.

———. 2000. *Consciousness Workshop*. Prescott, AZ Sedona, AZ: Veritas Publishing. (CD/DVD)

———. 2000. *Consciousness and A Course in Miracles*. (California.) Sedona, AZ: Veritas Publishing. (CD)

———. 2000. *Consciousness and Spiritual Inquiry: Address to the Tao Fellowship*. Sedona, AZ: Veritas Publishing. (CD)

———. 1997. *Research on the Nature of Consciousness*. Sedona, AZ: Veritas Publishing. (The Landsberg 1997 Lecture. University of

California School of Medicine, San Francisco, CA)

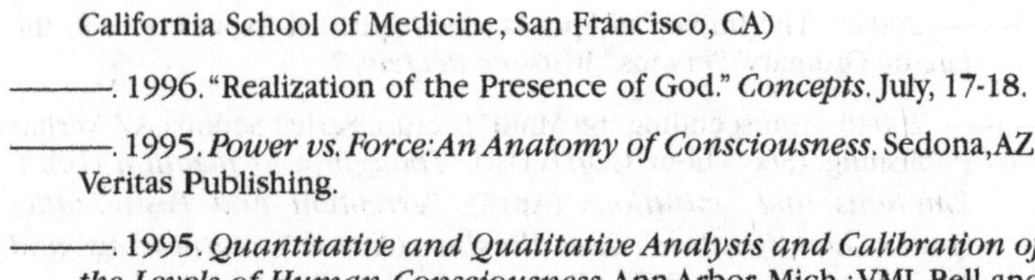

———. 1996. "Realization of the Presence of God." *Concepts*. July, 17-18.

———. 1995. *Power vs. Force: An Anatomy of Consciousness*. Sedona, AZ: Veritas Publishing.

———. 1995. *Quantitative and Qualitative Analysis and Calibration of the Levels of Human Consciousness*. Ann Arbor, Mich.: VMI, Bell and Howell Col.; republished 1996 by Veritas Publishing, Sedona, AZ

———. 1995. *Power Versus Force; Consciousness and Addiction; Advanced States of Consciousness: The Realization of the Presence of God; Consciousness: How to Tell the Truth About Anything,* and *Undoing the Barriers to Spiritual Progress*. Sedona, AZ: Veritas Publishing. (CD/DVDs.)

———. 1987. Sedona Lecture Series: *Drug Addiction and Alcoholism; A Map of Consciousness; Cancer; AIDS;* and *Death and Dying*. Sedona, AZ: Veritas Publishing. (CDs, DVDs.)

———. 1986. Office Series: *Stress; Health; Spiritual First Aid; Sexuality; The Aging Process; Handling Major Crisis; Worry, Fear and Anxiety; Pain and Suffering; Losing Weight; Depression; Illness and Self-Healing;* and *Alcoholism*. Sedona, AZ: Veritas Publishing. (CDs/DVDs.)

———. 1985. "Consciousness and Addiction" in *Beyond Addictions, Beyond Boundaries*. S. Burton and L. Kiley. San Mateo, CA: Brookridge Institute.

Hawkins, D. R., and L. Pauling. 1973. *Orthomolecular Psychiatry*. New York: W. H. Freeman and Co.

Hayakawa, S. 1971. *Our Language and Our World; Selections from Etc.: A Review of General Semantics*, 1953-1958. New York: Harper Collins.

Hayward, S. F. 2005. *Greatness: Reagan, Churchill, and the Making of Extraordinary Leaders*. New York: Crown Forum/Random House.

Hazlitt, W. (1945) 2004. *The Spirit of the Age*. Kila, MT: Kessinger Publishing.

Hefner, P. 2006. "Religion and Science: Separationness or Coinheritance?" *Zygon*, 11:4, December.

———. 2006. "The Mythic Grounding of Religion and Science." *Zygon* 41:2, June.

Heisenberg, W. 1958. *Physics and Philosophy*. New York: Harper

Henderson, B. 2006. *Einstein and the Emperor's New-Clothes Syndrome:*

The Exposé of a Charlatan. Private printing. (Contact: bob.bet@cox.net. [Cal. level 90]).

———. 1972. *Relativity - A Scientific Blunder*. Private printing.

Henson, V. D. 2006. "America's Freedoms." *Arizona Republic*, 8 July. (Progressive evolution of human civilization not a straight line but fluctuates with cycles of peace and war.)

Herrnstein, R. J. 1973. *IQ in the Meritocracy*. Boston: Little Brown

———. 2006. "Gods of Our Fathers." *Weekly Standard*. 11 December. (Founding fathers of U.S. Constitution were deists and theists; left legacy of the Enlightenment.)

Hilliker, J. 2006. "Sickness in Britain's Heart: How, via Relativism and Moral Decline Britain Learned to Hate Itself." *Philadelphia Trumpet*, Nov.-Dec. (British passivity to Islamic extremists.)

Hirsch, E., J. Katt, et al. 1988. *The Dictionary of Cultural Literacy*. Boston: Houghton Mifflin Co.

Hitchens, C. 2005. *Thomas Jefferson: Author of America*. New York: Eminent Lives/HarperCollins.

Hofstadter, R. 1959. *Social Darwinism in American Thought*. Boston: Beacon Press.

Holding, R. 2007. "Speaking Up for Themselves." *Time*, 21 May. (Schools harassed by lawsuits for attempts to set limits and maintain order.)

Holloway, C. 2006. "Losing Our Religion." *Science and Theology News*. July/August (Failure of Darwinism to provide morality to replace religion.)

Horowitz, D. 2007. *Indoctrination U: The Left's War Against Academic Freedom*. New York: Encounter Books. (Brainwashing of Students by Academia.)

———. 2006. *The Professors: The 101 Most Dangerous Academics in America*. Washington, DC: Regnery Publishing. (Postmodern elitism.)

———. 2004. *Unholy Alliance: Radical Islam and the American Left*. Washington, DC: Regnery Publishers.

Hostetler, B. 2006. *American Idols: The Worship of the American Dream*. Nashville, TN: B and H Publishing Group. (Media seduction.)

Hubbard, T. 2007. "Mental Representation: How Does It Relate to Consciousness?" *Journal of Consciousness Studies* 14:1-20, 37-66.

"Human Rights: Stand Up for Your Rights." (Editor). 2007. *Economist*, 24

March. (Amnesty Internet losing clout due to overreaching definitive from so-called "rights" to Socialism.)

Hunt, H. 2006. "The Truth Value of Mystical Experience." *Journal of Consciousness Studies*, 13:12 December. (Intellectual discourse of mystical states: philosophies; cal 435.)

Huxley, A. (1945) 2004. *The Perennial Philosophy*. New York: Harper Perennial Modern Classics.

Huxley, T. H. 1894. *Evolution and Ethics and Other Essays*. London: MacMillan.

Ignatius, D. 2006. "A Long War? Maybe not. Unless we add new fuel, the fires of hate will burn out." *Washington Post Writers Group/Arizona Republic*, 14 September. (Jihad just a passing fad.)

Illes, J. ed. 2005. *Neuroethics: Defining the Issues in Theory, Practice, and Policy*. New York: Oxford University Press. (Correlation with neurophysiology.)

Imam Training Video. 2007. *Fox News*, 3 November. (How to beat your wife.)

"In the Beginning." 2007 (Editor). *Economist*, 21 April. (Debate on creation versus evolution now global.)

"In the World of Good and Evil." 2006. (Editorial.) *Economist*. 16 September. (Influence of religion in U. S. politics and foreign.. policy.)

Issacson, W. 2007. Einstein: His Life and Universe. (Book review.) *Time*, 16 April.

Jacoby, S. 2004. Freethinkers: *A History of American Secularism*. New York: Metropolitan Books.

Jahnake, A. 2007. "Snide Bloggerspeak Loaded with Rude, Cowardly Words." *Arizona Republic*, 16 August. (Sees decline as tragic.)

James, W. [1802]1999. *The Varieties of Religious Experience. A Study in Human Nature*. New York: Modern Library.

Jaoudi, M. 1999. *Christian Mysticism East - West*. Costa Mesa, CA: Paulist Press.

Jarman, M. 2007. "Human Effort Beats Computers." *Arizona Republic*, 16 November. (Honeywell Corp. discovers brain monitors sensory input faster than can computers.)

"Jean Baudrillard." 2007. (Obituary.) *Economist*, 17 March. (Leftist French philosopher died at age 77. He wrote of symbolism and consumer society; book calibrates at 475. Very anti the U.S. as imperialist who deserved 9/11.)

Jenkins, M. 2007. "Tyranny in Universities." *Philadelphia Trumpet*, June. (Colleges dominated by exclusive presentations of Leftist theories and propaganda re moral relativism, Marxism, atheism, Darwinian theory. Conservatives commonly harmed and physically attacked.)

Jesser, N. A. 2007. "A Forum to Oppose Muslim Radicals." *Arizona Republic*, 14 August. (Struggle for dominance between Islamic political factions - "Islamism" vs. moderates.)

Johnson, D. 2006. "America and the America-Haters." *Arizona Republic*, 18 June.

Johnson, M. 2006. "Western Culture Must Regain Its Will to Survive." *Human Events*, 16 October.

Johnson, R.A. 1998. *Balancing Heaven and Earth*. San Francisco: Harper Collins.

Johnson, W., ed. 1973. *The Cloud of Unknowing*. New York: Doubleday.

Jung, C. 1955. *Modern Man in Search of a Soul*. New York: HBJ/Harvest Books.

———. 1938. *Psychology and Religion*. New Haven, CT: Yale University Press; Reprint edition.

Kanfer, S. 2002. "America's Dumbest Intellectual." *City Journal*, Summer. (Noam Chomsky)

Kant, I. [1781] 1999. *The Critique of Pure Reason*. New York: Cambridge University Press.

———. 1959. *Foundation of the Metaphysics of Morals*. New York: MacMillan.

Kantor, E. 2006. *The Politically Incorrect Guide to English and American Literature*. Washington, DC: Regnery Publishing.

Kasick, J. 2007. "Creation Museum Controversy." *Fox News*, 28 May. (Biblical literal interpretations vs. creationism and science.)

Kauffman, J. M. 2007. "Climate Change Reexamined." *Journal of Scientific Exploration* 21:4. (Claims of human-caused warming fallacious as there is no correlation between carbon dioxide levels and warming.)

Keane, D. 2007. "The Human Swarm." *Time*, 26 February. Letters to Editor. (Debate on global pollution/warning ignores critical factor of overpopulation.)

Keating, T. 1994. *Open Mind, Open Heart: The Contemplative Dimension of the Gospel*. (Reissue) New York: Continuum International Publishing Group

Keen, A. 2007. *The Cult of the Amateur: How Today's Internet is Killing Our Culture*. New York: Currency.

Kelly, G. 2006. "The Power of Culture: An Exploration of Collective Transformation." *Shift* 12, Sept-Nov. (Societal problems the result of ingrained cultural myths.)

Kenny, R. 2004. "The Science of Collective Consciousness." *Enlightenment*, May/June.

Kiblinger, W. 2007. "Evolution and Subjectivity." *Zygon* 42:1, March.

King, P. (2007). U.S. Rep. (R-NY). Comments made during interviews on Hannity and Colmes (*Fox News*). September.

Kinsley, M. 2006. "Do Newspapers Have a Future?" *Time*, 2 October.

Kirschnev, M. W. 2006. "Answers to Darwin's Dilemma: Molecular Versatility Facilitates Genetic Variation." *Science and Theology News*, May.

Kishner, H. 2004, 2006. *Holy War on the Home Front: Secret Terror Network in the U.S.* New York: Penguin.

Klein, J. 2007. "Beware the Bloggers Bile." *Time*, 18 June. (Fierce witless bullying by Far Left bloggers attack anyone not in lock step get savaged and ridiculed.)

Kluger, J. and C. Masters. 2006. "How to Spot a Liar." *Time*, 28 August. (Neuroscience of lie detection.)

Kohlmann, E. 2006. "America Greases al-Qaeda Media Machine." *msnbc.com*, 14 July.

Kohut, A. 2007. "Pew Research Reports Most Muslims in U.S. Nonviolent." *Arizona Republic*, 23 May. (Small minority of youngest Islamics favor suicide bombing.)

Kohut, A., and B. Stokes. 2006. *America Against the World: How We Are Different and Why We Are Disliked*. New York: Times Books. (Madeline Albright, Pew Research Center's Global Attitudes Project in 50 countries.)

Kolodiejchuk, B. 2007. *Mother Teresa: Come Be My Light*. New York: Doubleday. Correspondence of Mother Teresa. (Inner doubt similar to St. John of the Cross's "dark night of the soul" in the first century.)

Krishna, G. (1971). *Kundalini: The Evolutionary Energy in Man*. Boston: Shambhala.

Krattenmaker, T. 2007. "The Bible vs. Science." *USA Today*, 5 February. (Creationists weaken own case by claiming earth is only 6,000 years old. Science says 4.5 billion.)

Krauthammer, C. 2007. "Europe Wimps Out Again." *Washington Post Writers Group*, 8 April. (Glaring failure of multinationalism, multiculturalism, U. N., E. U. and Security Council.)

Kreeft, P. 2007. *Socrates, Machiavelli, Marx, and Sartre Lectures*. Ft. Collins, CO: Ignatius Press. (Philosophy.)

Kristol, W. 2007. "Lincoln's Wisdom." *Time*, 18 June. (Need for more patriotic surge of American society.)

Kuhn, T. 1996. *The Structure of Scientific Revolution*. 3rd ed. Chicago: University of Chicago Press.

Kupelian, D. 2005. *The Marketing of Evil: How Radicals, Elitists, and Pseudo-Experts Sell Us Corruption Disguised As Freedom*. Nashville, TN: WND Books/Cumberland House Publishing. (Corruption sold as freedom via the media.)

Kuroda, K. 2007. "Japan's Atomic Bomb." *International History Channel*, 10 March. (Revealed after 50 years that Japan was 30 days from bombing U.S. with nuclear bomb, before Nagasaki and Hiroshima. Revealed in 2001 after Kuroda's death.)

Kurtz, P. B., B. Karr, and R. Sandhu, Eds. 2003. *Science and Religion: Are They Compatible?* Amherst, NY: Prometheus Books

Kusher, Harold. 2002. *Who Needs God?* New York: Simon and Schuster.

Lamsa, G. 1993. *Holy Bible: From Ancient Eastern Manuscripts*. New York: HarperCollins. (Translation from the Eastern church Peshitta.)

Ladd, J., ed. 2002. *Ethical Relativism*. Lanham, MD: University Press of America.

Lasch, C. 1991. *Culture of Narcissism: American Life in an Age of Diminishing Expectations*. New York: W. W. Norton and Co.

La Tulippe, S. 2006. *Statism, Postmodernism, and the Death of the Western World*. http://www.lewrockwell.com/latulippe/

latulippe71.html

Lawrence, Brother. 2005. *Practice of the Presence of God*. Boston: Shambhala. Or at www.practicegodspresence.com/ brother-lawrence/index.html

Leery, M. 2004. "Get Over Yourself." *Psychology Today*. July/August.

LeGault, M. 2006. *Think!: Why Crucial Decisions Can't Be Made in the Blink of an Eye*. New York: Threshold Editions/Simon & Schuster. (Cultural debate.)

Lehr, J. and F Bennett. 2003. "It's the Sun." *Environmental and Climate News* 6:4 May. (Earth warming not environmental but due to heat of magnetic activity of sun's surface. Polar cone drilling documentation.)

Leo, J. 2004. "When Church's Head Left." *U. S. News and World Report*. 18 October.

Levin, A. 2007. "Old Dogs and Humans Can Learn New Tricks." *Psychology News*, 20 July. (Mature brains create new neurons.)

Levin, B. 2007. "Entitlement is Narcissism." Center for Study of Hate and Extremism [Homophobia). *O'Reilly Factor* Fox News, 15 February.

Levin, M. and R. Limbaugh. 2005. *Men in Black: How the Supreme Court Is Destroying America*. Washington, DC: Regnery Publishing.

Lewis, J. 2007. "Which God?" *Psychiatric Times* 24:4, April. (Implications of seeing God as punitive vs. forgiving and merciful.)

Lewis, J. R. 2001. *Odd Gods: New Religions and the Cult Controversy*. Amherst, NY: Prometheus Books.

Lexchin, J., L. Bero, et al. 2003. "Industry Sponsorship and Research Outcome." *British Medical Journal* 326, 1167-70.

Libet, B. et al. 1979. "Subject Referral of the Timing for a Consciousness Sensory Experience." *Brain* 102, 193-224.

Lief, J. 2006. "Letting Go." *Tricycle*, Fall.

Limbaugh, D. 2006. *Bankrupt*. Washington, DC: Regnery Publishing,

Lind, K. R. 2006. "Faith, Science, and Life: Toward a Coherent Cosmology." Shift, June-August.

Lindberg, T. 2007. *The Political Teachings of Jesus*. New York: HarperOne.

Livestro, J. 2007. "Holland's Post-Secular Future." *Weekly Standard*, 1-8 January. (Rebirth of grassroots Christianity.)

Locke, R. 2001. "Deconstructing Deconstructionism." *Front Page*, 28 November. (Deconstructionism as merely cultural Marxism with culture instead of economics and capitalists as the oppressors.)

Lokovoc, E. 2007. "Muslim Moderates/America." *Fox News*, 13 July. (Spokesperson for Muslim Public Affairs Council.)

Lomperis, J. and A. Wisdom. 2006. *Strange Yokefellows*. Washington, DC: Institute for Religion and Democracy. (National Council of Churches are beholden to the Ford Foundation for funding; biased.)

Long, G. 2004. *Relativism and the Foundations of Liberalism*. Exeter, UK:: Imprint Academic.

Longer, J. 2007. "Today's Anti-War Movement Relies on Socialism and the Past." (1960s). *Human Events*, 5 February. (Washington protest rally.)

Lovejoy, A. O. (1936) 2005. *Great Chain of Being: A Study of the History of an Idea*. Cambridge: Harvard University Press (New ed.)

Loy, D. 2006. "The Second Buddha." *Tricycle*, Winter. (Clarification of teachings of Nagarjuna and error of nihilism.)

Loy, J. "Salmon Rushdie's *The Satanic Verses*." www.jimloy.com/issues/rushdie.htm. (Bomb threats, violence, international violence, and book banning.)

Luntz, F. 2006. *Words that Work: It's Not What You Say, It's What People Hear*. New York: Hyperion.

Lynch, A. 2006, "Thought Contagion: Islam and Jihad from a Mimetic Perspective." http://www.youmeworks.com/thoughtcontagion.

———. 1999. *Thought Contagion: How Belief Spreads Through Society*. New York: Basic Books.

Lynds, P. 2003. "Zeno's Paradoxes: A Timely Solution." http://philsci-archive.pitt.edu/archive/00001197.

———. 2003. "Subjective Perception of Time and a Progressive Present Moment: The Neurobiological Key to Unlocking Consciousness." http://cogprints.org/3125/

———. 2003. "Time and Classical and Quantum Mechanics: Indeterminacy vs. Discontinuity." *Foundations of Physics Letters*, 16(4). (There is not any "instant" in time, nor is time a physical reality. Solution to Xeno's paradox. There is no "present moment" or determined relative position.)

Lyotard, F. (1984). *The Postmodern Condition*. Minneapolis: University of Minnesota Press.

MacCulloch, D. 2004. *The Reformation: A History*. New York: Viking Adult. (Calvinistic doctrine vs. Catholic Church.)

Macdonald, B. 2007. "Uncivil War." *Philadelphia Trumpet*, June. (U. S. paralyzed by political division and continuous conflict into a "house divided against itself," as stated by Abraham Lincoln.)

MacDonald, H. 2000. *The Burden of Bad Ideas: How Modern Intellectuals Misshape Society*. Chicago: Ivan R. Dee, Publisher

MacEachern, D. 2007. "Social Work School Breeding Relativists; Political Ideology Clouding educational Purpose." *Arizona Republic*, 23 September. (To get approved, colleges have to teach left-wing socialist/relativist political indoctrination.)

———. "Socialist Bent Taints Higher Education." *Arizona Republic*, 12 August. (Indoctrination of teachers by Far Left ideology as "social justice" now routine instead of a liberal arts education. Socialist dogma prevails.)

———. 2007. "Silencing Muslim Moderates." *Arizona Republic*, 10 April. (PBS drops documentary that views conflict between moderate and extremist Muslims as fundamentalist "Nation of Islam" threatens to sue.)

MacIntyre, A. 1981. *After Virtue: A Study in Moral Theory*. Notre Dame, IN: University of Notre Dame Press.

Mackay, C. [1841] 2003. *Extraordinary Popular Delusions & the Madness of Crowds*. Hampshire, UK: Harriman House.

MacMurray, J. 1991. *The Self As Agent*. Amherst, NY: Humanity Books (Prometheus).

Macoby, M. 2007. *Narcissistic Leaders: Who Succeeds and Who Fails*. Boston: Harvard Business School Press. (Applies only to business, not politics.)

Malach, R. 2006. "Perception Without a Perceiver." *Journal of Consciousness Studies* 13:9. (Neurological substrates.)

Malkin, M. 2006. "2006: Year of Perpetual Outrage." *Human Events*, 25 December. ('Religion of Peace' riots around the globe.)

———. 2006. "The Reuterization of War Journalism." *Human Events*, 14 August. (Media bias.)

Manji, I. 2007. "Thinking Does Not Negate Islamic Faith." *Arizona Republic*, 15 April. (She lives her life behind bulletproof doors and windows because of threats for speaking out for a moderate, rational position.)

———. "Bringing Islam into Today's World." *CNN*: Glenn Beck Show, 9 February.

———. 2005. *The Trouble with Islam Today: A Muslim's Call for Reform in Her Faith*. New York: St. Martin's Griffin. (Attempts to reform Islam to peacefulness have resulted in her being labeled as a heretic. She also authored the documentary Faith without Fear.)

Mansfield, H. 2007. "Atheist Tracts." *Weekly Standard*, 13 August. (Atheism fashionable as in eighteenth century France.)

———. 2006. "Democracy and Greatness." *Weekly Standard*, 11 December. (The value of excellence and dignity.)

Marcuse, H. 1996. *Eros and Civilization: A Philosophical Inquiry into Freud*. Boston: Beacon Press.

———. 1972. *Counterrevolution and Revolt*. Boston: Beacon Press.

———. 1964. *One Dimensional Man: Studies in the Ideology of Advanced Industrial Society*. Boston: Beacon Press.

Marzeles, L. F. 2007. *Life for the Reality Impaired*. Sedona, AZ: Purpose Publications.

Matthew, R. J. 2001. *The True Path: Western Science and the Quest for Yoga*. New York: Perseus Publishing. (Spirituality shifts brain dominance. Correlation of advanced physics with Vedas and Vedanta.)

Matthews, V., et al. 2006. "Short-term Effects of Violent Video Games: An MRI Study." *Medical News Today*, 29 November.

McLean, B. 2006. "The Power of Philanthropy." *Fortune*, 18 September.

McGowan, W. 2001. *Coloring the News: How Crusading for Diversity Has Corrupted American Journalism*. San Francisco: Encounter Books.

McGrath, A. 2006. "Breaking the Meme Fallacy." *Science and Theology News*, May. (Atheism of Dawkins and Dennett based on irrational meme of 'atheism', including Feuerbach, Crick, Watson, Marx, and Freud.)

Medina, J. J. 2007. "Mirroring in the Human Brain." *Psychiatric News*. September. (Empathy hardwired in brain neurons even in primates such as monkeys: sociological importance.)

———. 2007. "Functional MRI as a Lie Detector." *Psychiatric Times* 24:5, April. (Brain imagery reflects truthfulness.)

———. 2006. "Attention States." *Psychiatric Times*, July.

Meese, E., M. Spalding, and D. Forte. 2005. The Heritage Guide to the Constitution. Washington, DC: Regnery Publishing.

Mehlman, J. D. 1997. "Uncertainties in Projections of Human-Caused

Global Warming." *Science* 2278, 1416-17. 21 November.

Meier, B. 1998. "Judge Voids Study Linking Cancer to Secondhand Smoke." *New York Times*, 20 July.

Mekransky, J. 2007. "Love is All Around." *Tricycle*, Fall. (Recognition that love prevails and is often merely unrecognized.)

Merney, M. 204. "Experience Alterations in Gene Expression: Impact of Early Experience on Emotional Functioning." Dharamsala, India: *Mind and Life Institute*. 18-22 October. (Nature-nurture balance.)

Menezes, J. L. 1912. *The Life and Religion of Muhammad*. Harrison, NY: Roman Catholic books.

Merrill, T. W. 2006. "The Village Atheist: Daniel Dennett's Answers Avoid the Big Question." *Weekly Standard*, 21 August. (Dennett proposes professorial activism to destroy faith, spirituality, and religion.)

Merton, T. (1961) 1986. *Mystics and Zen Masters*. New York: Farrar Straus Giroux; Reissue.

Metzinger, T. 2000. *Neural Correlates of Consciousness: Empirical and Conceptual Questions*. Cambridge: MIT press.

Metzinger, T., ed. 1996. *Conscious Experience*. Exeter, UK: Schoningh: Imprint Academic.

Midgely, M. (1985) 2002. *Evolution as a Religion*. New York: Routledge.

———. 1993. *The Myths We Live By*. New York: Routledge.

Midkiff, T. 2008. "Preacher Thanks God for Evolution." *Sedona Red Rock News*, 31 January. (Rev. Michael Dowd, author of *Thank God for Evolution*, speaks nationally on Evolutionary Theology to resolve creationist-vs.-evolutionist controversy.)

Mikulus, W. 2007. "Buddhism and Western Psychology." *Journal of Consciousness Studies* 14:4, 4-49.

Mileson, K. 2006. *Our Energetic Evolution in Healing*. Steamboat Springs, CO: Energetics Research Publishers. (Includes basics of chakra energy system.)

Milgram, S. 2004. "The Perils of Obedience." http://home.swbill.not/ravseat/ perilsofobedience.html.

———. 1974. *Obedience to Authority*. New York: HarperCollins.

Miller, K. R. 2000. *Finding Darwin's God: A Scientist's Search for Common Ground Between God and Evolution*. New York: Cliff Street

Montini, E.. 2007. "From the Square Root of Our Free Speech." *Arizona Republic*, 17 May. (Professor censured for promulgating conservative opinions.)

Moaveni, A. 2007. "Intimidation in Tehran." *Time*, 20 September. (Resurgence of repression of women.)

Moran, M. 2007. "Schizophrenia Scientist Comes Full Circle." *Psychiatric News*, 15 June. (The brain creates its own reality.)

———. 2004. "Secrets of the Social Brain." *Psychiatric News*, July. (Maternal/social behavior releases oxytocin to the brain.)

Morgante, M. 2004. "DNA Co-Discoverer Dies." *Arizona Republic*, 30 July. (Scientific importance of Francis Crick.)

Morley, R. 2007. "The United Welfare States of America." *Philadelphia Trumpet*, October. (Big social welfare government is now a "big Mother Hen" nurturing 40-year-old children.)

———. "Return of the Slave Trade." *Philadelphia Trumpet*, April. (Globalization's downside.)

Morningstar, C. 1993. "How to Deconstruct Anything-My Postmodern Adventure." http://www.info.ucl.ac.be/~pvr/decon.html.

Mosly, I., ed. 2000. *Dumbing Down: Culture, Politics, and the Mass Media*. Exeter, UK: Imprint Academic.

Moyers, B. 2006. "On Faith and Reason." *PBS-TV*, 25 June.

Muhaiyaddeen, M. 2001. *The Resonance of Allah*. Philadelphia: The Fellowship Press. (Exploration of the Koran by a Sufi Sheikh.)

"Muhammed." 1986. *Encyclopedia Britannica*. Chicago, IL.

Muktananda, S. 1979. *Kundalini: The Secret of Life*. New York: Syda Foundation.

Muller, R. 2006. "Willing Paranoid Delusions." *Psychiatric Times*, December. (Delusional systems are psychologically self-serving.)

Murakami, K. 2004. "Laughter Regulates Blood Glucose Levels and Gene Expression." Dharamsala, India: *Mind and Life Institute*. 18-22 October.

"Muslim Protest Group Threatens to Shoot Anyone Who Accuses Them of Being Violent." 2006. *Fox News*, 12 December.

"Muslims in America." 2007. *Week*, 8 June. (100,000 Muslims in U.S. justify violence. They are 5% of the 2.35 million Muslims in the U.S.)

Nadean, R. and M. Kafatos. 2003. *The Nonlocal Universe:The New Physics and Matters of the Mind*. London: Oxford University Press.

Napolitano, A. 2006. *The Constitution in Exile: How the Federal Government Has Seized Power by Rewriting the Supreme Law of the Land*. Nashville, TN: Nelson Current

Nash, R. H. 1992. *Word of God and Mind of Men: Crisis of Revealed Truth in Contemporary Theology*. Phillipsburg, NJ: Presbyterian and Reformed Publishing Co.

Nasrin, T. 1997. "The Problem is not Islamic Fundamentalism but Islam Itself.: *Fri Tanke* No. 6, 22 October (Norwegian journal) via www.roiorgbooks/foxch24.htm 12/28)

Nelso, G. 2006. "Time Mag 'Person of the Year' is You!" *Arizona Republic*, 21 December. (Postmodern era narcissism and confusion about truth or values.)

Netanyahu, B. 2006. *CNN*: Glenn Beck Show, 23 November. Interview. (President of Iran plans nuclear apocalyptic disaster to precipitate the approval of the 12th Imam, the "mahdi" savior.)

Newberg, A. and M. Waldman. 2006. *Why We Believe What We Believe*. New York: Free Press. (Brain physiology.)

Newman, J. and A. A. Grace. 1999. "Binding across Time: The Selective Gating of Frontal and Hippocampal Systems Modulating Working Memory and Attentional States." *Consciousness and Cognition* 8:2, June, 196-212.

"New Wars of Religion, The." 2007. (Editorial) *Economist*, 3 November. (Major section on impact of religion and politics worldwide.)

Nilus, S., V. Marsdent, trans. [1897] 1997. *The Protocols of the Learned Elders of Zion*. (Available through http://www.amazon.com

Nolan, K. and C. Miday. 2006. "Secondhand Smoke Dangers and Risks Emphasized." *Arizona Republic*, 28 June.

Nor, M. S. 2006. "Nun Who Helped Sick Killed in Somalia." Associated Press. 18 September.

Novak, M. and J. Novak. 2006. *Washington's God*. New York: Basic Books.

Nowicki, D. 2006. "Snobsdale in Prime Time." *Arizona Republic*, 15 June. (TV show, "Tuesday Night Book Club," described by *Winnipeg Sun* as "Manipulative, phony, and despicable.")

Oakley, D.A., ed. 1985. *Brain and Mind*. New York: Methuen.

Obsession of the Threat of Radical Islam. 2006. *Fox News*, 4 October. (Documentary.)

O'Kelly, G. 2005. *Chasing Daylight.* New York: McGraw-Hill.

Olasky, M. and J. Perry. 2005. *Monkey Business: The True Story of the Scopes Trial.* Nashville, TN: Broadman and Holman.

O'Murchu, D. 1997. *Quantum Theology: Spiritual Implications of the New Physics.* National Book Network.

Oreido, L. 2006. "Is Christian Theology Suited to Enter the Discussion between Science and Humanism?" *Zygon* 11:4.

O'Reilly, B. 2006. *Culture Warrior.* New York: Broadway Books.

———. 2006. "The public information system has broken down; any rumor is reported with no basis in fact or truth." *O'Reilly Factor.* Fox News. (All media now discredited as well as the Internet.)

Orem, W. 2006. "Panspermia: Life from the Sky." *Science and Theology News*, May. (Earthly life began four billion years ago, but life pre-existed on earth.)

Organization for Economic Co-operation and Development (OECD). 2006. (U.S. Aid as compared to foreign countries.) http://www.oecd.org/

Orloff, J. 2004. *Positive Energy.* New York: Harmony Books (Random House).

Orwell, G. 1949. *1984.* London: Secker and Warburg.

Osario, S. 2007. "Fashion Victims." *CNN*: Glenn Beck Show, 29 March. (President of NOW deplores media sensationalism of gruesome murder scenes of scantily clad seductive women.)

O'Sullivan, J. 2006. *The President, The Pope, and the Prime Minister: Three Who Changed the World.* Washington, DC: Regnery.

Paniewozik, J. 2007. "The End of Fairy Tales?" *Time*, 21 May. (Postmodernism revision of intrinsic morality of classic children's stories.)

Parker, K. 2007. "U. S. Media goes Stark-Raving Tabloid." *Washington Post Writers Group*, 23 December. (Malevolence and unprovoked cruelty now commonplace.)

———. 2007. "A Different Kind of Rape." *Washington Post Writers Group*, 21 June. (Totalitarian politically correct groupthink is destroying America's institutions of higher learning, e.g., Duke University example: 58 professors' false accusation declaration still not retracted.)

———. 2007. "If This Is Evolutionary, We Still Have a Ways to Go." *Washington Post Writers Group*, 13 May. (Debate now politicized so know-nothings add their worthless two cents' worth to the debate.)

———. 2006. "Chavez's Wacky Ranting . . ." *Tribune Media Services/ Arizona Republic*.(118-member meeting of nonaligned movement with Castro.)

———. 2006. "Faith-Based Conspiracies." *Tribune Media Services/ Arizona Republic*, 9 August. (Religionist extremism.)

Paterik. S."U.S. Image Overseas May Sink Terrorism." *Arizona Republic*, 14 June.

Pauchant, T., ed. *Ethics and Spirituality at Work: Hopes and Pitfalls of the Search for Meaning in Organizations*. Westport, CT: Quorum Books.

Peck, M. S. 1983. *People of the Lie*. New York: Simon and Schuster. (Basis of evil is narcissism.)

Penrose, R. 1997. *The Large, the Small, and the Human Mind*. Cambridge: Cambridge University Press.

———. 1994. *Shadows of the Mind: A Search for the Missing Science of Consciousness*. New York: Oxford University Press.

———. 1989. *The Emperor's New Mind: Concerning Computers, Minds, and the Laws of Physics*. New York: Oxford University Press.

Peres, J. 2007. "Study: Brains of Liberals, Conservatives Work Differently." *Chicago Tribune*, 10 September. (Psychologist at New York University found difference in response of anterior cingulated gyrus.)

Perllis, R. H., C. S. Perlis, et al. 2005. "Industry Sponsorship and Conflict of Interest." *American Journal of Psychology* 162, 1957-60.

Peters, K. 2007. "Towards an Evolutionary Christian Theology." *Zygon* 42:1, March.

Peters, R. 2007. *Wars of Blood and Faith: The Conflicts That Will Shape the 21st Century*. Mechanicsburg, PA: Stackpole Books.

Peters, R. 2007. "Apathy Threatens U.S. Way of Life." *Arizona Republic*, 16 January.

Peters, R. 2006. "Jaded Journalism." *American Legion*, October. (U. S. media self-admitted leftist bias.)

Peterson, G. "Theology and Science Wars: Who Owns Human Nature?"

Zygon 11:4, December, 853-862.

Petitmangin, C. 2007. "Toward the Source of Thoughts." *Journal of Consciousness Studies* 14:3, 54-82. (Preconceptual "fringe" of awareness and source of subjective experience/awareness.)

Petras, R. 2006. "Visualize (and mentally rehearse) Success." *Arizona Republic*, 11 June.

"Philanthropic Research." 2006. *Wikipedia*. www.wikipedia.com.

Phillips, M. 2006. *Londonistan*. New York: Encounter Books.

Pinker, S. 2007. "The Mystery of Consciousness." *Time*, 29 January. (Neurophysiology and materialistic speculation; misidentifies (nonlinear) consciousness with linear content of consciousness [cal. 205].)

Pine, R., trans. 2002. *The Diamond Sutra: The Perfection of Wisdom*. New York: Perseus/Counterpoint Press.

Pipes, D. 2003 (2nd ed.) *The Rushdie Affair: The Novel, the Ayatollah, and the West*. Piscataway, NJ: Transaction Publishers.

Pitts, L. 2007. "Hollywood is (fill in the blank)." *Tribune Media Services*, 13 May. (Despite its ultra-liberal image, the business side of the movie industry is run by profit motive.)

———. 2006. "9/11? Oops! No such thing." *Tribune Media Services*, 17 September. (Media now report delusional fallacies as though they were factual news.)

———. 2004. "Facts? We don't need no stinkin' facts." *Tribune Media Services*, 29 December. (Because of media bias, whole segments of society live in an "alternate reality.")

Plato. 2004. "*Theaetutus*." London: Penguin Books.

Plum, F. 1991. "Coma and Related Global Disturbances of the Human Conscious State." In Jones, E. and P. Peters (eds.) *Cerebral Cortex*, Vol. 9. New York: Plenum Press.

"Politics of Global Warming, The." (Editor). 2007. *Philadelphia Trumpet*, April.

Polkinghorne, J. 2006. "Space, Time, and Causality." *Zygon* 41:4, December, 975-984.

———. 2005. "The Continuing Interaction of Science and Religion." *Zygon* 40:1.

Poniewozik, R. 2007. "The End of Fairy Tales?" *Time*, 21 May.

(Postmodernism revision of intrinsic morality of classic children's stories.)

Principe, L. 2007. "Science and Religion," Lecture series, *The Great Courses*. Chantilly, VA: The Teaching Co.

Popper, K. R. and J. C. Eccles. 1983. *The Self and the Brain*. London: Routledge.

Powell, R. 1996. *Dialogues on Reality*. San Diego: Blue Dove Press.

Puhakka, K. 1999. "Form and Formless in Spiritual Practice." Esalen Center Conference 28 Nov. - 2 Dec.

Pyle, R. 2006. "N.Y. Subway Threat Was Real, Says Senator Chas. Schumer." Associated Press, 19 June.

"Radicals vs. Moderates: British Muslims at Crossroads." 2007. *CNN World News*, 18 January.

Rather, D. 2007. "Media Owns Dumbing Down." *Fox News*, 11 June. (By using sexpots and gossip instead of significant news: catering to sensationalism/glamour instead of responsible integrity.)

Ratzinger, J. (Pope Benedict XVI). 2007. *Jesus of Nazareth: From the Baptism in the Jordan to the Transfiguration*. New York: Doubleday. (Relationship with God is through mystical faith rather than just the authority of the Church.)

Rauchi, G. A. 1971. *Contemporary Philosophical Alternatives and The Crises of Truth*. New York: Nijhoff Publishers.

Ravitch. D. 2003. *The Language Police*. New York: Knopf.

Rawls, T. 2007. "Boycott Honors Freedom." *Arizona Republic*, 31 January. (Dissent is highest form of patriotism.)

Regenerus, M. 2007. *Forbidden Fruit: Sex and Religion in the Lives of American Teenagers*. New York: Oxford University Press.

Reinbert, S. 2006. "Survey Finds Faith a Boon in Living to be 100." *Arizona Republic*, 16 August.

"Researching Philanthropy - Top 100 US Foundations by Total Giving." 2006. *The Foundation Center*. http://www.case.edu/artsci/funding/resources/ basics/documents/top_fdns_US.pdf

Richmond, R. 1979. Personal communication.

Rimbach, D. 2004. "Doctors Recognize Faith's Role in Recovery." *Science and Theology News*, July/August.

Rippe, D. 2007. "Unraveling the Secret." *Shift*, June. (Hermetic tradition/understanding consciousness.)

Robb, R. 2007. "Where to, Lady Liberty?" *Arizona Republic*, 19 January. (Freedom House Study: Civil liberty based on economic freedom, not just politics.)

Rodwell, J., trans. [1909] Republished 2001. *The Koran*. North Clarendon, VT: Tuttle Publishing. (Includes 114 Sura.)

Rorty, R. 1990. *Objectivity, Relativism, and Truth: Philosophical Papers*. New York: Cambridge University Press.

Rose, D. 2006. *Consciousness: Philosophical, Psychological, and Neural Theories*. New York: Oxford University Press. (Academic review.)

Rose, G. 2001. *When You Reach the End of Your Rope...Let Go*. Los Angeles: Awareness Press. ("O-Ring" muscle-test method.)

Rosedo, C. "From Fragmentation to Wholeness: Quantum Physics and Urban Ministry." Philadelphia, Penn.: Dept. of Urban Studies, Eastern University. www.rosado.net/pdf/QP_Urban_Ministry.pdf

Rosenbaum, R. 2007. "Turning Yoga into New-Age Mumbo Jumbo." *Week*, 6 April. (Commercialization of spiritual practices.)

Rosenblum, B. and F. Kuttner. 2007. *Quantum Enigma: Physics Encounters Consciousness*. New York: Oxford University Press. (Without an observer, no universe exists.

Rosenfield, I. 1993. *The Strange, Familiar, and Forgotten: An Anatomy of Consciousness*. New York: Vintage.

Rothstein, E. 2007. "Creation Museum." *New York Times* quoted in *Week*, 8 June. (Answers in Genesis ministry in Kentucky alleges world is only 6,000 years old.)

Roughgarden, J. 2006. *Evolution and Christian Faith: Reflections of an Evolutionary Biologist*. Washington, DC: Island Press.

Rowe, J. 2007. "The Rankings Revolt." *Time*, 2 April. (Colleges question validity of college ranking criteria [published annually by U.S. News & World Report].)

Rushdie, S. 2006. "The Threat of Islam: Personal Experience." *CNN*: Glenn Beck Show, 11 October. Interview. (Leader of Iran hopes to precipitate apocalyptic scenario to bring about return of the 12th Iman, the Mahdi.)

———. 1989. *The Satanic Verses*. New York: Viking.

Russ, H. 1989. *The Fingerprint of God: Recent Scientific Discoveries*

Reveal the Unmistaken Identity of the Creator. New Kensington, Pa.: Whitaker House.

Rutten, T. 2007. "Will Anyone Stand Up to the Islamists?" *Los Angeles Times* quoted in *Week*: "Best Columns of the U.S.," 6-13 July. (Salmon Rushdie knighting Jihad brought no defense from Western writers who bizarrely view disapproval of Islamic violence as perhaps "insensitive" but which is actually moral cowardice.)

Sebanz, N. 2007. "The Emergence of Self." *Journal of Consciousness Studies* 14:1-2, 234-251. (Sense of self as causal agent.)

Sadleir, S. 2004. *Self-Realization*. Laguna Beach, CA: Self-Awareness Institute.

———. 2000. *Looking for God: A Searcher's Guide to Religious and Spiritual Groups of the World*. New York: Perigee Trade.

Sagan, C. 2006. *The Varieties of Scientific Experience: A Personal View of the Search for God*. New York: Penguin Press HC.

Salzberg, S. 2006. "I Feel Your Brain." (Interview with Daniel Goleman). Tricycle, Winter edition. (Reviews basic concepts of social intelligence, mirror neurons, and brain hand-wired for empathy.)

Sannella, L. 1987. *The Kundalini Experience: Psychosis or Transcendence*. Lower Lake, CA: Integral Publishing.

Saraswati, Swami Dayananda. 1875. *Wahi: The Supernatural Basis of Islam*. Not in print. (Discusses trance state of Wahi.)

Schacter, D. L. 1998. "Memory and Awareness. *Science* 280, 59-60.

Scheuer, M. 2007. *Through Our Enemies' Eyes: Osama bin Laden, Radical Islam, and the Future of America*. Rev. Ed. Dulles, VA: Potomac Books.

———. 2004. *Impersonal Hubris: Why the West Is Losing the War on Terror*. Dulles, VA: Potomac Books. Previously published anonymously in 2002 as *Through Our Enemies' Eyes: Osama bin Laden, Radical Islam, and the Future of America* (revised). (Former head of the CIA's bin Laden unit tries to clarify basis of mutual misunderstanding by U. S. and militant Islam.)

Schmidt, T., and L. Cullen. 2006. "Today's nun has a veil - and a blog." *Time*, 20 November. (Not satisfied with current culture of sex, money and freedom, young women increasingly turning to religious vocation.)

Schmitt, G. 2007. "Pax Americana: A Debate on the Wisdom of Global Primacy. *Weekly Standard*, 12 March. (Review of A Debate by C.

Layma and T. Thayer on American hegemony, pro and con.)

Schorow, S. 2006. "In the Beginning Was the Bible." *Science and Theology News*, May. (Importance of knowledge of the Bible to understand society from law to literature, sociology, education, and history.)

Schroeder, G. L. 1997. *The Science of God: The Convergence of Scientific and Biblical Wisdom*. New York: Free Press.

Schwartz, L. 2006. "Intelligent Evolution." *Shift*, June-August.

Scott, A. 2004. "Reductionism Revisited." *Journal of Consciousness Studies* 11:2. (Nonlinear science.)

Searle, J. R. 2004. *Mind: A Brief Introduction*. New York: Oxford University Press.

———. 1992. *The Rediscovery of the Mind*. Cambridge: MIT Press.

———. 1990. *The Mystery of Consciousness*. New York: New York Review Books.

Sears, A. and C. Osten. 2005. *The ACLU vs. America: Exposing the Agenda to Redefine Moral Values*. Nashville, TN: B and H Publishing Group.

Seewald, P., ed. 2006. *Pope Benedict XVI: Servant of the Truth*. Fort Collins, CO: Ignatius Press.

Shapiro, B. 2004. *Brainwashed: How Universities Indoctrinate America's Youth*. Nashville, TN: WND Books/Cumberland House Publishing.

Shea, N. and J. Hoffman. 2006. "Teach Your Children Well." *Weekly Standard* 11:45, 14 August. (Arabic promulgation of the hate propaganda of the infamous *Protocols of the Learned Elders of Zion*, including systematic indoctrination of children.)

Shelar, J. 2004. "The Power of Prayer." *Newsweek*. 22 November. (Prayer as native to the human mind.)

Sheldrake, R. 2004. "Morphic Fields." *Shift*, December 2004 to February 2005.

———. 1982. *A New Science of Life*. Los Angeles: J. P. Tarcher.

———. 1981. "Formative Causation" *Brain-Mind Bulletin* 6, 3 August.

———. 1981. Essay in *New Scientist* 90, 18 June.

Siegel, B. 1986. *Love, Medicine and Miracles: Lessons Learned about Self-Healing from a Surgeon's Experience with Exceptional Patients*. New York: Harper

Smart, J. J. C. 2004. "Consciousness and Awareness." *Journal of*

Consciousness Studies 11:2, 41-50.

———. 1980. "Time and Becoming." *Time and Cause*, n.d.

Smith, C. 2006. "Tax Benefits and Abuses of Having Church Status." http://www.rothgerber.com/newslettersarticles/ff026.asp (Fourteen necessary requirements and factors.)

Smith, S. 2006. "Perception is Reality." *Fox News*, 15 August. (Middle-east news; Muhammad year 269 attack on Jews.)

Smoley, R. 2002. *Inner Christianity: A Guide to the Esoteric Tradition*. Boston: Shambhala.

Somers, H. 1992. *Een Andere Mohammed*. Antwerp: Hadewijch.

Sowell, T. 2007. "Today's Lesson: Keep Your Cool." *Creators Syndicate*, 4 September. (Dumbed-down education has resulted in people ready to vent emotions and parrot slogans but unable to utilize reason or logic.)

———. 2006. "Political Messiahs Spread the Word." *Arizona Republic*, 21 December. (Politics now the new religion and savior of man.)

Spencer, R. 2007. "Islamic Supremacism in Britain." *Human Events*, 29 January. Advocates Sharia law and suppression of women.)

———. 2007. "Pakistan Bans the Truth." *Human Events*, 15 January. (The Truth about Muhammad banned even though based on all Islamic sources.)

———. 2006. *The Truth about Muhammad*. Washington, DC: Regnery Publishing.

———. 2006. "Deck the Infidels." *Human Events*, 25 December. (Worldwide Jihadism.)

———. 2006. "Why Khaybar Should Concern the West." *Human Events*, 14 August.

———. 2005. *The Myth of Islamic Tolerance*. Amherst, NY: Prometheus Books.

Spong, J. S. 2005. *The Sins of Scripture: Exposing the Bible's Texts of Hate to Reveal the God of Love*. San Francisco: HarperSanFrancisco.

Sraves, L. 2004. "New Ways to Know God." *Science and Theology News*, July/August.

Stacknev, S. 2006. "Arizona Bar Works to Boost Diversity in Workplace." *Arizona Republic*, 15 June. (Social engineering by race, sex, etc.)

Stapp, H. 2007. *Mindful Universe: Quantum Mechanics and the Participating Observer.* New York: Springer-Verlag Publishing.

———. 2006. "Science's Conception of Human Beings as a Basis for Moral Theory." *Zygon* 41:3, September.

———. 2004. "Quantum Physics and the Psycho-physical Nature of the Universe." Esalen Institutional Conference and Survival of Bodily Death, 2-7 May. (Prakriti is secondary to Purusha and is in accord with quantum physics theory.)

———. 2001. "Quantum Theory and the Role of Mind in Nature." *Foundational Physics* 31, 1465-99.

www-physics.lbl.gov/~stapp/vnr.pdf

———. 1999. "Attention, Intention, and Will in Quantum Physics." *Journal of Consciousness Studies* 6 (8-9), 143-164.

Stapp, H. and D. Bourget. 2004. "Quantum Leaps in Philosophy of Mind." *Journal of Consciousness Studies* 11:12, December.

Stark, M. 2006. "Neurotransmitters: Pharmacology and Synergy." *Psychiatric Times*, 23:12. October.

Starke, W. 2007. "The Digital Generation." *Unity*, September-October. (Substitution of virtual reality for direct experience results in symbolizations.)

Steenbrink, K., trans. 2006. *Dutch Colonialism and Indonesian Islam: Contacts and Conflicts 1596-1950.* 2nd Rev. Ed. Amsterdam: Editions Rodopi BV

Steinhauer, S. R. 2006. "Pupillary Response: Cognitive Psychophysiology and Psychopathology." Pittsburgh, PA: University of Pittsburgh School of Medicine. (Extensive references.)

Stenger, V. 2007. *God: The Failed Hypothesis. How Science Shows That God Does Not Exist.* Amherst, NY: Prometheus Books.

Stennard, F. 2006. "Experimenting with the Divine." *Science and Theology News*, May.

Stern, S. 2007. "Radical Math at the DoE." *City Journal*, 11 May. ("Radical Math," a new avenue for Marxist indoctrination of grade-school students…to "current social injustice," etc.)

Stewart, J. 2007. "The Future Evolution of Consciousness." *Journal of Consciousness Studies* 14:8, 58-92. ("Global Workplace Theory" embraces adaptation as focus.)

Steyn, M. 2006. *America Alone: The End of the World as We Know It*. Washington, DC: Regnery. (Collapse of Western civilization due to internal collapse of will.)

Stoeger, W. R. and G. B. Coyne, Eds. 1993. *Quantum Cosmology and the Laws of Nature: Scientific Perspectives on Divine Action*. Notre Dame, IN: University of Notre Dame Press.

Stossel, J. *Myths, Lies, and Downright Stupidity: Get Out the Shovel-Why Everything You Know is Wrong*. New York: Hyperion. (Media influence.)

Stove, D. and R. Kimball. 2006. *Darwinian Fairytales: Selfish Genes, Errors of Heredity and Other Fables of Evolution*. New York: Encounter Books; Reprint edition.

Sturme, D. 2007. "Person or Subject?" *Journal of Consciousness Studies* 14, No. 5-6, pp. 77-100. ("I am," "I exist" are only statements that are beyond doubt. Issue on personhood.)

"Sword of Islam, The." 2007. http://www. www.masada2000.org/islam.html; http://www.strategypage.com/the_war_in_iraq/

Sullivan, A. 2006. *The Conservative Soul: How We Lost It, How to Get It Back*. New York: HarperCollins.

———. 2006. "When Not Seeing Is Believing." *Time*, 9 October. (The value as well as the downside of radical religious faith.)

Sultaw, W. 2006. "We are Hostages to Our Own Religion." Danish TV DR 2 via Y Net News.com, 6 October.

———. 2005. "L. A. Psychologist Clashes with Algerian Jihadist over Islamic Teachings and Terrorism." *Front Page*, 30 July. Aired on al-Jazeera TV, 26 July. (Basic incompatibility of Islam and the Western world.)

"Survey of Young People." 2007. Associated Press on *MTV*. (Shows friends and family are most associated with happiness; money ranked much lower.)

Svebak, S. 2007. "Sense of Humor Results in People Living Longer, including Patients with Cancer." *American Psychosomatic Society*. Budapest, March. (Study of 54,000 Norwegians.)

Swarup, R. 1993. *Hindu View of Christianity and Islam*, 107. New Delhi: Voice of India.

Swineburne, T. 2006. "Return to Sender." *Science and Theology News*, May. (Efficacy of healing by prayer versus Divine Will, and benefits of sickness and suffering.)

Szegedy-Maszak, M. 2004. "How We Talk to God." *Newsweek*, 20 November. (Scientific study of prayer and healing.)

Talbot, M. 1992. *Holographic Universe*. New York: Harper Perennial.

Targ, R. and J. Katra 2003. "Close to Grace: The Physics of Silent Transmission." *Spirituality & Health*, July/August.

Templeton, J. H. 1981. *The Humble Approach: Scientists Discover God*. (Rev. ed.) W. Conshohocken, PA: Templeton Foundation Press.

Templeton, J. H., and R. Dunlap. 2003. *Why Are We Created?* W. Conshohocken, PA: Templeton Foundation Press.

Theise, N.D. 2006. "From Bottom Up." *Tricycle*, Summer. (Emergence and complexity theory.)

Thomas, C. 2007. "Dodging a Bullet at [Fort] Dix." *Los Angeles Times Syndicate*, 10 May. ("Political Correctness" opens door to Jihadists.)

———. 2007. "Shameless Pursuit of Voter Disgraces Both Parties." *Los Angeles Times Syndicate*. 6 February. (Nonintegrity of politics.)

———. 2006. "Violence Breeds Violence." *Los Angeles Times Syndicate/Arizona Republic*, 13 October. (Violence celebrated worldwide by media.)

———. 2006. "Scandal? Can't even Spell It." *Los Angeles Times Syndicate/ Arizona Republic*. (Morality under attack from philosophy of relativism.)

———. 2006. "Radical War, Radical Rules." *Los Angeles Times Syndicate/ Arizona Republic*, 15 August. (Euphemisms versus facts.)

———. 2006. "Spin distorts truth of moving incident." *Los Angeles Times Syndicate/Arizona Republic*, 6 June

———. 2006. "The Death of Ideology." *Los Angeles Times Syndicate/ Arizona Republic*, 23 May. (Dearth of Scopes Trial legal database.)

Thompson, C. 2007. "Hokum and Looney Snake Unwary on Internet." *Arizona Republic*, 3 January. (Fallacious memos and stories abound.)

Thompson, D. F. 1993. "Understanding Financial Conflict of Interest in Research." *New England Journal of Medicine* 329, 573-6.

Thompson, E. 2004. "Neuroplasticity and Neurophenomenology." Dharamsala, India: *Mind and Life Institute*. 18-22 October. (Necessity for first-person subjective experiential reports.)

Thornhill, R. and C. Fincker. 2007. "Evolution and Human Behavior." *Arizona Republic*, 22 May. (Effect of childhood rearing on political preferences and character traits. Conservatives had happier, more secure childhoods.)

Tiebout, H. 1999. *Collected Papers*. Center City, MN: Hazelden Foundation. (Includes "Surrender vs. Compliance" and "The Act of Surrender.")

Tisdale, S. J. 2006. "Beloved Community." *Tricycle*, Fall.

Tong, V. 2007. "Americans give record $295 billion for charity." Associated Press, 25 June. (America most generous nation in the world.)

Tooley, M. 2006. "God's Left Hand." *Weekly Standard*, 13 November.

Towles, E. 2006. "Prop. 201 Facts Do Not Add Up." *Arizona Republic*, 9 October. (Scientific refutation of supposed dangers of secondhand smoke.)

Trivers, R. 1985. *Social Evolution*. Menlo Park, NY: Benjamin-Cummings Publishing Co.

Underhill, E. 1986. *Practical Mysticism*. Columbus, OH: Ariel Press.

"Use of 'CE' and BCE' to Identify Dates, The." 2005 Religious Tolerance Organization. May. http//www.bbc.co.uk.

Ushen, R., and R. Edwards. 1994. *Postmodernism and Education*. London: Routledge.

Vadum, M. 2006. "Terrorists Legal Team." *Human Events*, 2 October. (Record of Center For Constitutional Rights [CCCR] pro-Communism and Islamo-fascism.)

Valdez, L. 2006. "Religion is a Good Thing Up to a Point." *Arizona Republic*, 26 November. (Social protest regarding religious garb exhibitionism.)

Valencia, G. 2007. "A Difficult Subject on Campus." (Essay on decline of the Harvard Law School from the Socratic method to biased politicalization, submitted to Yavapai College, Cottonwood, Arizona.)

———. 2007. Coined the term "media terrorists" to describe far-left hate web sites and political organizations.

Van Biema, D. 2007. "Her Agony." *Time*, 3 September. (The hidden value of doubt - Mother Teresa.)

———. 2007. "The Pope's Favorite Rabbi." *Time*, 4 June. (Dialog between Pope and Jacob Neusner re Judaism and Christianity.)

———. 2007. "The Case for Teaching the Bible." *Time*, 2 April. (Important subject for literacy and education.)

———. 2007. "Blunt Bishop." *Time*, 19 February. (Anglican Church split over liberalism; Nigerian bishop Patel Akinola rejects liberal "sins."

Van Biema, D. 2006. "God vs. Science." Time, 13 November.

Van Biema, D. and C. Mayer. 2007. "Looking for the Light." *Time*, 18 June. (Anglican Church split between liberals and conservatives. Archbishop of Canterbury seeks reconciliation.)

Van Biema, D. and J. Israely. 2006. "The Passion of the Pope." *Time*, 27 November. (Pope Benedict's visit to Turkey. Vatican vs. Islamic violence and nonrationality.)

Van Biema, D. and J. Chu. 2006. "Does God Want You to be Rich?" *Time*, 18 September.

Van Till, H. J., D. A. Young, and C. Manninga. 1988. *Science Held Hostage: What's Wrong With Creation Science and Evolutionism*. Downers Grove, IL: Intervarsity Press

"Vicious about Virtue." 2007. [Editor] *Economist*, 23-29 June. (Religious police extremism in Saudi Arabia: extreme cruelty and even death to citizens to enforce Sharia.)

Vitz, P. C. 1995. "The Psychology of Atheism." *Truth Journal*. http://www.leaderu.com/truth/1truth12.html

Vitz, P. C. and J. Gartner. 1984. "Christianity and Psychoanalysis: Part 1." *Journal of Psychology and Theology* 11, 4-18. (Jesus as the anti-Oedipus.)

———. 1984. "Christianity and Psychoanalysis: Part 2. *Journal of Psychology and Theology* 12, 82-89. (Jesus is the transformer of the superego.)

Vivekananda, S. 2003. *Complete Works of Swami Vivekananda*. (Vol. 1. "Raja Yoga, Ch. 7: "Dhyam and Samadhi.") Hollywood, CA: Vedanta Press

W. Pseud. Bill. 1998. *The Language of the Heart*. New York: AA Grapevine.

Walton, S. 1993. Personal correspondence regarding his business principles.

Warraq, I. 2002. *What the Koran Really Says: Language, Text, and Commentary*. Amherst, NY: Prometheus Books. (Scholarly, authoritative, documented, with erudite contributors - 800 pages.)

———. ed. 1998. *The Origins of the Koran: Classic Essays on Islam's Holy Book*. New York: Prometheus Books.

———. 1995. *Why I Am Not A Muslim*. New York: Prometheus Books.

(Critical analysis of Islam.)

Warren, R. 2002. *The Purpose Driven Life: What on Earth Am I Here For?* Grand Rapids, MI: Zondervan.

Watson, B., trans. 1997. *The Vimalakirti Sutra*. New York: Columbia University Press.

———. trans. 1993. *The Lotus Sutra*. New York: Columbia University Press.

Webb, G. 2006. "Circumstantial Evidence." *Science and Theology News*, July/August. (Analyzing the Scopes Trial.)

Weiser, J. 2006. "What Luther Wrought." *Weekly Standard*, 28 August. (Protestant vs. Catholic wars and counter-reformation in theology and politics.)

Weiss, S. and K. Wesley. 2006. *Postmodernism and Its Critics*. University of Alabama, Dept. of Anthropology. http://www.as.ua.edu/ant/Faculty/murphy/pomo.htm

Wells, G., et al. 2000. "From Lab to the Police Station: A Successful Application of Eyewitness Research.: *American Psychologist* 55, No. 6: 581-598.

Werss, D. 2007. "Keith Ellison: Lying to the Infidels." *Human Events*, 3 January. (Islamic law, Sharia, condemns lying to non-Muslims and negates all non-Muslim governments. Ellison claims Koran as authority and teaching negates allegiance to U. S. law.)

Westhelle, V. 2006. "Are Science and Humanism Suited to Enter the Ancient Quest of Christian Theology? *Zygon* 11:4, December, 843-852.

Wheat, R. 2007. "Beware Which Wolf You Feed." *Arizona Republic*, 20 January. Letters to Editor. (Choice between good and evil Cherokee.)

Whelen, E. 2006. "A View from the Bench." *Weekly Standard*, 4 December. (Abuse of judicial activism to bypass voters.)

Wilber, K. 2004. "The Perennial Philosophy. *Unity*. July/August.

———. 1997. *The Eye of the Spirit*. Boston: Shambhala.

Wilcox, R. 1985, 1995. *Japan's Secret War: Japan's Race Against Time to Build Its Own Atomic Bomb*. New York: Marlowe and Co.

Wilkinson, T. 2006. "Pope Makes Apology for Remarks." *Los Angeles Times*, 18 September.

Williams, B. (Archbishop). 2006. "Creationism Should Not be Taught in Schools. It is a Mistake." *Science and Theology News*, April.

Williams, G. 2007. Personal correspondence about faith in God and liberty.)

Williams, R. 2005. *Why Study The Past?: The Quest For The Historical Church*. Grand Rapids, MI: Wm. B. Eerdmans Publishing Company.

Wilson, E. 1975. *Sociobiology: The New Synthesis*. Cambridge: Harvard University Press.

Witham, L. 2003. *By Design: Science and the Search for God*. San Francisco: Encounter Books.

Woodfield, A. 1976. *Teleology*. New York: Cambridge University Press.

Wright, R. 1992. "Science, God, and Man." *Time*, 28 December.

Yost, B. 2005. "Doctors See Positive Effect of Humor on Health." *Arizona Republic*, 27 April.

Yost, B. and S. Felt. 2006. "Belief in Miracles a Matter of Faith?" *Arizona Republic*, 25 December. (2003 Harris Poll reveals 84% of Americans believe in reality of miracles.)

Young, G. 2006. "Preserving the Role of Conscious Decision Making in the Initiation of Intentional Action." *Journal of Consciousness Studies* 13:3, 51-68.

Zaslow, G. 2007. "The New 'Greatest' Generation." *Wall Street Journal*, cited in *Week*, 7:309.

Zimbardo, P. G. 2007. *The Lucifer Effect: Understanding How Good People Turn Evil*. New York: Random House. (Situational influences that turn into atrocities.)

———. 2004. "The Stockholm Syndrome." http://www.yahoodi.com/ peace/ stockholm.html.

———. 1977. *Influencing Attitudes and Changing Behavior: an Introduction to Method Theory and Applications of Social Control and Personal Power*. New York: McGraw-Hill.

Zimen, J. M. 2000. Real Science: What It Is and Means. New York: Cambridge University Press.

———. 1978. *Reliable Knowledge: An Exploration of the Grounds for Belief in Science*. New York: Cambridge University Press.

Zmirak, J. 2006. *ISI Guide to All-American Colleges: Top Schools for Conservatives, Old-Fashioned Liberals, and People of Faith*. Wilmington, DE: Intercollegiate Studies Institute.

Zoll, R. 2006. "Survey: Americans are more religiously active than thought."

Associated Press, 12 Sept. (Baylor University study.)

———. 2006. "Episcopal Church Elects First Woman Bishop." Associated Press, 19 June.

ABOUT THE AUTHOR

Biographical and Autobiographical Notes

Dr. Hawkins (1927–2012) was an internationally known spiritual teacher, author, and speaker on the subject of advanced spiritual states, consciousness research, and the Realization of the Presence of God as Self.

His published works, as well as recorded lectures, have been widely recognized as unique in that a very advanced state of spiritual awareness occurred in an individual with a scientific and clinical background who was later able to verbalize and explain the unusual phenomenon in a manner that is clear and comprehensible.

The transition from the normal ego-state of mind to its elimination by the Presence is described in the trilogy Power vs. Force (1995) which won praise even from Mother Teresa, The Eye of the I (2001), and I: Reality and Subjectivity (2003), which have been translated into the major languages of the world. Truth vs. Falsehood: How to Tell the Difference (2005), Transcending the Levels of Consciousness (2006) and Discovery of the Presence of God: Devotional Nonduality (2007) continue the exploration of the ego's expressions and inherent limitations and how to transcend them.

The importance of the initial work was given recognition by its very favorable and extensive review in *Brain/Mind Bulletin* and at later presentations such as the International Conference on Science and Consciousness. Many presentations were given to a variety of organizations, spiritual conferences, church groups,nuns, and monks, both nationally and in foreign countries, including the Oxford Forum in England. In the Far East,Dr.Hawkins was a recognized "Teacher of the Way to Enlightenment" ("Tae Ryoung Sun Kak Dosa").

In response to his observation that much spiritual truth has been misunderstood over the ages due to lack of explanation, Dr.Hawkins presented monthly seminars that provided detailed explanations which are too lengthy to describe in book format. Recordings are available that end with questions and answers, thus providing additional clarification.

The overall design of this lifetime work is to recontextualize the human experience in terms of the evolution of consciousness and to integrate a comprehension of both mind and spirit as expressions of the innate Divinity that is the substrate and ongoing source of life and Existence.This dedication is signified by the statement "*Gloria in Excelsis Deo!*" with which his published works begin and end.

Biographic Summary

Dr. Hawkins practiced psychiatry since 1952 and was a life member of the American Psychiatric Association and numerous other professional organizations. His national television appearance schedule included *The McNeil/Leher News Hour*, *The Barbara Walters Show*, *The Today Show*, science documentaries, and many others.

He was the author of numerous scientific and spiritual publications, books, CDs, DVDs, and lecture series. Nobelist Linus Pauling coauthored his landmark book, *Orthomolecular Psychiatry*. Dr. Hawkins was a consultant for many years to Episcopal and Catholic Dioceses, monastic orders, and other religions orders.

Dr. Hawkins lectured widely, with appearances at Westminster Abbey, the Universities of Argentina, Notre Dame, and Michigan; Fordham University and Harvard University; and the Oxford Forum in England. He gave the annual Landsberg Lecture at the University of California Medical School at San Francisco. He was also a consultant to foreign governments on international diplomacy and was instrumental in resolving longstanding conflicts that were major threats to world peace.

In recognition of his contributions to humanity, in 1995, Dr. Hawkins became a knight of the Sovereign Order of the Hospitaliers of St. John of Jerusalem, which was founded in 1077.

Autobiographic Note

While the truths reported in this book were scientifically derived and objectively organized, like all truths, they were first experienced personally. A lifelong sequence of intense states of awareness beginning at a young age first inspired and then gave direction to the process of subjective realization that has finally taken form in this series of books.

At age three, there occurred a sudden full consciousness of existence, a nonverbal but complete understanding of the meaning of "I Am," followed immediately by the frightening realization that "I" might not have come into existence at all. This was an instant awakening from oblivion into a conscious awareness, and in that moment, the personal self was born and the duality of "Is" and "Is Not" entered my subjective awareness.

Throughout childhood and early adolescence, the paradox of existence and the question of the reality of the self remained a repeated concern. The personal self would sometimes begin slipping back into a greater impersonal Self, and the initial fear of non-existence—the fundamental fear of nothingness—would recur.

In 1939, as a paperboy with a seventeen-mile bicycle route in rural Wisconsin, on a dark winter's night I was caught miles from home in a twenty-below-zero blizzard. The bicycle fell over on the ice and the fierce wind ripped the newspapers out of the handlebar basket, blowing them across the ice-covered, snowy field. There were tears of frustration and exhaustion and my clothes were frozen stiff. To get out of the wind, I broke through the icy crust of a high snow bank, dug out a space, and crawled into it. Soon the shivering stopped and there was a delicious warmth, and then a state of peace beyond all description. This was accompanied by a suffusion of light and a presence of infinite love that had no beginning and no end and was undifferentiated from my own essence. The physical body and surroundings faded as my awareness was fused with this all-present, illuminated state. The mind grew silent; all thought stopped. An infinite Presence was all that was or could be, beyond all time or description.

After that timelessness, there was suddenly an awareness of someone shaking my knee; then my father's anxious face appeared. There was great reluctance to return to the body and all that that entailed, but because of my father's love and anguish, the Spirit nurtured and reactivated the body. There was compassion for his fear of death, although, at the same time, the concept of death seemed absurd.

This subjective experience was not discussed with anyone since there was no context available from which to describe it. It was not common to hear of spiritual experiences other than those reported in the lives of the saints. But after this experience, the accepted reality of the world began to seem only provisional; traditional religious teachings lost significance and, paradoxically, I became an agnostic. Compared to the light of Divinity that had illuminated all existence, the god of traditional religion shone dully indeed; thus spirituality replaced religion.

During World War II, hazardous duty on a minesweeper often brought close brushes with death, but there was no fear of it. It was as though death had lost its authenticity. After the war, fascinated by the complexities of the mind and wanting to study psychiatry, I worked my way through medical school. My training psychoanalyst, a professor at Columbia University, was also an agnostic; we both took a dim view of religion. The analysis went well, as did my career, and success followed.

I did not, however, settle quietly into professional life. I fell ill with a progressive, fatal illness that did not respond to any treatments available. By age thirty-eight, I was *in extremis* and knew I was about to die. I didn't care about the body, but my spirit was in a state of extreme anguish and despair. As the final moment approached, the thought flashed through my mind, "What if there is a God?" So I called out in prayer, "If there is a God, I ask him to help me now." I surrendered to whatever God there might be and went into oblivion. When I awoke, a transformation of such enormity had taken place that I was struck dumb with awe.

The person I had been no longer existed. There was no personal self or ego, only an Infinite Presence of such unlimited power that it was all that was. This Presence had replaced what had been 'me', and the body and its actions were controlled solely by the Infinite Will of the Presence. The world was illuminated by the clarity of an Infinite Oneness that expressed itself as all things revealed in their infinite beauty and perfection.

As life went on, this stillness persisted. There was no personal will; the physical body went about its business under the direction of the infinitely powerful but exquisitely gentle Will of the Presence. In that state, there was no need to think about anything. All truth was self-evident and no conceptualization was necessary or even possible. At the same time, the physical nervous system felt extremely overtaxed, as though it were carrying far more energy than its circuits had been designed for.

It was not possible to function effectively in the world. All ordinary motivations had disappeared, along with all fear and anxiety. There was nothing to seek, as all was perfect. Fame, success, and money were meaningless. Friends urged the pragmatic return to clinical practice, but there was no ordinary motivation to do so.

There was now the ability to perceive the reality that underlay personalities: the origin of emotional sickness lay in people's belief that they *were* their personalities. And so, as though of its own, a clinical practice resumed and eventually became huge.

People came from all over the United States. The practice had two thousand outpatients, which required more than fifty therapists and other employees, a suite of twenty-five offices, and research and electroencephalic laboratories. There were a thousand new patients a year. In addition, there were appearances on radio and network television shows, as previously mentioned. In 1973, the clinical research was documented in a traditional format in the book, *Orthomolecular Psychiatry*. This work was ten years ahead of its time and created something of a stir.

The overall condition of the nervous system improved slowly, and then another phenomenon commenced. There was a sweet, delicious band of energy continuously flowing up the spine and into the brain where it created an intense sensation of continuous pleasure. Everything in life happened by synchronicity, evolving in perfect harmony; the miraculous was commonplace. The origin of what the world would call miracles was the Presence, not the personal self. What remained of the personal 'me' was only a witness to these phenomena. The greater 'I', deeper than my for-mer self or thoughts, determined all that happened.

The states that were present had been reported by others throughout history and led to the investigation of spiritual teachings, including those of the Buddha, enlightened sages, Huang Po, and more recent teachers such as Ramana Maharshi and Nisargadatta Maharaj. It was thus confirmed that these experiences were not unique. The *Bhagavad-Gita* now made complete sense. At times, the same spiritual ecstasy reported by Sri Rama Krishna and the Christian saints occurred.

Everything and everyone in the world was luminous and exquisitely beautiful. All living beings became Radiant and expressed this Radiance in stillness and splendor. It was apparent that all mankind is actually motivated by inner love but has simply become unaware; most lives are lived as though by sleepers unawakened to the awareness of who they really are. People around me looked as though they were asleep and were incredibly beautiful. It was like being in love with everyone.

It was necessary to stop the habitual practice of meditating for an hour in the morning and then again before dinner because it would intensify the bliss to such an extent that it was not possible to function. An experience similar to the one that had occurred in the snow bank as a boy would recur, and it became increas-ingly difficult to leave that state and return to the world. The incredible beauty of all things shone forth in all their perfection, and where the world saw ugliness, there was only timeless beauty. This spiritual love suffused all perception, and all boundaries between here and there, or then and now, or separation disappeared. During the years spent in inner silence, the strength of the Presence grew. Life was no longer personal; a personal will no longer existed. The personal 'I' had become an instrument of the Infinite Presence and went about and did as it was willed. People felt an extraordinary peace in the aura of that Presence. Seekers sought answers but as there was no longer any such individual as David, they were actually finessing answers from their own Self, which was not different from mine. From each person the same Self shone forth from their eyes.

The miraculous happened, beyond ordinary comprehension. Many chronic maladies from which the body had suffered for years disappeared; eyesight spontaneously normalized, and there was no longer a need for the lifetime bifocals.

Occasionally, an exquisitely blissful energy, an Infinite Love, would suddenly begin to radiate from the heart toward the scene of some calamity. Once, while driving on a highway, this exquisite energy began to beam out of the chest. As the car rounded a bend, there was an auto accident; the wheels of the overturned car were still spinning. The energy passed with great intensity into the occupants of the car and then stopped of its own accord. Another time, while I was walking on the streets of a strange city, the energy started to flow down the block ahead and arrived at the scene of an incipient gang fight. The combatants fell back and began to laugh, and again, the energy stopped.

Profound changes of perception came without warning in improbable circumstances. While dining alone at Rothman's on Long Island, the Presence suddenly intensified until every thing and every person, which had appeared as separate in ordinary perception, melted into a timeless universality and oneness. In the motionless Silence, it became obvious that there are no 'events' or 'things' and that nothing actually 'happens' because past, present, and future are merely artifacts of perception, as is the illusion of a separate 'I' being subject to birth and death. As the limited, false self dissolved into the universal Self of its true origin, there was an ineffable sense of having returned home to a state of absolute peace and relief from all suffering. It is only the illusion of individuality that is the origin of all suffering. When one realizes that one is the universe, complete and at one with All That Is, forever without end, then no further suffering is possible.

Patients came from every country in the world, and some were the most hopeless of the hopeless. Grotesque, writhing, wrapped in wet sheets for transport from far-away hospitals they came, hoping for treatment for advanced psychoses and grave, incurable mental disorders. Some were catatonic; many had been mute for years. But in each patient, beneath the crippled appearance, there was the shining essence of love and beauty, perhaps so obscured to ordinary vision that he or she had become totally unloved in this world.

One day a mute catatonic was brought into the hospital in a straitjacket. She had a severe neurological disorder and was unable to stand. Squirming on the floor, she went into spasms and her eyes rolled back in her head. Her hair was matted; she had torn all her clothes and uttered guttural sounds. Her family was fairly wealthy; as a result, over the years she had been seen by innumerable physicians and famous specialists from all over the world. Every treatment had been tried on her and she had been given up as hopeless by the medical profession.

A short, nonverbal question arose: "What do you want done with her, God?" Then came the realization that she just needed to be loved, that was all. Her inner self shone through her eyes and the Self connected with that loving essence. In that second, she was healed by her own recognition of who she really was; what happened to her mind or body didn't matter to her any longer.

This, in essence, occurred with countless patients. Some recovered in the eyes of the world and some did not, but whether a clinical recovery ensued didn't matter any longer to the patients. Their inner agony was over. As they felt loved and at peace within, their pain stopped. This phenomenon can only be explained by saying that the Compassion of the Presence recontextualized each patient's reality so that he or she experienced healing on a level that transcended the world and its appearances. The inner peace of the Self encompassed us beyond time and identity.

It was clear that all pain and suffering arises solely from the ego and not from God. This truth was silently communicated to the minds of the patients. This was the mental block in another mute catatonic who had not spoken in many years. The Self said to him through mind, "You're blaming God for what your ego has done to you." He jumped off the floor and began to speak, much to the shock of the nurse who witnessed the incident.

The work became increasingly taxing and eventually overwhelming. Patients were backed up, waiting for beds to open although the hospital had built an extra ward to house them. There was an enormous frustration in that the human suffering could be countered in only one patient at a time. It was like bailing out the sea. It seemed that there must be some other way to address the causes of the common malaise, the endless stream of spiritual distress and human suffering.

This led to the study of the physiological response (muscle testing), which revealed an amazing discovery. It was the 'wormhole' between two universes—the physical world and the world of the mind and spirit—an interface between dimensions. In a world full of sleepers lost from their source, here was a tool to recover, and demonstrate for all to see, that lost connection with the higher reality. This led to the testing of every substance, thought, and concept that could be brought to mind. The endeavor was aided by my students and research assistants. Then a major discovery was made: whereas all subjects went weak from negative stimuli, such as fluorescent lights, pesticides, and artificial sweeteners, students of spiritual disciplines who had advanced their levels of awareness did not go weak as did ordinary people. Something important and decisive had shifted in their consciousness. It apparently occurred as they realized they were not at the mercy of the world but rather affected only by what their minds believed. Perhaps the very process of progress toward enlightenment could be shown to increase man's ability to resist the vicissitudes of existence, including illness.

The Self had the capacity to change things in the world by merely envisioning them; Love changed the world each time it replaced non-love. The entire scheme of civilization could be profoundly altered by focusing this power of love at a very specific point. Whenever this happened, history bifurcated down new roads.

It now appeared that these crucial insights could not only be communicated with the world but also visibly and irrefutably demonstrated. It seemed that the great tragedy of human life had always been that the psyche is so easily deceived; discord and strife have been the inevitable consequence of mankind's inability to distinguish the false from the true. But here was an answer to this fundamental dilemma, a way to recontextualize the nature of consciousness itself and make explicable that which otherwise could only be inferred.

It was time to leave life in New York, with its city apartment and home on Long Island, for something more important. It was necessary to perfect 'myself' as an instrument. This necessitated leaving that world and everything in it, replacing it with a reclusive life in a small town where the next seven years were spent in meditation and study.

Overpowering states of bliss returned unsought, and eventually, there was the need to learn how to be in the Divine Presence and still function in the world. The mind had lost track of what was happening in the world at large. In order to do research and writing, it was necessary to stop all spiritual practice and focus on the world of form. Reading the newspaper and watching television helped to catch up on the story of who was who, the major events, and the nature of the current social dialogue.

Exceptional subjective experiences of truth, which are the province of the mystic who affects all mankind by sending forth spiritual energy into the collective consciousness, are not understandable by the majority of mankind and are therefore of limited meaning except to other spiritual seekers. This led to an effort to be ordinary, because just being ordinary in itself is an expression of Divinity; the truth of one's real self can be discovered through the pathway of everyday life. To live with care and kindness is all that is necessary. The rest reveals itself in due time. The commonplace and God are not distinct.

And so, after a long circular journey of the spirit, there was a return to the most important work, which was to try to bring the Presence at least a little closer to the grasp of as many fellow beings as possible.

The Presence is silent and conveys a state of peace that is the space in which and by which all is and has its existence and experience. It is infinitely gentle and yet like a rock. With it, all fear disappears. Spiritual joy occurs on a quiet level of inexplicable ecstasy. Because the experience of time stops, there are no apprehension or regret, no pain or anticipation; the source of joy is unending and ever present. With no beginning or ending, there is no loss or grief or desire. Nothing needs to be done; everything is already perfect and complete.

When time stops, all problems disappear; they are merely artifacts of a point of perception. As the Presence prevails, there is no further identification with the body or mind. When the mind grows silent, the thought "I Am" also disappears, and Pure Awareness shines forth to illuminate what one is, was, and always will be, beyond all worlds and all universes, beyond time, and therefore without beginning or end.

People wonder, "How does one reach this state of awareness," but few follow the steps because they are so simple. First, the desire to reach that state was intense. Then began the discipline to act with constant and universal forgiveness and gentleness, without exception. One has to be compassionate towards everything, including one's own self and thoughts. Next came a willingness to hold desires in abeyance and surrender personal will at every moment. As each thought, feeling, desire, or deed was surrendered to God, the mind became progressively silent. At first, it released whole stories and paragraphs, then ideas and concepts. As one lets go of wanting to own these thoughts, they no longer reach such elaboration and begin to fragment while only half formed. Finally, it was possible to turn over the energy behind thought itself before it even became thought.

The task of constant and unrelenting fixity of focus, allowing not even a moment of distraction from meditation, continued while doing ordinary activities. At first, this seemed very difficult, but as time went on, it became habitual, automatic, requiring less and less effort, and finally, it was effortless. The process is like a rocket leaving the earth. At first, it requires enormous power, then less and less as it leaves the earth's gravitational field, and finally, it moves through space under its own momentum.

Suddenly, without warning, a shift in awareness occurred and the Presence was there, unmistakable and all encompassing. There were a few moments of apprehension as the self died, and then the absoluteness of the Presence inspired a flash of awe. This breakthrough was spectacular, more intense than anything before. It has no counterpart in ordinary experience. The profound shock was cushioned by the love that is with the Presence. Without the support and protection of that love, one would be annihilated.

There followed a moment of terror as the ego clung to its existence, fearing it would become nothingness. Instead, as it died, it was replaced by the Self as Everythingness, the All in which everything is known and obvious in its perfect expression of its own essence. With nonlocality came the awareness that one is all that ever was or can be. One is total and complete, beyond all identities, beyond all gender, beyond even humanness itself. One need never again fear suffering and death.

What happens to the body from this point is immaterial. At certain levels of spiritual awareness, ailments of the body heal or spontaneously disappear. But in the absolute state, such considerations are irrelevant. The body will run its predicted course and then return from whence it came. It is a matter of no importance; one is unaffected. The body appears as an 'it' rather than as a 'me' as another object, like the furniture in a room. It may seem comical that people still address the body as though it were the individual 'you', but there is no way to explain this state of awareness to the unaware. It is best to just go on about one's business and allow Providence to handle the social adjustment. However, as one reaches bliss, it is very difficult to conceal that state of intense ecstasy. The world may be dazzled, and people may come from far and wide to be in the accompanying aura. Spiritual seekers and the spiritually curious may be attracted, as may be the very ill who are seeking miracles. One may become a magnet and a source of joy to them. Commonly, there is a desire at this point to share this state with others and to use it for the benefit of all.

The ecstasy that accompanies this condition is not absolutely stable; there are also moments of great agony. The most intense occur when the state fluctuates and suddenly ceases for no apparent reason. These times bring on periods of intense despair and a fear that one has been forsaken by the Presence. These falls make the path arduous, and to surmount these reversals requires great will. It finally becomes obvious that one must transcend this level or constantly suffer excruciating 'descents from grace'. The glory of ecstasy, then, has to be relinquished as one enters upon the arduous task of transcending duality until one is beyond all oppositions and their conflicting pulls. But while it is one thing to happily give up the iron chains of the ego, it is quite another to abandon the golden chains of ecstatic joy. It feels as though one is giving up God, and a new level of fear arises, never before anticipated. This is the final terror of absolute aloneness.

To the ego, the fear of nonexistence was formidable, and it drew back from it repeatedly as it seemed to approach. The purpose of the agonies and the dark nights of the soul then became apparent. They are so intolerable that their exquisite pain spurs one on to the extreme effort required to surmount them. When vacillation between heaven and hell becomes unendurable, the desire for existence itself has to be surrendered. Only once this is done may one finally move beyond the duality of Allness versus Nothingness, beyond existence or nonexistence. This culmination of the inner work is the most difficult phase, the ultimate watershed, where one is starkly aware that the illusion of existence one here transcends is irrevocable. There is no returning from this step, and this specter of irreversibility makes this last barrier appear to be the most formidable choice of all.

But, in fact, in this final apocalypse of the self, the dissolution of the sole remaining duality of existence and nonexistence-identity itself-dissolves in Universal Divinity, and no individual consciousness is left to choose. The last step, then, is taken by God.

—*David R. Hawkins*

Hay House Titles of Related Interest

YOU CAN HEAL YOUR LIFE, the movie,
starring Louise L. Hay & Friends
(available as a 1-DVD program, an expanded 2-DVD set, and an online streaming video)
Learn more at www.hayhouse.com/louise-movie

THE SHIFT, the movie,
starring Dr. Wayne W. Dyer
(available as a 1-DVD program, an expanded 2-DVD set, and an online streaming video)
Learn more at www.hayhouse.com/the-shift-movie

BEYOND HAPPINESS: Finding and Fulfilling Your Deepest Desire, by Dr. Frank J. Kinslow

CHOICES AND ILLUSIONS: How Did I Get Where I Am, and How Do I Get Where I Want to Be?, by Eldon Taylor

THE HONEYMOON EFFECT: The Science of Creating Heaven on Earth, by Bruce H. Lipton, Ph.D.

MIND OVER MEDICINE: Scientific Proof That You Can Heal Yourself, by Lissa Rankin, M.D.

THE TAPPING SOLUTION: A Revolutionary System for Stress-Free Living, by Nick Ortner

We hope you enjoyed this Hay House book. If you'd like to receive our online catalog featuring additional information on Hay House books and products, or if you'd like to find out more about the Hay Foundation, please contact:

Hay House, Inc., P.O. Box 5100, Carlsbad, CA 92018-5100
(760) 431-7695 or (800) 654-5126
(760) 431-6948 (fax) or (800) 650-5115 (fax)
www.hayhouse.com® • www.hayfoundation.org

Published in Australia by: Hay House Australia Pty. Ltd., 18/36 Ralph St., Alexandria NSW 2015
Phone: 612-9669-4299 • *Fax:* 612-9669-4144
www.hayhouse.com.au

Published in the United Kingdom by: Hay House UK, Ltd., The Sixth Floor, Watson House, 54 Baker Street, London W1U 7BU
Phone: +44 (0)20 3927 7290 • *Fax:* +44 (0)20 3927 7291
www.hayhouse.co.uk

Published in India by: Hay House Publishers India, Muskaan Complex, Plot No. 3, B-2, Vasant Kunj, New Delhi 110 070
Phone: 91-11-4176-1620 • *Fax:* 91-11-4176-1630
www.hayhouse.co.in

Listen. Learn. Transform.

Get unlimited access to over 30,000 hours of Hay House audio!

Today, life is more hectic than ever—so you deserve on-demand and on-the-go solutions that inspire growth, center your mind, and support your well-being.

Introducing the *Hay House Unlimited Audio* mobile app. Now, you can listen to the experts you trust and the titles you love—without having to restructure your day.

With your membership, you can:

- Enjoy over 30,000 hours of audio from your favorite authors.
- Explore audiobooks, meditations, Hay House Radio episodes, podcasts, and more.
- Listen anytime and anywhere with offline listening.
- Access exclusive audios you won't find anywhere else.

Try FREE for 7 days!

Visit **hayhouse.com/unlimited** to start your free trial and get one step closer to living your best life.